DENNIS RODMAN with JACK ISENHOUR
I SHOULD BE DEAD BY NOW

The Wild Life and Crazy Times of the NBA's Greatest Rebounder of Modern Times

Dennis Rodman
with Jack Isenhour

Epilogue by Kent McDill

SPORTS
PUBLISHING

To all my kids—

Without your love and support,
life would not be worth living.

Thank you for understanding
what Daddy is all about.

Sports Publishing books may be purchased in bulk at special discounts for
sales promotion, corporate gifts, fund-raising, or educational purposes. Special
editions can also be created to specifications. For details, contact the Special
Sales Department, Sports Publishing, 307 West 36th Street, 11th Floor, New
York, NY 10018 or sportspubbooks@skyhorsepublishing.com.

Sports Publishing® is a registered trademark of Skyhorse Publishing, Inc.®,
a Delaware corporation.

Visit our website at www.sportspubbooks.com

10 9 8 7 6 5 4 3 2

Library of Congress Cataloging-in-Publication Data is available on file.

Cover design by David Ter-Avanesyan
Cover photo by Getty Images

ISBN: 978-1-68358-427-8
ebook ISBN: 978-1-61321-415-2

Printed in the United States of America

CONTENTS

PROLOGUE

Chicago, May 23, 2005. It's 10:45 p.m., and I'm running late—
not the first time. The changeover from Dennis into "Dennis
Rodman" is taking a little longer than usual. It's a top problem.
I've got the tails of a solid black, button-front shirt tied off just
below my nipples revealing the tattoo of two charging bulls, the
ripped stomach, the pierced navel, but it's still not right.

This top problem had come up about five o'clock after this
pretty white girl showed up at our suite at the Allegro Hotel toting
a manila grocery bag—a fucking grocery bag—full of sequins, buttons, seamstress supplies, with the job of converting a T-shirt sup-
plied by the event sponsor, a leading rum company, into some kind
of Dennis-Rodman-fabulous top. Well the T-shirt hadn't made it,
and somebody got on the phone trying to track it down while the
pretty white girl pulled out this stack of hats. I'd asked for a pinstripe. I try the thing on, and it's sitting on top of my head like a
donut perched on a bowling ball. The pretty white girl says something like, "You need an extra large." No shit—most six-foot-eight
guys would be wearing your larger sizes. I would have said something, but I was too busy checking out her piercings.

She's got nose rings, lip rings, earrings, brow rings—silver metal
sticking out everywhere. And she's got multicolored hair that looks
like woven cotton candy, and she's wearing jeans, a T-shirt, a jacket,
and a pair of platform shoes in some neon color—seems like it was
lime green—that looked like the gold ones I wore with the psyche-
delic Cleopatra outfit for my New Year's Eve bash back in 1997.
Long story short, this is a girl who would look good on my arm—
if I had a taste for pretty white girls.

That's a joke.

So the pretty white girl is talking, and she says the folks who sent her over said that the "rum company" T-shirts were too big—that "they would just hang on me." This came from people who'd been in the same room with Dennis Rodman.

Let me give you an idea just how fucking dumb that is:

We're riding up to the suite in a packed elevator, and the guy behind me—this six-foot-something reporter who's following me around—is bitching that my butt is hitting him in the chest. He could just nod and bite a chunk out of my ass. So Dennis Rodman is tall. There's more. I've been lifting weights religiously for about 20 years now, and so Dennis Rodman is also wide. There's not an extra-large T-shirt on the planet that would be hanging on my ass.

The pretty white girl is going on, something about mesh T-shirts, cut-outs so my tattoos—front, back, arms, and side—will show, and I'm counting the girl's piercings, trying to figure out who has more, me or her, not that you can ever be sure with your clothes on and your legs crossed. It's looking like she's the winner.

Anyway, all this turns out to be a waste of time. The T-shirt never arrives, and I tell the pretty white girl to forget about the mesh shirt. So, left to my own wardrobe devices, it's now 10:50 p.m. in Chicago; I'm still late, still having a top problem. I stroll into the suite living room and ask Darren—Darren Prince, my friend and agent, the guy who's going to negotiate my way back in the NBA—how the top looks. Now Darren is a great agent, but when it comes to fashion, he's just another clueless white guy.

"Okay, whatever," he says.

The boy just don't get it.

"Should I wear the shiny shirt?" I ask.

Darren looks stumped. He checks out his watch. It's his job to get me places on time when he's not negotiating my way back into the NBA.

Fuck it. I throw the shiny black shirt on over the tied-off black shirt, and we're out the door.

These days Dennis is content to ride around in your standard full-sized passenger car, but "Dennis Rodman" is still riding in style. And tonight not even a limo will cut it. At first, I think the thing is some new model of Bentley or Rolls. But this sleek silver car with copper highlights, which looks like an SUV on steroids, is something called a Maybach, an upscale Mercedes retailing for about $350,000, the driver tells us. The driver is upscale himself. He's a Harvard graduate—a basketball player no less—who played in the CBA. An Ivy League graduate is driving around Dennis Rodman, a proud dropout from Southeastern Oklahoma State. How fucked up is that?

What I like about the Maybach is it has plenty of legroom, and for a guy who is all legs, that matters. Not that I'll be getting one any time soon. While I'm doing all right, my days of swapping Bentleys when they get dusty are over—at least for the moment.

So the driver sees a little open road—in downtown Chicago, mind you—and decides to demonstrate the Maybach's power. He stomps on the car's zero-to-sixty-in-four-seconds gas, and it feels like falling backwards off the high dive. Damn! I'll take two.

Minutes later, we pull up to a club called Reserve located in a brick building just across the street from the EL—elevated train. The professional autograph people are at the curb waving shit they want signed, but we bypass them as the security guy leads us around to the side. We're out of the car and up a set of steep, dimly lit stairs to the back entrance. There's a five-minute wait while the security people get it together, then the door flies open to a wall of noise.

The place is fucking slammed, people shoulder to shoulder, pushing, shoving, screaming when they spot me. The dance music is ear-splitting. First time I saw a crowd like this, I thought, "No way we're getting through," but, like always, the security guys surround us—me, my two bodyguards, one of the bodyguard's girlfriends, her friend, and the reporter bringing up the rear—then make their move. Reaching out with horizontal arms held shoulder high, they keep us in, outsiders out, as we steadily snake our way through the crowd to a small stage where the DJ whips the crowd into a frenzy. Out of nowhere, four dancers appear and fall in line behind me.

The dancers are stenciled from the bikini line to the neck with body paint—some kind of rum-company motif that seems to be different for each girl. They've also got fake black tattoos running up and down their arms and legs. Then there's the pasties. I'm not sure what they're made of—looks like smoky plastic, just like at the strip club the night before. But if seeing open-air nipples is your thing, better stay out of Chicago.

The DJ shouts something. People scream. I shout something. People scream. The DJ steps aside, I take off my shirt—what top problem?—revealing what a lifetime of weightlifting can do for a skinny freak's body. People scream.

Folks are always asking me what I did to get this buff body. What kind of steroid cocktail am I using? None. What kind of top secret, super-athlete diet I'm on? None. While I do eat sushi for lunch most every day, the only real diet I'm on is a steady diet of pain. I work out at least an hour a day, six days a week, 52 weeks a year. Who says Dennis Rodman isn't disciplined?

Back at Reserve, I spin around, showing off the X-rated tattoo that fills up most of my back—a spread-eagled beauty pleasuring herself. People scream. I put my arms around the shoulders of the four dancers—two on each side—who are now toasting me with shot glasses full of the rum company's latest offering. I wave around a black bottle of the stuff, just like the 19 I autographed that afternoon back at the hotel. The crowd goes wild.

Welcome to "Rodman World," a daylight-to-dawn adult amusement park.

The good folks at a Chicago-based event marketing agency have paid me five figures to help launch the rum company's newest. "Promotional work," Darren calls it.

Basically, I show up, let them use my name and picture for advertising, posters, invitations, whatever, and make media appearances. This morning I did two television shows, two radio interviews, and talked to a bunch of newspaper reporters.

Back in the day, corporate America thought I was too unreliable, too flaky for this kind of work. They wouldn't get near my ass. Now I'm still edgy, off the wall, daring, this, that, but it's all dressed up, and you can count on me to show up sober and more or less on time. Not that you should be looking for me in the next Disney

World campaign. But if your image is a little bit out there, a little bit renegade, Dennis Rodman is your man.

Take GoldenPalace.com, the online gambling casino. I've just signed a lucrative, three-year deal with those guys that—among other things—has me running with the bulls in Pamplona, cruising across America in a customized Lamborghini, and hosting something called a "wife-carrying competition" in Finland. You call this work? Shit, I should be paying them. The sober, but still edgy Dennis also has a deal with The Upper Deck Company, the world's largest sports licensing and memorabilia company, as well as with adidas, which you know about. Hard to believe: adidas. I can remember a time when I would have kissed their collective asses just for the free shoes and workout gear.

Meanwhile, back at Reserve, everyone is getting his money's worth. The crowd, the media, the hype—America's number-one bad ass is endorsing this rum company's bad-ass drink. It's a perfect match. And until Darren negotiates my way back into the NBA, I'll be paying the tab being "Dennis Rodman," America's fuck-the-world, number-one bad boy—the man who puts the "free" in freedom. Anybody don't like it, they can kiss my black ass. That's the rap.

There'll be a second stop downstairs at Reserve after the security guys do the snake-through-the-crowd routine again, one body guard taking a pretty good two-handed lick from a drunk woman who didn't like being pushed aside. The guy didn't even flinch. Soon we move back upstairs and are seated in a roped-off VIP area.

I sit in one corner of a U-shaped sectional sofa. I'm separated from the crowd by a couple of security guards and a coffee table loaded with carafes of rum, ice, glasses, lemons, limes, mixers, whatever. Behind me and to the right, another security guy is sitting on a ledge. There's room for two visitors to sit beside me—one on the left and one on the right. My people occupy the seats farther down the couch on both sides: the roving reporter, my security guy, two of his women friends, and another security guy. They've got me surrounded.

The four dancers show up on the ledge—more of a runway—behind me, still doing their thing. After a while, they turn into little more than writhing wallpaper, and folks are more likely to stare out the plate glass window at a passing elevated train. Meanwhile the video screen behind my head is playing a rum commercial featuring guess who? over and over. Music blaring. A beautiful girl in a short, strapless, black velvet dress is handing out glasses with double shots of the new rum.

Shirt back on and shades in place, I settle in, light up a cigar, and host a continuing round of visitors. The usual. I sign autographs, pose for photographs, chat with the people the security and marketing people let through—friends, strangers, media—I do a T.V. interview. I yap. They yap. Flash bulbs. People in. People out. Girls. Men. Women. Young. Old. No boys. Not everybody makes the cut. Over to my left, sitting on the other side of the reporter, some gorgeous young girl, brunette, stares at me, fucking *stares* at me, all but drooling, for like half an hour straight—you have to admire the focus—before she gives up and goes on her way.

One of the dancers bends over and shouts, "Havin' a good time?"

"Oh yeah!" somebody yells above the noise.

"Well, I'm sweating my ass off," she says.

From what I can see, that's a fucking shame.

There's one thing missing from the picture these days. A few years ago, a reporter from *The New York Times* reported that he saw me down 19 shots in four hours before he stopped counting. Back then I was determined to treat every day like it was New Year's Eve and the Mardi Gras. You name it—sex, booze, fun—too much was never enough. Since I wasn't hurting anybody but myself, I figured, "No harm, no foul." No more.

In October 2003, the boozing started getting in the way of some things I wanted to do more than party (I can't believe that just came out of my mouth). The "party animal" had turned into a just plain old "animal," and I was in danger of losing everything if I didn't rein in the beast.

It all came to a head in—where else—Las Vegas.

CHAPTER ONE

FEAR AND MOANING
IN LAS VEGAS

I should be dead—crippled anyway. My brain scrambled. If it's true that God "takes care of drunks and fools," then he must bend over backwards to take care of drunken fools. It happened in Las Vegas, and it came at a very bad time.

Things were falling into place. Following a fling with showbiz, I was finally coming home to mama—the NBA. It hadn't been easy. After I bailed out of "Lost" Angeles in 1999, and Dallas shit-canned my ass in 2000, I had been making a living as an actor and entertainer, partying worldwide for a fee and hosting a series of wild parties for a DVD titled *Stripper's Ball*. In my free time, I partied free. Why? Because I could. By this time, I had reworked the old "Work hard, play hard" slogan to fit my new lifestyle. Without basketball in my life, it now read, "Play hard, then play hard some more." Not a bad life, but the Dallas thing had left a bad taste in my mouth.

Dallas owner Mark Cuban had hired me to be Bad Boy Rodman—the rock star who would put butts in seats and put the then-pathetic Mavericks on the map. I even agreed to live in Cuban's guesthouse, so his security guards could keep an eye on me 24/7 (I couldn't wipe my ass without three guards surrounding the

1

toilet). So how did the guy repay me? After 12 games, less than a month on the job, I was dumped. Why?

Well, maybe it had something to do with the one-game suspension by the league, the two ejections, the DUI, the 4-9 record, or the fact I challenged NBA commissioner David Stern to a fistfight—somebody needs to whip his arrogant white ass. Whatever. So did Cuban call me with the news? No. I found out about my release on ESPN. But Mark has gotten my back in the media over the past few years, saying that bringing Dennis Rodman onto a NBA team has many more positives than negatives.

After that, I soured on the NBA and spent a little over a year fucking around, being "Dennis Rodman," getting paid to have a good time. I knew I'd made it when people first started paying me to party. I mean, I'm partying anyway—why not take the cash? Life was good. But the more I thought about what happened in Dallas, the more pissed I got. I didn't like the way I went out. I wanted to make my farewell to the NBA on my terms. So when I signed with Darren, my number-one priority was to get back on the court. And on July 18, 2003, I held a news conference in L.A.

"The reason why we are here is to formally announce I officially want to come back to the NBA," I told the reporters, "basically to finish my career the way I want to."

I dressed down for the occasion: Reebok baseball cap, shortsleeved gray shirt over a white tee, and jeans. I still had the hoop earrings, shades, nose studs, and lip ring. Like I told them, comeback or no comeback, "I'm gonna be Dennis Rodman."

My comeback would give people a little reminder that Dennis Rodman was not only the proud poster boy for the stripper, biker, *WrestleMania* crowd, but one of the best professional basketball players of all time. I still can't believe they left me off the list of the 50 greatest NBA players. I mean, John Stockton? Shit. Listen to my stats. Five championships (more than all but 11 other players), seven rebound titles (second only to Wilt), two-time NBA Defensive Player of the Year, seven-time member of NBA defensive first team, and two-time NBA all-star. Telling you this shouldn't be my job, but who else is going to do it?

Reality Check: You sit around waiting for somebody else to crown you king, you'll end up a lady in waiting—waiting to take one up the ass.

After dozens of phone calls, months of wrangling, the good news had come in October of 2003. Darren called to say the Denver Nuggets were going to take me on. No long-term contract, no big NBA money—just ten grand a game—but my size-15 foot was in the door.

Not everybody was thrilled. A Denver reporter complained to ESPN about the increased workload. "Now you're on Rodman watch," he said. "Now you have to check the police blotter every morning when you wake up before you go to work."

Whatever ... I was psyched—not that the pending deal slowed down my partying. If anything, I cranked it up a notch, figuring what had worked for me during five championship seasons should keep on working with the Denver-fucking-Nuggets, not exactly the NBA elite.

While I was 42 at the time, I felt like I hadn't lost a step—on the court or in the clubs. So on Sunday, October 19, I was partying at Josh Slocum's (later "Rodman's"), my restaurant in Newport Beach, California. It was like 3:30 in the morning, and I had been tossing back one Grey Goose and cranberry juice after another followed by shots of Jägermeister chased with Coors Light. (How's that for product placement?) Now I had been doing this for like eight, nine, 10 hours—who's counting?—when I got a wild hair up my ass. Let's go to Vegas!

Soon the Dennis Rodman party mobile—a black Ford 350 XLT club cab pickup truck—pulled out of the Josh Slocum parking lot and headed east on highway 55. On board were driver Mike Diaz and a bodyguard in front, and me sprawled in back sucking down more Coors Light.

A couple of hours down the road; we made what was supposed to be a quick gas stop at this Mobil station just off the main drag in Barstow. Then I was recognized (it might have had something to do with my picture being plastered all over the hood of the truck). Anyway, I got to yapping with this guy and pulled a classic "Dennis," giving him my shoes, a nice pair of white canvas Chuck Taylor All-Stars with red trim. Then I tried to make a deal for the station's tow truck. I'm always doing stuff like that—take off my shirt and give it to somebody, buying this, buying that. Luckily the tow-truck deal fell through, and we were back on the road with my new favorite group, the country band Rascal Flatts, still blaring on the stereo, the same song playing over and over. Turned out the fucking thing had been stuck on repeat ever since we left Newport Beach. I was too drunk to care, and Mike and the bodyguard were afraid to do anything, having seen me in action when people bitched about me playing country music at my restaurant. It's basically, "If you don't like it, get out." So Rascal Flatts it was, for like three straight hours.

We made it to Vegas around 7:00 a.m. and pulled into the far side of the empty parking lot at Treasures Gentleman's Club and Restaurant—a brand-new, $30-million strip club open 24 hours a day. In the *Las Vegas Sun*, one of the owners described the place as "an upscale nightclub in an elegant, tasteful environment."

Mike woke me up so I could get it together before we made our big entrance. I did what I could with my Levi shorts, oversized T-shirt with a Josh Slocum's logo, knee-high basketball socks, and black rubber sandals—beachwear—just right for Treasures' "elegant, tasteful environment."

We drove around front to valet park. At first glance, the twin-towered joint, in what looks like sandstone, reminds you of a mosque or something, but there ain't nothing for the religious faithful inside. Just tits and ass and a nice USDA choice 16-ounce "bone-in cowboy ribeye served with garlic mashed potatoes, sautéed vegetables, topped with spicy shoestring fried onions" if you decide to try out the "gourmet" restaurant.

When we walked in, the place was all but empty. No customers, no strippers, no bartenders or waitresses, just a couple of guys who seemed like they were really glad to see me. They stalled, giving us a quick tour of the place, as if I'd never been there before. I don't know if "state of the art" is what you'd call it, but, as the man said, Treasures does offer a full range of gentlemen's services: strippers, booze, and lap dances. Why a strip club? I'll have to go along with Vegas writer Al Mancini, who allowed as how "bare breasts complement just about any leisure activity."

They rounded up a bartender, a waitress, and a couple of strippers, and soon I was back to my steady diet of Grey Goose and cranberry juice, music blaring, girls stripping down to g-strings before getting very friendly with their poles. There might even have been a lap dance or two. After like an hour of this, the girls were bored; I was bored. So I swapped seven $100 bills for 700 ones and treated my new favorite strippers to a Dennis Rodman forte. I took the 700 ones, stepped up on stage with the girls and started throwing wads of cash up in the air creating what the *Las Vegas Sun* would call a "green shower." The girls seemed to like it.

But even that wasn't enough to hold my interest for long. On a normal night there were—what?—a couple dozen girls in the place, other customers all around raising hell. And here we sat: me, Mike, and the bodyguard, coming up on Sunday School time, with the waitress, two strippers, and a bartender who wanted to go home—seven of us all together—in this big, empty room that seats maybe 150 people. It was bleak. Time to move on. Next stop: Cheetah's strip club.

As we were on the way out the door, this Treasures manager, bouncer, whatever, came walking in. "Hey, you're Dennis Rodman," he said. He laid his motorcycle helmet on the hostess counter, and that got us to talking bikes. He had just bought a new one for like $5,000. He was really proud of the thing; thought he got a good buy; wanted me to see it.

I have a thing for motorcycles. I got my first bike, a Kawasaki 1100, about 15 years ago and haven't been without one since. I even posed on a Harley for the cover of my autobiography, *Bad As I*

Wanna Be, but—seeing as how I was buck naked—nobody said much about the bike.

Anyway, I love motorcycles. So why not make this guy's day? So just after 8:00 a.m., I led my little entourage of Mike, the bodyguard, the manager, and one of the strippers outside to look at the cycle. It was a red and black beauty with an attitude—a rocket with handlebars.

"You ride?" the owner asked.

"Yeah, I can ride," I said.

"You all right to ride?"

"I'm good."

Not.

Now, I had no helmet—the guy left his inside—no leathers, just the shorts, sandals, and T-shirt, but I hopped on anyway. As for the owner, well … "Dennis Rodman" is a hard guy to refuse.

So I started her up, did a few lazy figure-eights in this huge parking lot, nice and easy. Around about now was when I should've thanked the guy for his trouble, hopped off, and gone about my business. I didn't do that. I had been awake for like 20 hours, been drinking steady for at least 12, had maybe a half-hour's sleep, and haven't had anything much to eat since I left Newport Beach. I was not a guy who should be operating heavy machinery. What's more I was only days away from my last DUI (that one on water in my boat, Sexual Chocolate), and this was far from my first regrettable rendezvous with a motorcycle.

I ran into a tree the first time I ever got on a bike back in my college days in Oklahoma and had suffered through four motorcycle accidents in all—including the one in 1995 when I separated a shoulder and missed 14 games with the Spurs. And even though I was only a few days away from realizing my dream of returning to the NBA, the booze and I decided that Dennis Rodman, the great one, was bulletproof.

So I was making these lazy figure-eights in the parking lot. At that speed, it was like reining in a horse that's trying to take off on you. What's Dennis Rodman know about horses? Well, I may have grown up on the streets of Dallas and made a name for myself in

Chicago, but during my college days, I lived and worked on a farm in Bokchito, Oklahoma, where I rode a horse or two. The temptation is always to give the horse his head, ride that mother wherever he takes you.

Ya-fucking-hoo!

And since there's no temptation (except drugs) that Dennis Rodman won't give in to, not only would I give this bike her head, I would show her who was the fucking boss.

Wheelies, bro, wheelies.

The great Dennis Rodman wouldn't just be cruising around, he'd be doin' wheelies in the parking lot of the Treasures Gentlemen's Club and Restaurant in Las-fucking-Vegas, Nevada. How cool is that?

So wheelies it would be on Sunday, October 19, around 8:35 a.m. Pacific Daylight Time. I revved the engine and popped the clutch. Bye-bye. The thing got away from me. I veered into the curb on the left, crashed through a hedge, and the bike took off in the opposite direction headed straight for a light pole. The cops told the *Las Vegas Sun* I was going 70 miles per hour—that's bullshit— claimed the thing threw me, then took off on its own. More bullshit. Wish it had. Actually, I was on the motherfucker all the way as the cycle rammed head on into the opposite curb, popped up in the air, and slammed into the light pole. The handlebars snapped off, the front end disintegrated, and the bike came down on my shins.

"When the motorcycle fell on him," Mike Diaz said later, "it was like a bomb hit him. I thought he was dead. I honestly thought the man had gone head first into the pole. It had hit so hard, so quick, I thought he was dead."

Later one television reporter said he saw the imprint of my knees in the bike's gas tank. I can believe that. The motorcycle was totaled. As for me, it looked like I was going to be spending a little time in the body shop.

After the crash, Mike and the bodyguard ran over and hauled the bike off of me. I was lying on the pavement in a total daze, blood everywhere, but I still managed to say, "Don't worry. It's gonna be all right."

The stripper ran up and was like, "Oh my God! Oh shit!" She was just all panicky. Panicky. Who could blame her? As Mike describes it, my right leg was "butterflied to the bone" from just below the kneecap to the middle of my shin. I thought it looked more like a split banana. Whatever. It was fucked up. The other shin, said Mike, "looked like it was just burnt up and like somebody took a razor blade and scraped all the skin off."

"You need a doctor," the bike owner said.

No shit. 911 time. Meanwhile somebody was yelling, "No cops! No cops!"

Yeah, right.

They wrapped my shins up in T-shirts to stop the bleeding, and in minutes, a fire truck, an ambulance, and a single cop on a motor-cycle arrived. They hauled my sorry black ass to the University Medical Center. Mike, the bodyguard, and one of the strippers fol-lowed along in the truck. So did the cop toting my DUI. Of all the things I've done in Vegas, it was the first time ever the cops had shown up—first time *ever*.

And while I would swear I wasn't drunk, and all my reps would back me up, shit, if they'd struck a match, my ass would've burst into flames. I admitted as much to Leno a month later. How drunk was I? I would call Darren and ask him to wire me another ten grand so I could keep partying when I got out of medical stir.

We got to the hospital and, as I was lying there all fucked up, hurting like hell—the booze starting to wear off—people began gathering around. It was like, "Hey, what's going on, Dennis?"

Showtime.

People are taking pictures, asking for autographs, this and that. The "Dennis Rodman Total Entertainment Franchise" was now open for business from a gurney in a Las Vegas hospital.

When they finally got around to stitching me up—more than 70 stitches—the medical staff was amazed that I wouldn't let them use Novocain. Not a big deal. For some reason, pain doesn't really affect me as much as other people. I deal with it in the beginning, and then once my body gets adapted to it, I'm cool. So I was just sitting there casually talking to my assembled fans while they were sewing my "butterflied" shin back together.

Meanwhile, my driver, Mike Diaz, was fielding phone calls. "They wore my phone out," he said. Agent Darren Prince was telling him to get my ass out of Vegas.

"He has a workout with the Denver Nuggets in two days," Darren said. "I know Dennis. He can suck it up. He can play."

Now, Mike, he didn't want to be the one to tell Darren, "That ain't happening."

"You'll have to talk to Dennis," he said.

The second caller was Thaer Mustafa from Newport Beach. Thaer, a Palestinian-American, calls himself my "babysitter." Actually, he's my right-hand man in California and, after he declared a jihad on my ass for slipping out of town without telling him, he told Mike not to talk to the media.

"Do not tell anybody anything period, regardless of who they are, reporters, nothing," said Thaer. "You know nothing. You saw nothing. You know nothing. You saw nothing."

By the time Mike and the bodyguard got in to see me (at about three that afternoon), I was holding court with a dozen or so people who had gotten word that Dennis Rodman was in the house. There were firemen, nurses, doctors joking around, amazed I didn't take any Novocain, laughing because I hadn't been wearing any underwear, and when the nurses cut off my shorts, they got a little more—a lot more—than they bargained for.

This was not the first time I was the star attraction at a hospital. Any celebrity will attract that kind of staff attention, and that's especially true if you have a condition that is the least bit interesting from a medical standpoint. Take a "broken dick."

You get a broken dick by bending a rock solid hard-on at a right angle. The result is ruptured blood vessels and a big ole scary mess. Now this has happened to me three times, and it sounds bad, but it's not all that serious, and it really doesn't hurt that much. But bro, it looks bad. It looks really, really bad.

The first time I broke my dick was on the Fourth of July at this lake down along the Texas-Oklahoma border. I was doing what I do with my lady friend, we got crosswise, and suddenly my dick was spurting blood like a water hose. She was screaming, "Oh my God! Oh my God! Something's happened! Something's happened!" Everybody came running in to see what the ruckus was. Now I don't embarrass easy, but hell. ... The girlfriend was trying to shut it off, squeezing my dick with a towel. Meanwhile, the damn thing was swelling up like four, five, 10 times its normal size.

The last time I suffered from this ailment was in New York City, and I ended up with my dick in a sling in the emergency room of this huge hospital. They must have announced it on the public address system, because everybody—and I mean *everybody*—who worked in the damn place was dropping by to check out my "rare" condition. I, of course, was the life of the party, proud to share my very special, educational dick with all of these medical professionals—all in the interests of science, of course.

Time to say goodbye to my new best friends at the University Medical Center in Vegas. Since my Levi shorts and T-shirt were history, the nurses gave me these green medical scrubs to wear, the pants hitting me about mid-calf like Capri pants. Mike picked up a couple of prescriptions for pain and swelling, and I limped out of there. Soon, Mike, the bodyguard, the stripper and I were back in the truck, making our escape. Thaer was on Mike's cell, still ranting, telling him, "You got Dennis in the truck, get him the hell out of Vegas right now." Well Mike works for me, and I call the shots, so Cheetah's it was. Out of the hospital 20 minutes, and I was back in a strip club throwing down one Grey Goose and cranberry juice after another, still partying.

Most people after an accident, drunk or sober, would've just said, "Fuck it, let's go home and relax."

But without the daily routine of playing basketball—the endless round of practices, meetings, travel, games—I had been partying non-stop for a couple of years, and my body was on automatic pilot—automatic partying pilot—and it just wouldn't stop. It just wouldn't stop. It just kept feeding itself, saying, "We're gonna keep on going. We're gonna keep on going. We're gonna keep on going."

And keep going we did. That's me. I take it to the limit. I take it as far as I can take it.

So we were at Cheetah's strip club, and all the girls wanted to do their thing. They're thinking, "Dennis Rodman, king of the strip clubs, is in the house, and we know what he wants. Couch dances!" Not this time. You'd think they would've noticed something wasn't quite right when I limped in dressed in hospital scrubs. Of course, it was dark in there. Maybe they thought the outfit was just another Dennis Rodman fashion statement. Whatever. Mike and the bodyguard did a good job of keeping them off me. They were like, "Don't touch this man! He's all fucked up."

Meanwhile, this awesome stripper, who had been with us the whole time from inside Treasures through the motorcycle accident to the hospital and now to Cheetah's, got up on stage and did her thing. I think she really cared about me and wanted to make sure I was all right before she took off. She was what you might call "a stripper with a heart of gold." Other nights it could go the other way. You could end up with your run-of-the-mill, star-fucking gold digger—you just never know. Any woman I meet, same basic questions. That's what fame and money can do to you—and them. Not that I give a shit one way or the other.

I think most people who meet me really like me. They think I'm a true motherfucker, honest, down to earth, and pleasant to be around. Others are just there for the ride. To them the money and fame are more attractive than I am, and when I realize that, it's like "Fuck!" But whatever somebody's motive is, I can roll with it.

I learned a long time ago that worrying about that shit—trying to judge people—can cut into a man's party time. Anyway, it doesn't matter if a particular person uses you or not. If it won't be this person, it'll be that person. If it won't be that person, it'll be this person. Go down the line. But whatever happens, by my way of thinking, you can't let that kind of cynical bullshit rule your life. You should always leave the door open.

Reality Check: Trust first, and ask questions later.

After a couple of hours at Cheetah's, the booze had really kicked in, and I was ready to move on; so we took off for the Hard Rock, got a couple of rooms. The stripper said her goodbyes, and Mike and the bodyguard thought they were done for the night. Wrong. Next stop: the circular bar above the Hard Rock casino where I bought rounds of drinks for everybody. People were cracking up just looking at me. I could hardly walk; I was still in those funky green hospital scrubs, and I was still partying. Mike kept saying, "How do you do this? How do you do this?" I was just used to it. It was normal for me. It was what I did. By now it's about 11:00 p.m., and I decided I wanted to go to the strip club across the street—that's the last thing I remember.

By then, I had been partying for almost 48 hours straight—a good showing, but well short of my record of three days. I had wrapped up that binge by passing out in the Ruth's Chris Steak House in Vegas. Another proud moment.

When I began to sober up the next day, I realized that I was fucked in a million different ways. First, not even Dennis Rodman could play ball anytime soon with the mangled shins and banged-up knees. Second, the Vegas slogan, "What happens here stays here," was not working for me. If you're "Dennis Rodman," what happens here or anywhere, ends up on the AP wire, in every fucking newspaper, and on every television station at home and abroad—including Denver, home of the Nuggets.

Reality Check: If you're famous, you're news 24/7, especially when the news is bad.

As if the regular media weren't bad enough, it just so happened that this was during the time ESPN was taping the reality show *Rodman on the Rebound.* The idea was to document my comeback to the NBA (what a joke that turned out to be). My close friend and agent Darren Prince calls up the sons-of-bitches at ESPN and gets them to fly to Vegas and get some video of me at the lowest point of my life. It wasn't pretty. He later told me he hoped that when I saw the tape it would shock me into sobriety. I later told him that—fucked-up shins or not—he was lucky his skinny white ass had been in West Orange, New Jersey.

Since I was a kid, I have always prided myself on being disciplined in the things that really matter—in the weight room, on the court (forget the refs), in how I play the game—defense, rebounding. Off court was my business; but suddenly things had changed.

My partying had made a liar out of Darren. For months, he had been telling every NBA general manager who would listen that Dennis Rodman had cleaned up his act. Based on that half-truth, he had the Denver deal lined up. And if that had gone south, he had the ear of Phil Jackson, who was then coaching L.A. for the first time. But now I was too hot to handle. Two years of Darren's work, and my comeback, were down the drain. So I was thinking maybe I ought to cut down a bit, and I promised Thaer I would do just that, as soon as I got past the Radio Music Awards.

After the motorcycle accident, Darren was so worried about my partying he called in the cavalry, my former bodyguard, Wendell "Big Will" Williams, a six-foot-four-inch, 400-pound black man. When Wendell talks, people, including Dennis Rodman, tend to listen. Wendell was coming out of bodyguard retirement to make sure I did what I was supposed to do when I was supposed to do it. He started out strong at the Radio Music Awards in Las Vegas. It was exactly a week after the Treasures motorcycle crash.

Despite my usual protests—"I don't want to do this. This is bullshit. It's not gonna help my career"—that afternoon Wendell managed to get me, sober no less, to this series of round-robin interviews with every fucking radio station in America.

"So tell me about Madonna, Dennis?"

"What's Michael Jordan really like, Dennis?"

"Where's your dress, Dennis?"

This went on for hours before the actual awards show that night, and Wendell wouldn't let me drink. Afterwards it was like I'd just run a marathon, and I went out by the pool to relax with a cool one while he went upstairs to shower. When Wendell got back down, I was wasted. This was all new to him. In the three years since he'd worked with me, I'd started spending much more time with my friend Herr Jägermeister, and this was his first time to see Dennis Rodman, daytime drunk.

So I went through the "I don't want to go to any awards ceremony," "It's bullshit," "It's not gonna help my career" routine, and he reminded me that they were paying me good money to be there. Money I'd already spent. So he dragged me into the auditorium.

I don't remember much of this, but Wendell says I was like some wino on skid row. He was holding me up, I was ranting, but my speech was so slurred nobody could understand what the fuck I was saying. The producers of the show got wind I was drunk, cancelled my award presentation, and even denied me a backstage pass. I went backstage anyway, falling-down drunk. A couple of years before, stars like Al Pacino and Meryl Streep were coming up to me, seeking me out, and now B-level celebrity hacks were turning their backs, avoiding me. I saw Puff Daddy giving an interview and started pinching him on the ass. He blew me off, and his crew was like, "Get him the fuck away from us!" Wendell pulled me aside. Then security showed up and drug my ass out of there—no backstage pass. "Fuck this place!" I shouted to Wendell. "Fuck this! Let's go. Let's go." So where were we going? A strip club. Where else?

After the Radio Music Awards, everybody was on my ass. Darren was on my ass. Wendell was on my ass. Thaer was on my ass. Even my wife, Michelle, was on my ass. After the motorcycle accident and my skid-row drunk performance at the Radio Music Awards, ESPN sat Michelle down for an interview.

"I'm done. I'm ready for a divorce," she told the interviewer.

This from a woman who has "Mrs. Rodman" tattooed just above her butt in letters about an inch high.

"He doesn't care about himself; he doesn't care about his kids; he doesn't care about me. He has no respect for himself."

It got worse.

"Not only am I gone, and his kids are gone, but his career is gone. He pretty much has lost everything."

She still wasn't done.

"He doesn't want the last thing to be said about him was that he was some drunk has-been. He definitely doesn't want that."

So by the end of October 2003, I was royally fucked. The wife and family were gone, Darren, Will, and Thaer had one foot out the door, and my NBA dream was over. Hell, even the "Dennis Rodman" entertainment franchise was in danger.

Reality Check: After almost a decade of steady party-ing, I wasn't having the party—the party was having me and having me good.

There was some good news.

Whenever I go through something traumatic like the Treasures motorcycle accident, something so emotionally and physically draining, I have like an out-of-body experience. And shortly after the accident, I found myself sitting there, taking a look across the room at what remained of Dennis Rodman, and I was left wondering: "How exactly did this happen? How did I get here? Is there any way out?"

CHAPTER TWO

THE ACCIDENTAL CELEBRITY

It was 1998 in Chicago, my third year with the Bulls, and I was white hot. I was the second most famous player in the NBA, right behind a guy named Michael Jordan. I was getting dozens of phone calls a day from charities, promoters, producers—everyone wanting a piece of my ass. I had an agent, bodyguards, and hangers-on. I had a Ferrari, a garage full of motorcycles, and even a rock star tour bus to ferry my partying friends and me from club to club after hours. I don't even know how much money I was making—millions—and I was spending it as fast as—sometimes faster than—I made it.

Feel like going to Vegas? Rent a private jet. Want a new car? How 'bout a Bentley? Girlfriend want a new wardrobe? Jewelry? Boob job? No fucking problem. I had it all and then some.

Ever heard that phrase "wretched excess"?

I was living it.

Meanwhile I was getting more famous by the day. Shit, Barbara Walters, Barbara-fucking-Walters, had come begging my ass for an interview. How did this happen? How did this skinny ex-janitor from nowhere become the hottest thing on the planet? It all started in a parking lot in Detroit.

For those of you who came in late, early one morning back in the spring of 1993, after I'd been with the Detroit Pistons for seven years, I ended up sitting in my pickup truck in this concrete wasteland that was the parking lot of Detroit's basketball stadium, the Palace of Auburn Hills. I had a rifle in my lap, and I was trying to decide whether I should blow my brains out.

There was a lot on my mind. Coach Chuck Daly, who had been like a father to me, was gone, shoved aside; the world championship Detroit team was being taken apart piece by piece; and my daughter, Alexis, was living a couple of thousand miles away in California. My ex-wife, from a marriage that lasted exactly 82 days, had decided she didn't want me in their lives. While I'd fulfilled most of my dreams in the NBA—won a couple of championships, a series of rebounding and defensive honors—I was suffering from a severe case of "is-that-all-there-is?" syndrome. Somehow, it wasn't enough, and what was worse, the real Dennis Rodman had been lost while I struggled to become an NBA poster boy. I decided that was going to change and put the rifle down. From then on, I was going to do what I wanted, when I wanted. "Dennis," the geek from the Oak Cliff projects in Dallas, was dead, and "Dennis Rodman" was born. Not that I knew what that meant. Not then. I fell asleep in the parking lot. Come daylight, the cops arrived, hauled me off to see a shrink, who pronounced me sane, and the media did what the media does.

I asked Detroit for a trade, ended up in San Antonio, and even before the season began, the new "Dennis Rodman" reared his lovely head. The occasion was the preseason opening of the brand new Alamodome. I showed up with blond hair to a cheering crowd. It was the Spurs' first clue that there was something seriously wrong with Dennis Rodman. Bottom line for the front-office suits: the motherfucker is crazy.

I loved it.

While I was a bit of a celebrity in Detroit, I was never the star on-court or off. "Isiah Thomas" was the name above the title, and I didn't even get top billing as the baddest of the bad boys. That honor went to center Bill "you-best-have-major-medical" Laimbeer, a white guy who left opponents like Scottie Pippen wondering if driving to the basket was worth the risk of ending their career. But, like it or not, in San Antonio my ever-changing hair color attracted a ton of attention from the public and the NBA, and I would end up center stage, sharing the limelight with teammate David Robinson, the Naval Academy graduate with the "Mr. Clean" image.

I also got my first tattoo in San Antonio, and the NBA didn't approve of that, either. I don't even know how many tattoos I have now, maybe 100, up and down my arms, legs, back, chest, and neck, covering about three-quarters of my body. The "tats" pretty much tell my life story beginning with the first—a picture of my daughter Alexis on my left forearm—running through a tribute to my current wife Michelle on the right side of my neck.

The hair and tattoos were a huge issue then, but now they're no big deal, thanks to a trailblazing Dennis Rodman. Like I told *The New York Times*, "Even all the boring white guys got tattoos now," not to mention all those pretty little middle-class girls with flowers etched on their pretty little white asses.

Over the years, even the NBA has developed a sense of humor about my hair, and on its web site, under the heading "Dennis Rodman," they actually report the Spurs 1993-94 won-loss record based on my hair color (Blond was the clear winner at 35-14). As for tattoos, a book called *In the Paint: Tattoos of the NBA*, reports more than two-thirds of the league is "tatted out." Rasheed Wallace of Detroit has a fine collection. Hair? Anything goes. Ben Wallace, also of Detroit, alternates between this wild-ass fro (he says he hasn't had a haircut in five years) and corn rows, which now are seen all over the league. I think Allen Iverson got that one going.

Back in the day, my hair and tattoos not only pissed off the NBA establishment, they were the first little steps toward moving the name of Dennis Rodman out of the cultish world of professional basketball and into the consciousness of mainstream America. Not that I cared. I wasn't looking for fame. I was just being "Dennis."

That first year with the Spurs, I would get a taste of national—hell, international—celebrity when I dated Madonna for like six months. If you believed the media accounts, that was more about Madonna than me—just another "boy toy" was the way it played out. But it was a whole lot more than that. Madonna wanted to have my babies.

Here's how far it went. One time I was in Las Vegas at the craps table doing my thing, and I got this frantic, "Somebody died!" kind of phone call from New York City. I picked up the phone, and Madonna was like, "I'm ovulating! I'm ovulating! Get your ass up here!"

So I left my chips on the table, *on the table*, flew five hours to New York, and did my thing. We got done, and she was standing on her head trying to get the full benefit, just like any girl trying to get pregnant. I flew back to Vegas and picked up my game where I left off.

Crazy shit.

Madonna had first called the Spurs' office out of the blue wanting to get hold of me. This was in 1993. I was, like, "Whatever." I knew who she was and everything, but I didn't like her music—too bubblegum—didn't like her videos, didn't like anything about her—her media image anyway. And I didn't know what the hell this white megastar wanted from me.

Turned out the real Madonna was a cool individual. She had her shit together. And she wasn't just in it for stud services. She wanted to get married—at least I think she did. She organized this intervention along with six female friends—the "Madonna Mafia" I called them. So Madonna was sitting right in the middle of this bunch, and she nodded at me and asked, "So you think I should marry this guy? He looks like a keeper."

I felt like I was on trial. I didn't even look at the fools. I mean nobody was asking *me* if I wanted to get married. Turned out the Madonna Mafia was cool with the idea, but I blew them off. I wasn't in love with her. And anyway, if I had married Madonna, my career would have come second. Madonna was like a fucking industry. She was General Motors.

Looking back, I sometimes wonder what would have happened if we had gone through with it. Can you imagine? You've got the bad girl and the bad, bad boy. We would have been the hottest Hollywood couple of all time—the Hollywood couple everyone wanted to see and hear about. Paparazzi heaven. Every day it would have been like:

"What are they doing now?"

"What's going on?"

"Who's zoomin' who?"

All that shit.

Madonna and Dennis, Dennis and Madonna, MaDennis, Denonna, one scandal after another. Dennis is over here doing this, and Madonna's over there doing that, and they collide in the middle. Shit, we would have made Brad and Jen and what's-her-face Jolie look like punks.

Maybe the strangest thing about my time with Madonna was when I realized she wasn't any bigger than I was—on the street at least. When we would walk somewhere, maybe go to Rodeo Drive in L.A., it was as if she were with me. I wasn't with her, okay? It was more like, "Dennis Rodman!" Then, "Oh, Madonna, whatever." It was always like that. She was old news to the paparazzi. I was the new kid on the block.

One Detroit teammate would claim all my marketing success was a result of ideas I'd picked up while hanging around with Madonna. (Trust me, we didn't spend a lot of time talking about marketing.)

Actually, I started dying my hair about six months before I ever met the woman. The reaction to the hair thing would eventually lead some people to start calling me a marketing genius. That's cool. But at the time, it had nothing to do with marketing.

So what was it about?

There are all kinds of amateur shrinks out there making up stuff about Dennis Rodman. One guy accused me of acting out as a way of getting a fix on how valuable I was as a player. The more shit management put up with, his theory went, the more it boosted my ego. He was like, "Think the Spurs' management would have let some sub do the rainbow hair? Son-of-a-bitch would have been gone by nightfall." So maybe the guy was right, but that shit's way too deep for me.

So how do *I* explain it? A couple of ways. First off, ever spent any time in San Antonio? As a black man? I was bored shitless. Secondly, everything I did in San Antonio was part of creating a new, free Dennis Rodman, the total makeover I had promised myself in that parking lot in Detroit. So one day, just because I felt like it, I got the hair dyed blond. The rest is marketing history—that simple, that complicated.

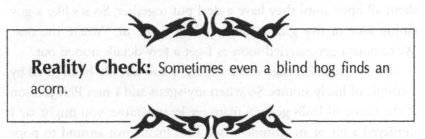

Reality Check: Sometimes even a blind hog finds an acorn.

During my two years in San Antonio, management and David Robinson were determined to tame—to save—Dennis Rodman. But I didn't cooperate. Figuring "if it ain't broke, don't fix it," I kept on dying my hair, painting my fingernails, getting tattoos, hanging out with weirdoes, fine-tuning the new me. So it didn't work out for them.

Thank God.

My first year with the Spurs, I won the league rebounding title for the third year in a row and made the NBA All-Defensive second team. Thanks to my play, David Robinson was free to concentrate on offense, and he led the NBA in scoring with almost 30 points per game. The next year, I again won the rebounding title, the Spurs had the best regular-season record in the league (62-20), and Robinson was named league MVP.

But by the end of that second year, I was in a pitched battle with the Spurs' management, self-appointed den mothers Gregg Popovich, then the general manager, and head coach Bob Hill. It was especially bad with Popovich. We fought, cussed each other out, and just couldn't get along. So San Antonio decided they'd had enough of the blond one—something about "distractions." (Management had seemed particularly pissed when Madonna had shown up at games—at least when they weren't kissing her ass.) So in one of the most lopsided trades in the history of professional sports, they swapped me to Chicago for Will Perdue, a journeyman, seven-foot center out of Vanderbilt best known for, well … nothing … nothing at all.

Not that the trade came easy.

When I became available, many teams seemed interested. Now the way the business works, teams have many options, and they keep them all open until they have a deal put together. So it's like a guy dating four or five girls at once, telling them all, "You're the one. We're gonna get married soon as I get a few details ironed out."

By the time Chicago came calling, I had already been jilted by a couple of likely suitors. So when my agent and I met Phil Jackson at the home of Bulls general manager Jerry Krause, you might say I displayed a bit of an attitude when Phil finally got around to popping the question.

"Dennis, we've decided we want to make a trade for you," Phil said. "Would you like to play here?"

"I don't give a fuck if I play here or not," I said.

And that's how I started the most incredible three years of my life. On court, I would be hooking up with the unretired Michael Jordan and Scottie Pippen to win three consecutive NBA championships, while off-court I would become the toast of Chicago.

While all this was going on with San Antonio and Chicago, I had been working on my autobiography with *San Francisco Chronicle* sportswriter Tim Keown. Entitled *Bad As I Wanna Be*, the book hit bookshelves in the spring of 1997, and that changed everything. The transformation began in Chicago with a simple book signing that turned into a media event.

CHAPTER THREE

BOOK SMARTS

hicago, Saturday, May 4, 1996. It was the morning of my first book signing for *Bad As I Wanna Be*, and I wanted to do something different. So a few of my gay, transvestite friends brought over some clothes and accessories, and we got creative.

It was like, "Okay, here we go, put this on, put that on. That looks good. Wear that. Let's check that out." This cross-dresser named Jo Jo dyed my hair, and Mimi Marks, one of Chicago's best known female impersonators, came up with the idea of putting me in full make-up. I'm like, "Okay, whatever."

I trusted Mimi to make me up not only because he made his living as a female impersonator, but because he actually lived his life as a woman. And he was hot—the spitting image of Marilyn Monroe. So when it came to putting make-up on a man, Mimi was the best.

Mimi, like Jo Jo, was not somebody I hired to trick me out for the book signing. They were friends. In Chicago, I was always hanging around with a "different" collection of people—gay guys, drag queens, and ex-cons hiding behind aliases—pretty much a bunch of "lowlifes." I loved them.

Then, as now, Mimi was a legend in Chicago. He was such a skilled female impersonator he fooled most guys—not just on stage, but up close. Back in the day, whenever I had out-of-town guests, I would take them to the Baton Club, where Mimi worked. Mimi would come over, and I'd say, "Hey, check out this girl." Nine times out of 10, somebody would end up hitting on him. Mimi would just play along. But after a while, if the guy was getting a little too close, I was like, "Oh shit! Hold on, bro, she's not really a she—it's a guy." That's how good Mimi was. People have asked me if Mimi was the best female impersonator of the bunch. Mimi was the best of many bunches. Who better to make me look presentable?

So Mimi slathered on the make-up while I tried on a fuchsia feather boa. After a couple of hours, the makeover was complete, and another friend said, "Hey, why don't you cruise down to the bookstore on my Harley?" Cool. So I threw the feather boa over my shoulders, hopped on the cycle, and set off for the book signing in something borrowed, something fuchsia.

I drove to the store (wrong way down a one-way street, of course) and was greeted by a thousand or so people, assorted media, and cops on horses. People started jumping out of their cars, running   around,   saying, "Oh my God!" While I wasn't in drag (somebody reported I was wearing a skirt), my get-up did show I was in touch with my feminine side. I had on full make-up with silver eye shadow and lipstick that matched my silver hair, nails, tank top, and motorcycle boots. I rounded out the ensemble with long, dangly earrings, tight black leather pants, and the fuchsia boa.

The media went ape shit, and I would make the front page of the *Chicago Sun-Times*, "The Rebounder Wore Rouge"; and the Sunday *Chicago Tribune*, "Eccentric Bull Transcends Even Jordan's Popularity." I had been in Chicago less than a year, and I was topping Michael Jordan. I would even become a landmark.

Here's how that happened.

Me, Michael Jordan, and a Cubs player by the name of Ryne Sandberg had a deal with this men's clothing store, and they painted a huge mural of the three of us on the side of a building just off the freeway near downtown. I was in the middle wearing this suit with no sleeves, arms folded. Every time I would change the color of my hair in real life, they would change the color of my hair on the mural using these big plywood cutouts shaped like my fro. After a while, this got to be such a huge thing that, in the mornings, when the radio stations were doing traffic reports, they would say shit like, "Well, from O'Hare to Dennis, it's 15 minutes," or "From Dennis to downtown, it's five."

The mural became a tourist attraction, people pulling over to the side of this busy highway to take pictures. Eventually it got to be such a traffic hazard that the Illinois Depart of Transportation made them paint over it. Unreal. I still don't know what it was. I think people just embraced me because they saw I wasn't afraid to do anything; that I just didn't give a shit.

◆ ◆ ◆ ◆

The clothes, the make-up, the dressing in women's clothing weren't new things I dreamed up for the Chicago book signing. This was part of my life and had been for a few years. Most people don't know that in San Antonio I wasn't just spending time with hairdressers during *daytime* hours. I was going to gay bars, wearing women's clothes to clubs all the time—women's tops, women's this, women's that—doing all these weird things I wanted to do. I freed my mind. The gay community embraced me. They didn't look at me and freak out. They were like, "Okay, great! Wow! He had the balls to do that, being an athlete, being a macho man or whatever. He has that soft feminine side." They knew I wasn't gay—knew that it was just Dennis being "Dennis."

Not that anybody heard about it. San Antonio wasn't Chicago or New York. There weren't inquiring reporters lurking on every street corner. So the media was a day late and a dollar short. But the truth is, I put together the new Dennis Rodman in San Antonio, took him on the road to Chicago, and then, most famously, to New York. Still none of it was part of any big marketing plan. I simply liked to wear a bit of women's clothing in public. That was it.

End of story.

I've never had a problem with gays and lesbians. If somebody comes up to me and says, "I'm gay," I don't give a rat's ass. We're all the same emotionally. I'm always asking guys who turn their nose up at gays, "Aren't you curious? Haven't you ever thought about being with a man?" And it's like, "No way, dude! Never! That shit's disgusting." Then I say, "How do you know it's disgusting if you haven't thought about it?"

Reality Check: Love is love.

If I had discovered I was gay when I started fooling around with that gender-bending shit, I wouldn't have waited to come out of the closet. I would've said straight out, "I'm gay—live with it." What were they going to do, throw me out of the NBA? If you're good, you're good. If you can play, you can play. That's the way it seems to work in women's sports.

Many girls who play tennis and golf are gay. Many girls who play basketball and softball are gay. People aren't surprised when women athletes are lesbians. It's the stereotype—you know: the butch, athletic woman. The stereotype for men is just the opposite. For men, the athlete is supposed to be a macho guy, not some sissy. All that's bullshit. There are a lot of lipstick lesbians and macho gays out there, not to mention sissy heteros. But while your average sports fan is basically saying "Whatever," to lesbian athletes, they don't have that same indifference toward gay males on the playing field.

I'm different. In my case, I honestly believe it really wouldn't have mattered if I were gay. I was so bizarre to begin with; I think people would have left me alone. Half of them thought I was gay anyway. Anybody else, I don't know. Now if it had been me who was HIV positive instead of Magic Johnson, it would have been a different story.

Back then everybody thought any sign of AIDS was a death sentence, and the NBA circled around Magic, stood by him, just as they should have. There were questions, of course.

"Is he gay?"

"Has he been with men?"

But Magic was so macho, was so loved, that for many people he was living proof that AIDS was not a gay disease, that straight people could get it, too. If it had been me that tested HIV positive, they would have kicked my ass out of the league in a heartbeat—made an example of me.

"See, that's where that kind of lifestyle can lead."

"The wages of sin are death."

"It ain't freedom, it's license."

Bullshit like that.

It's the kind of thing that happens when a very large, high-profile, black male athlete shows up in midtown Manhattan decked out in a wedding dress.

◆ ◆ ◆ ◆ ◆

A couple of months after the 1995-96 season ended (the Bulls won the championship over the Seattle Supersonics in six games while I won a fifth straight rebounding title), I went on Letterman and Howard Stern to announce I was going to be married. I didn't say exactly whom I was marrying, but a rumor started making the rounds that it would be Stacy Yarborough—this New York stripper I'd been dating. Whatever. I invited the media to come by my book signing at Barnes and Noble in New York City to find out.

I first got the idea of marrying myself while I was in Europe filming my first movie, Jean-Claude Van Damme's *Double Team*. Why? Who the fuck knows? I played around with the idea for a while, and then I thought, "I'm doing this New York book signing anyway, why not combine the two?" After that, the idea just kept growing and growing, and it was out of control by the time I made it to New York in late August of 1996.

I flew in a $3,000-per-hour make-up artist from London and bought an expensive dress (I wasn't writing the checks, so I don't

remember what it cost, but the *New York Post* reported it was
$10,000). When I was done with my outfit, there was no doubt. This
time I was definitely in drag—as "in drag" as you can get—wearing,
as the *The New York Times* put it, "a lacy white wedding dress," with
"a veil over [my] neatly coiffed, bright orange hair." Actually, it was
a wig, and I'd call the color "strawberry blond." As for the dress, it
was sleeveless—my shoulders are one of my best features—with a
band collar and matching long white gloves. The *Times* didn't mention that I was carrying an armload of white lilies.

Pretty fancy.

On the way down in the elevator, headed for the horse-drawn
carriage and eight beautiful groomswomen I'd hired for the occasion, I ran across Aerosmith's Steven Tyler, the first outsider to see
the outfit. I knew Tyler because we used to hang out when I came
back east. He looked me up and down.

"Dennis?" he said in a very low voice.

"Steven," I said, matching his tone.

"You go, man," he said. "I'll be watching."

Outside, I managed to get both me and the dress through the
door of the tour bus, which was to take me over to the horse and
carriage. Last chance to back down. Everything I had done in public up to then—the rainbow hair and tattoos in San Antonio, the full
make-up and boa in Chicago—was what one might call "out-
landish" or "eccentric." But this was something else all together. This
cross-dressing, female-impersonating jag wasn't just more fun and
games. It was a bold leap into homo-world, "Run-for-your-life-
queers!" shit, and there was no turning back once I crossed that line.
There was a reason no active, male professional athlete in any major
sport had ever come out of the closet. So this was risky, and it could
go either way.

Fuck it.

I stepped into the horse-drawn carriage and, with eight beautiful women in tuxedos walking alongside, took off down Fifth
Avenue. At first, people were curious, but not all that excited. Then
I got out of the carriage about five blocks away from the book store
and started walking, barefoot no less. Fifth Avenue is a street bor-

dered by high rises and, at street level, it looks like a concrete ravine. I remember hearing a clamor, looking up at the sheer gray walls, and seeing dozens of people opening windows, looking out.

Then people began congregating around me, checking out what they thought was a very tall black woman in a wedding gown, and instead of going about their business, they started walking along with me, trying to figure out what I was doing. It was like, "What the fuck is that?"

Then they started to put it together. "That must be the girl Rodman is marrying."

So they kept on following the big ugly black girl just to see what would happen. Soon there were hundreds of people clogging the street. Chaos. I hadn't expected that. I mean this was New York; they'd seen it all. I was like, "Goddamn!" Not even the police escort could control the crowd that came out to greet the "bride," and it got so crazy the cops shut down the street.

The cops shut down Fifth Avenue for Dennis Rodman.

By the time I got to the Barnes and Noble bookstore at Rockefeller Center, there were media everywhere, must have been 200 reporters and photographers going nuts.

I signed books until I chipped a nail. The media ended up treating it more like a freak show than the end of civilization as we know it. So ... I got away with it. What had started out as a joke, ended up a slam dunk. I had made it in "if-you-can-make-it-there, you-can-make-it-anywhere" New York City, and I did it by just being myself.

Bad As I Wanna Be would make a home for itself on *The New York Times* bestseller list for 20 weeks and end up selling over a million copies. At the time, you may not have known anything about basketball, but if you weren't living in a cave, if you were alive, love him or hate him, you had heard of Dennis Rodman. That fame was the cost I had to pay for fulfilling the dream that began in that parking lot in Detroit.

That last year in San Antonio, first year in Chicago, I had transformed myself into this beautiful individual. Free. Unafraid. At the same time, accidentally, thanks to the media, I became more than just a basketball player. Now I was more like a rock star. Some of the media called me an "outlaw," like it was Dennis Rodman against the world. It was never like that. It had always been "me against me." The old, conservative Dennis versus the new, free Dennis.

Before San Antonio, I had no energy to get up and go to work, to go play basketball. I had to find some reason to get up in the morning, to keep me motivated. That something came in going to the gay clubs, meeting new people, letting myself go wherever my imagination took me. And I did it for me, not as part of some marketing plan meant to make me famous. That was a happy—or maybe unhappy—accident.

On the happy side, fame means I'll be remembered not only for being a hell of a basketball player, but, more importantly, as a guy who did something that only a handful of people have done. I freed people up to do, say, feel, and dress the way they want.

Fuck the consequences.

That's the happy side. You can be a positive influence; you can change people's lives. And who wouldn't like being treated like a rock star everywhere they went? But there's a lot of bad shit, too. I can't scratch my ass without drawing a crowd. And while fame will get me a table at the restaurant ahead of you, it also gets me an audience for every bite I chew. I can't live a normal life.

Then there's the trust thing. After you get burned a few times, you figure everyone you meet is asking, "What's in it for me?" At its worst, you do so much to insulate yourself from the public, from real people, that you have no normal human contact at all. There's just your yes-boys, your "Go-get-me-this!" people, who are so afraid to say "no" to you, to speak their minds—afraid you'll say, "Fuck you! Get out of my life!" There's no real relationship. There's just ass-kissing and more ass-kissing.

As for real relationships, of all the so-called "friends" I've had over the course of the last 20 years, 99 percent of them have fucked me over—abused my power, sold stories to the tabloids, stolen from me.

Here's just one story:

I was in Atlantic City gambling, shooting craps, girls hanging all over me, and, while I may have been drunk, I wasn't fooling around. The house had advanced me $25,000 in $500 and $1,000 chips. Came my turn to roll, I was so drunk I had to hold onto the table to keep from falling down and I was bouncing the dice off people's heads, chests, stomachs, even onto the floor. Everybody was laughing, having a good time. It was like, "Isn't that Dennis a fun guy?"

Suddenly, I stopped.

"I'm missing a $1,000 chip," I said.

People from the casino started scrambling, crawling under the craps table, and looking all around on the floor, even asking me to go through my pockets. They couldn't find anything and decided I must have miscounted. No way. As my then-bodyguard, George Triantafillo, will tell you, when I'm gambling, drunk or not, I know exactly what is going on, every nickel on the table—what belongs to me, what belongs to the house, what the odds are on every roll. Sometimes I think I should have been a bookie.

So George went over to talk to the pit boss, told him, "If Dennis says he's lost or somebody's stolen a $1,000 chip, trust me, it's gone."

The guy was skeptical, but then George asked him, just for curiosity's sake, to "check out the 'eye in the sky.'"

Well the video from several security cameras showed that the girl who was still standing on my right—the brunette I had planned on sleeping with that night—had palmed the $1,000 chip and then cashed it in at cashier number nine. This after she'd told me that she was going to the bathroom. George whispered the news in my ear.

All I said was, "Get my money."

George waited a few minutes, then pulled the girl aside on some pretense, and called her out. She denied it, repeating, "I didn't steal shit! I didn't steal shit!" Right about then, George told her she was the star of her own casino video. Now she was sweating.

"If I give you the money, will you let me go?" she asked.

"Sure, no problem," George replied.

She jammed a hand down the front of her pants and dug 10-$100 bills out of her panties. George counted the money and then escorted her over to the two suits from casino security.

"You told me you were going to let me go," she said.

"Yeah, and you told me you didn't steal the chip," George said. "I guess we're both liars."

Reality Check: Life's a bitch, Bitch.

✦ ✦ ✦ ✦ ✦

I was a late bloomer. For me, all the sucking up started in college. For guys like Shaq, it begins in junior high school. If you're good on the basketball floor, you'll have many "friends," because they see the potential down the road. Then you start noticing how things change. Suddenly you're a whole lot smarter—nobody disagrees with you—you're a lot better looking, and women who wouldn't piss on you if you were on fire suddenly want to date you. You can do no wrong. The money you haven't made yet starts making friends on its own. Later when you finally realize the money and fame are more attractive than you are, it's like "Fuck!" But you can't dwell on it.

As for all you "Hey-let's-go-party-with-Dennis!" suck-ups out there, when you hang out with somebody just because of money or fame, and not because you like the person, you can lose yourself. When you're living the ass-kissing life, all of a sudden your views, your ideas, your opinions, and your thoughts get buried, and you have lost contact with yourself, downgraded yourself, sold your soul. The bottom line is: you're hurting yourself a whole lot more than you're hurting me.

CHAPTER FOUR

EVERY DAY IS
NEW YEAR'S EVE

I first hooked up with bodyguard George Triantafillo at the photo shoot for the cover of *Bad As I Wanna Be*. My agent at the time, Dwight Manley, asked George to work the shoot, trying to head off any trouble since there was nudity involved.

"Do *I* have to be naked?" George asked.

"No," replied Manley.

"Then I'm in."

Born and raised in Chicago, George is a burly guy, over six feet tall, who looks like he belongs in the "City of Broad Shoulders." We hit it off from the first, and he would soon become not only my full-time bodyguard, but my friend. A cop from a family of cops, his job was to protect me from the public—and myself—as I continued to try to live every day as if it were New Year's Eve.

During my three seasons with the Bulls, George was the hurdle you had to jump to get to me, whether you were my agent, a crazy-ass fan, or Phil Jackson himself. He was the bad guy if someone wanted an autograph, and we didn't have time to stop, the guy who got me to places on time and always answered the door. He was the guy who dropped women off at the curb with 20 bucks for cab fare at the first sign of trouble, and perhaps most importantly, he was the sober guy who did my thinking for me in the wee hours. (George swears my ass would have never gotten within 10 yards of that motorcycle at Treasures if he'd been around. He's probably right.) George also came up with the litmus test for when it was time to call it a night.

At some point late in some wasted evening, George would come up to me and say, "So Dennis, what's the state fish of Hawaii?" If I could pronounce it, we kept on partying. If I couldn't, we went home. Now this would be no big deal if we were talking about the Illinois state fish (the bluegill), or the California state fish (the golden trout). But the state fish of Hawaii is something called the *humuhumunukunukuapuaa*. Many a night, I just took it on home without even giving it a shot.

The Dennis Rodman party train had started out small—George, a few friends, and me—ferrying from one club to another until dawn in my pickup truck or Hummer. But in time, I became like a pied piper. We'd pick up a handful at supper, another bunch at a club, and before the night was over, there'd be a couple dozen of us raising hell. I got tired of everybody having to follow us in cabs—it interrupted the flow of the party—so I bought an R.V. first, and then, in my last year in Chicago, I got us a tour bus like the ones rock stars have—you know, with couches, a television, sound system, bar, and a bedroom in back. Now 20 or 30 of us could party non-stop all night long. Maybe we'd go to St. Louis to see the Rams play; or Joliet to gamble; or Detroit to see my favorite group, Pearl Jam. When you hopped on that bus, best pack a bag, it might be a three-day trip. Whatever. Whenever. If we didn't have a game the next night, I was partying. After a game, I was partying. Off-season, I was partying—lots of drinking, gambling, and, of course, women.

Most men spend the better part of their life chasing women. But if you're a famous NBA superstar like "Dennis Rodman," you aren't chasing—you're picking and choosing. Bottom line: if you're an NBA star, you never have to sleep alone. That ain't bragging; it's just the truth. And that changes everything. The whole man-woman thing is out of kilter. And while you might be living every man's dream, odds are if you sleep with 20,000 women like Wilt Chamberlain—My ass! Do the math—or a more modest couple of thousand like me, some freaky shit is going to happen.

Here are a couple of stories:

One night, George and I were at Crobar, this hot club in Chicago, and I got hooked up with this young lady. White. Blond. Beautiful. The usual. Normally, I'd just take her home to my house in Northbrook, but it was late, and that's like a 30-minute drive, so I asked George to get us a suite at the Ambassador East.

We took off in the pickup; the girl and me, and George, who drove, since I was hammered. He soon noticed that this guy was following us in a red Camero. George ran a few lights, made a few quick turns—the standard stalker/paparazzi drill—then double-parked in front of the Ambassador East. By now, it was like 4:30 a.m. So we were at the front desk getting the key to the suite and George spots the red Camero guy standing in the lobby about 30 feet away. George went over to check him out.

He flashed his badge. "May I help you?" he asked.

"Yeah," the guy said, "That's my girlfriend. That girl with Rodman."

"Wait right here," said George, without missing a beat. He came back over to talk to the girl. Turned out the guy was telling the truth.

"How long you been dating?" George asked the girl.

"Oh, we live together," she said.

I swear to God. They were fucking *living* together. I figured ol' Dennis was going to be sleeping alone that night.

"Should I let you go?" I asked the girl.

"No, no, no, no, no," she said. "I'm going with you."

Okay.

So now I was feeling sorry for the red Camero guy, not sorry enough to run the girl off, but you know … sorry. I gave the key to the suite to George, and he took it over to the boyfriend. I could get another room. Well, the guy accepted the key. No shit.

The girl and I went to our room and did what we did. The next morning, George, the girl and I were grabbing a little breakfast at the restaurant Third Coast, right around the corner from the hotel, and I spotted the boyfriend a couple tables away. So I asked George to pay for the guy's breakfast—least I could do. The boyfriend accepted.

Breakfast over, the girl gave me a big wet kiss and her number. "Call me," she said, and walked over to rejoin the boyfriend. Well, the red Camero guy stood up and started toward our table. I was thinking, "Oh shit!" (I wasn't afraid of the guy, I was afraid of the lawsuit).

George was tensing up as the boyfriend offered me his hand and said something like, "What a great fucking honor it is to meet you … You're the coolest guy. Chicago really needs you. Thanks for being who you are. Keep it real."

No shit.

Then the guy took his girlfriend's hand, and the last I saw of them, they were strolling down Dearborn arm in arm.

Freaky ain't it? It's been almost eight years, and I'm still trying to figure out what that was all about.

Reality Check: Fame changes everything.

Here's another freaky story. I've always had this thing about hijacking bridesmaids' parties. I must have horned in on a dozen of them over the years.

So one night I saw this group of girls out on the town in Chicago. Bridesmaids! I started buying them drinks; we hooked up; and after a while, the bride was all over my ass—the *bride*. As if that wasn't bad enough, turned out one of the bridesmaids was the groom's sister. I figured this was going nowhere. Whatever, we were having a good time. That was a few hours before the bride fucked my brains out. Now I've always wondered if the bride went through with the wedding. If she did, you know the sister-in-law *owned* her ass for as long as that marriage lasted.

Reality Check: Fame warps everything.

Some people hear these stories and say, "Dennis, you were wrong to sleep with that bride and the wayward girlfriend. Why didn't you do the right thing and send them packing?"

That's not my choice to make. If some woman wants to have sex with me for whatever reason—I'm irresistible, a last fling, revenge against an unfaithful husband, temporary insanity—who am I to say "No"? If they want to betray all that is holy by fucking the devil himself, that's their decision. If I say "No," I'm saying that this helpless little girl is incapable of making her own decisions. My approach has always been, "If you're willing, let's go." There is one exception: If I know you, know your husband or your boyfriend, I won't do it.

Other than that, bring it on.

And, by the way, back in the day, Dennis Rodman was the safest "devil" to screw in Chicago. That's because George was always close enough to hear a "No!" or a "Don't!" or any last-minute change of heart. And before my feet hit the floor, he would come charging in the bedroom and do the father-knows-best drill, dragging the girl's ass out the door. All for "her own good," of course. Actually, that's a pretty good example of another thing they accuse me of: treating women like a piece of meat.

I'll admit to that. And how do you think women treat Dennis Rodman? Hello—like a life-support system for a dick. So in my world, there ends up being a kind of crazy, *bassackwards* brand of equality that even a feminist might embrace. In Rodman world, *everybody* is treated like a piece of meat.

That's cool. I know women don't come to me looking to live happily ever after in a two-bedroom brick rancher with a white picket fence. They come to me so they can say, "I slept with Dennis Rodman." Then they get on back home to Opie. And so there's no doubt, I make it clear up front.

"We're just gonna have sex. That's it. Done."

So everybody knows what's up going in. Take it or leave it. That's the way it is. Everybody gets what they want—sounds like a perfect arrangement to me.

◆ ◆ ◆ ◆ ◆

Sometimes in party mode (maybe I've had 10, 15, 20 shots of Jägermeister) things have happened—not that I regret, I don't regret anything—but things have happened that probably wouldn't have happened if I were sober. I'm thinking in particular of this benefit sponsored by an upscale strip club where things got a little crazy. Some people called it an orgy. I'm not going to tell you the name of the club or even the city, except to say it wasn't Chicago.

Why?

In your typical strip club, there is lots of good, nasty fun: topless, maybe even buck-naked girls dancing, lap dances, rivers of booze. And unless you're tucking a few bucks into a stripper's garter belt or whatever, there's a "no touch" rule. But, if you believe the cops, this club was—for sports VIPs at least—nothing but a highpriced whorehouse, and we weren't even in Nevada.

Four of us flew up there from Miami on a private jet for a benefit the club was having the next day for some charity, somewhere. It was me, George, this big-name entrepreneur, and his son, whom we'll call "Joe" and "Joe Jr." I got hammered on the plane and commenced playing the big shot, making promises to Joe, who was an older guy around 60.

"You're gonna have the time of your life," I said. "I'm gonna get two girls to go down on you."

George sometimes calls me "a corruptor," and this time perhaps he was right. We went straight from the plane to the club. I'm known all over the world for going to strip joints—you might say I'm a recognized connoisseur. So every bouncer, every manager, every *yahoo* in the place came out to meet me at the door. It was like, "Oh my God! Dennis Rodman's here!" I was the man of the hour. I could go in there and get anything I wanted. It was like waving a magic wand and—shazam!—I got my wish.

They led us upstairs to this private, dimly lit room, and when we all got inside, they closed the curtains. There were already a dozen naked girls in there, maybe more—nothing but writhing flesh. I chatted up the woman in charge of "negotiable services," and soon two girls went over and delivered on my promise to Joe. Joe Jr., a kid in his early twenties, couldn't take it, and he had to leave the room. Can't blame him. George laughed, and I said, "What are you laughing at?" and sicced a couple of girls on him. Then I got three girls for myself.

After a while, Joe Jr. wandered back in the room. Not that he was having a good time. He was sitting there, straight up in his seat, eyes big as saucers, frozen, watching all this way nasty shit going on. The boy was in shock. I tried to snap him out of it, "introduced" him to one of the girls. It didn't help. Turned out the kid was germophobic, and he dashed out of there to the bathroom where he scrubbed his hands for 15 minutes.

The next day the charity thing kicked off with a golf outing. It was a shotgun start, and all these pretty girls—there were like three women for every man—were spread out all over the course doing hostess duty for all these big-name sports celebrities. I won't tell you who they were, but let's just say there were future hall of famers from three or four sports on hand—all for some charity, somewhere. Anyway, the shotgun went off, and so did the girls' clothes. They went topless. They went bottomless. They were making golf balls disappear. This was right in the middle of this suburban golf course. Even I was impressed. Somebody called the sheriff.

Party's over.

So we went back to the private room at the strip club where the owners said they were donating the day's proceeds to some charity, somewhere. The more I drank, the more enthusiastic I got. It was for a good cause, right? I was running up a major tab—$5,000-$10,000—for girls, booze, champagne, food. After a while, an AFOed—"all-fucked-out"—George was just sitting there in a room full of beautiful naked women eating buffalo wings, proving once again that you *can* get too much of a good thing.

Night over, I was out about $50,000, but it was for a good cause, right? I even got to take a couple of girls home: "the woman in charge of negotiable services" and a sweet young thing who would later tell the cops I paid her $500 for the privilege. No way, I have never paid for sex. Don't have to.

As I told the district attorney, a stripper's job is to please you and satisfy you the best way she knows how. And sometimes she might end up having sex with you, but not in a way where she's going to be a whore. It's like meeting a girl at a club, at the grocery store. I mean if she wants to screw you, she's going to screw you. Money has nothing to do with it.

As for all this shit being demeaning to women, I don't buy it. I don't do anything that the woman doesn't want me to do. Strippers are there for one reason—to make money. They do it by fulfilling male fantasies. It's tit for tat (yeah, that's on purpose), and it's the most straightforward relationship a man will ever have with any woman. I pay you this. You do that. There's no bullshit.

I treat a woman as she is. If she wants to work in a strip joint, I treat her just like that—take anything I can get. If she has a "respectable" job, I treat her like a respectable woman. That's the way I break these girls down—no big mystery. If I'm treating you like what you are, what you chose to be, how can that be demeaning, disrespectful? It would be disrespectful if I treated you like something you're not. Say I treated a whore like a Sunday school teacher. Hell ... the bitch would starve to death.

Reality Check: Act like a piece of meat, get treated like a piece of meat.

Back in my suite at the hotel, "the woman in charge of negotiable services" won out, and the sweet young thing bailed, ending up in the next room with George. "You mind if I come sleep with you?" she asked. "It's pretty wild in there." A couple of minutes later she was sound asleep in his arms. Later, George was like, "So what's wrong with my ass? Not even a stripper will screw me." Turns out she wasn't all that interested. The sweet young thing and "the woman in charge of negotiable services" were lesbian lovers. You can't make this shit up.

I told one on George, now here's one on me. I was so drunk, I don't remember any of this, but George swears it's true. One night I was in the rear bedroom of my rock 'n' roll tour bus with a young lady. George was outside just watching the bus rock "like a ship at sea," as he tells it. Well, the rocking stopped too soon, based on past experiences, and George came charging onto the bus to find out what was wrong. The girl was standing there stark naked in the bedroom.

"Hey! I'm naked here," she said.

"Shut the fuck up!" George said as he hustled over to check me out. I was sitting on the bed, passed out, head down, with a full hard-on propping up my chin (as George tells it.)

George shook me and saw I was still breathing.

"I think he overdosed," the girl said.

"Bullshit. He just passed out," said George, knowing I never do drugs.

"No, guys can't keep it up when they pass out," she said.

"This guy can," said George.

George called for his backup, another one of Chicago's finest, and the guy walked in the bedroom.

"Hey! I'm naked here," the girl said.

"Shut the fuck up!" he said.

George decided to get me dressed and haul me into the hotel to sleep it off. So they dressed me in these baggy pants, shirt, Birkenstocks, but they couldn't do a thing with my member that was making a goddamn circus tent in the front of my pants. What the hell? They were dragging my ass down the aisle of the bus when I woke up. Now I couldn't walk, I could barely talk, but I still wanted to stay with the girl. I wanted to keep partying.

"Sure. No problem," said George. "So tell me, Dennis. What's the state fish of Hawaii?"

That's what it's like when you live every day like it's New Year's Eve—lots of fun, lots of great stories. And I lived that life for almost 10 years. But after a while—a long, long while—I began to realize that there was a New Year's Day following New Year's Eve. A day I'd been sleeping through.

CHAPTER FIVE

WHO LOVES DENNIS RODMAN?

The question was simple enough: "Who loves Dennis Rodman, and who does Dennis Rodman love?" But it got me stammering.

"Who loves Dennis Rodman?" I finally asked, stalling.

I really don't know who loves Dennis Rodman. My kids for sure—at least the two little ones, Dennis Jr.—"D.J.," we call him—and Trinity. But they're so young, four and three; they're blind right now. They just know daddy, daddy, daddy.

They don't know "Dennis Rodman."

As for Alexis and Chance, my 16-year-old daughter and seven-year-old son, they are part of my life just one day a month—payday. Other than that, we haven't been in contact for a long, long time. I still love them both, but if they love me, they aren't showing it. There are scars—literally—when it comes to Alexis. When she was a toddler, she grabbed my right earring, splitting the ear wide open. It hurt like hell for a minute, and I still have a big notch in my ear lobe. In those days, Alexis was the light of my life, but now she won't even talk to me. Oprah tried to get us back together on her show a few years ago, and that turned into a disaster. My publicity-hound ex-wife wouldn't let Alexis come on stage unless she was included, and I ended up crying on national television.

Love has too often been just another word for "pain" in my life. What is love anyway?

I hear tell you're supposed to learn that as you're growing up—not in my family. My father, Philander (that's not a typo), who was career Air Force, disappeared when I was three. People tell me he's living in the Philippines and reportedly brags about having a couple of dozen children. What an asshole.

As for my mother down in Texas, I could never say, "I love my mother." I don't know what that is—have never known—to be honest. My mother never hugged me, or my two younger sisters, Debra and Kim. Never even gave us a hug. That's just how she was—I don't hold it against her. She worked as many as four jobs at once, usually managing to keep us living a lifestyle I guess you'd call "lower middle class," and all three of us kids made it to college on basketball scholarships. My sisters even graduated. I mean the woman was busy. Maybe she loved us; she just didn't know how to show it. She had her own problems with love, seemed to be always be hooking up with some sorry-ass man. We would hear her crying all the time in the bedroom by herself. We didn't know what to do. We were kids, you know? We didn't know why she was crying.

And there are unhealed wounds—tough love gone wrong, you might say. When I was 19, my mother let me cool my heels in jail overnight when I got caught stealing some watches. Later, she kicked me out of the house, trying to shock some sense into me, and I was homeless for months. She was just a hardcore black woman. Now I know "it was for my own good," but I'm not sure I will ever be able to forgive or forget.

Today I guess you could call my family "estranged." My mother has never even seen my three youngest kids, and I can't remember the last time the family spent Christmas—or any holidays—together. I was 20-something. I've always said that I'm not going home until I make something of my life. And even after all I've done, I don't think I've accomplished enough to sit down and talk to my mother about anything.

Reality Check: You have to get love to give love.

In some ways, I've turned out like my mother. I don't show love on the outside. I don't show it. I've been so scarred and calloused. Another one of those amateur shrinks said, after looking at the way I deal with women, the way I treat women, I may be taking out the anger I feel for my mother on women in general. I don't think so. First off, I'm not mad at my mother. It's more like indifference. Second, I've had many bad things happen with women that don't have a damn thing to do with my mother.

As I said, before I made it in the NBA, I thought women were shit, and they returned the favor. I didn't have any money, no car, this, that, so they weren't interested. That left me feeling vindictive. Then I made the pros, and all those girls who didn't like me came back all of a sudden and wanted to date me. I thought that was bullshit.

These days I like to say women are adaptable. They may come into a relationship humble and poor, but they adapt really quickly. You end up in court, and it's like, "I gotta live a certain way. I gotta have this, I gotta have that."

"What do you mean, you gotta have that? You didn't have shit when I met you."

Men have no choice but to sit there and take it. Whoever came up with the divorce laws in this country ought to have their ass kicked.

Who do I love? Coaches Chuck Daly and Phil Jackson, Lakers owner Jerry Buss, and James Rich, the head of the Oklahoma family I lived with during my college years. Each has been like a father to me—the "four wise men" I call them. Put them all together, and they are the winter, spring, summer, and fall of fatherhood. These were guys who set me straight when I needed setting straight—who hung with me when they didn't have to. I can say I love them. Do they love me back? You'll have to ask them.

Friends? I've never had the ability to have one true friend forever. And I'm not sure the word "love" applies. I have trusted friends and counted on them, but love? Get back to me when the money and fame are a distant memory.

I guess when somebody's time runs out, making a list of who loved them and who they loved would be one way of tallying up a life, measuring success and failure. As for me, right now, I can say my children loved me, and I loved them back; a segment of the public loved me, the image anyway, it still does, although I'm not sure that counts. They don't really know me. My family? Forget it. Women? That is probably my biggest failure in the love department. While I hope it will happen with my wife Michelle, so far, I haven't been able to get anything to last. Dennis Rodman can tell you how to sleep with dozens of women in one year, but don't ask him how to sleep with one woman for a dozen years.

In the market for an orgasm? I'm your man.

Want to set up housekeeping? I don't have a clue.

"Who loved Dennis Rodman, and who did Dennis Rodman love?"

When I look back over all the people I have known in my life, only one name keeps popping up in both columns with no qualifiers, no asides, no doubt. While I may have fucked it up completely—from the tarmac of the Orange County Airport to the wedding chapel in Las Vegas through our headline-making brawl at the Bentley Hotel in South Beach—I have to say it was all done with a certain bad-boy-meets-bad-girl, lives-noisily-ever-after, up-yours, can't-you-see-that-we're-busy, Dennis-Rodman style. I mean we may have become a punch-line on the late-night talk shows, but if you'd been there beside us, known what was really going on, you would have been cheering for us. For as messed up as it was, this was purely and simply a love story: a funny, sexy, touching, and, in the end, heartbreaking love story.

"Who loved Dennis Rodman, and who did Dennis Rodman love?"

Tara Leigh Patrick, a.k.a. Carmen Electra—the love of my life. Our tale begins in Los Angeles.

CHAPTER SIX

CARMEN-CHANTED EVENINGS

Once upon a fucking time in Los Angeles, I met Carmen Electra. It happened at Billboard Live, a dance club in West Hollywood. This was in early 1998, midway through my last season with the Bulls, when we were in town to play the Lakers. I was upstairs at the club, standing at the bar working on a Coors Light, when "Joe Jr.," the kid you may remember from the orgy, walked up to me rubbing his chin like someone had just busted him in the chops.

"What's wrong?" I said.

"My hard-on just hit me in the chin," he said. "Carmen Electra's here."

"Who's that?" I asked.

I'd never even heard of her.

"The *Baywatch* babe," said Joe Jr. "She's so beautiful. She's gorgeous."

Whatever.

By then I was used to meeting beautiful girls, even bored with it.

They comes.

They goes.

But Joe Jr. persisted and talked this friend of ours, Floyd Ragland, "Mr. Social" we called him, into chatting up Carmen. A few minutes later, Floyd escorted her over to the bar.

"This is Carmen Electra," he said.

A striking brunette a few inches over five feet with a body to kill for, I could see what Joe Jr. meant. Not that it was love at first sight. I don't do love at first sight—lust maybe, but not love. It's not in me.

"How you doing?" I said, and she looked like she wasn't any more thrilled meeting me than I was meeting her. I'm guessing I wasn't the first athlete she'd met. She hung around for a minute and then disappeared.

Whatever.

I wasn't looking for a girlfriend. I wasn't looking for true love, let alone a wife. I wasn't even looking for a one-on-one relationship. Far from it. Never had one. Didn't see any need for one. I was perfectly happy with my girl-at-every-NBA-franchise lifestyle. At that moment, Carmen Electra was just another beautiful woman in a long line of beautiful women.

But later, like two or three o'clock in the morning, we went downstairs and somehow Carmen ended up sitting in my lap. How? Don't know. I was hammered. Anyway, Carmen is a talking machine, and we were talking, talking, talking, and having a good time. Nothing much physical was going on. We hung out until like five in the morning.

I would learn later that Carmen, born Tara Leigh Patrick, about 26 years before, was one of five children from a nice, middle-class family that lived in the Cincinnati area. She had spent her childhood training to be a performer and moved to La-La Land when she came of age in the early 1990s. It took her all of two weeks, by one account, to hook up with the artist again known as Prince, who would launch her career. Early highlights were an album on Prince's Paisley Park label in 1993, a nude pictorial in *Playboy* in 1996, and a couple of television shows. Then came the *Baywatch* gig.

Come time to go at Billboard Live, I thought Carmen and I had clicked, and I was sure of it when she blew off the girlfriend who was with her. This wasn't one of your typical, "catch-a-cab, see-ya-later" deals. The girlfriend had managed to fall on her ass and break her arm, yet Carmen ended up accompanying me to my favorite late-night haunt, a snazzy joint called "Fat Burger." So I guess you could say my first one-on-one date with Carmen Electra was at the Fat Burger. Fitting.

Then the really strange things started to happen.

First, Carmen said her good nights and went home alone. When I woke up the next morning, it dawned on me: she hadn't given me her phone number. No, I didn't ask for it—I don't have to—girls usually want to give me their numbers. I'd come home after a long night of partying with a scrap of paper in one pocket, a napkin in another, a stray matchbook in a third—phone numbers every-where—in pencil, pen, lipstick.

"Don't worry about the number, dude," a friend said at break-fast. "My cousin knows her."

So Carmen and I hooked up again the next night at a club called Garden of Eden on Hollywood Boulevard. She and another girlfriend showed up, I took their coats, and about that time a friend of mine cruises in—surprising me with this girl I'd been dating. I handed her the coats, and while she was trying to figure out what to do with them in coatroom-challenged L.A., Carmen and I slipped out the door and into my Rolls.

Nothing strange about that—standard Dennis.

What was strange was that, although I had a game the next day, I ended up staying up all night talking, again; and she ended up going home alone, again. For two nights in a row, the notoriously quiet ladies man named Dennis Rodman had talked himself silly and slept alone. Stranger still, I was cool with it. Something was hap-pening. I invited her to the game that night, but she didn't show.

I don't know what it was. Maybe it was because, at that time in my life, I was having sex with lots of different women. So many that, sometimes, it became like a job, y'know? With Carmen, it was different. It was nice to be hanging with someone, waiting for the right time, the right place, the right moment.

A week or so later, I invited Carmen to meet me in Las Vegas. At the time, when I was in Vegas, I was dating this stripper—a beautiful blonde who worked at my favorite strip joint, O.G.'s, Olympic Gardens. So there was one Dennis and two babes—three actually, since Carmen again brought a girlfriend. The trick was keeping everybody separated. When we went to dinner, bodyguard George Triantafillo handled the seating arrangements. If it was a long, rectangular table, George would put me in the center and the girls at each end. If it was a round table, he'd surround me with guys, and put the girls at 12 and six, so they wouldn't get into a conversation. Every now and then, I would get up and make the rounds, making sure everybody was happy. There was still nothing much physical happening with Carmen. We had kissed, but that was about it. We didn't sleep together, and George made sure her room was on a different floor to head off any potential problems when I hooked up with my stripper friend come bedtime.

In those days, juggling women was commonplace. Many times George and I would go to O'Hare, and I'd drop off one girl at one terminal and pick up a second at another—shuttled them in and out. Wherever I went, I always "brought sand to the beach," as George used to put it. I'd fly in a girl I was comfortable with, keep her there until I found somebody local, and then ship the first one back home. As often as I traveled, there would be different girls three or four times a week.

When Carmen came along, there was not only women juggling, there was schedule juggling as we tried to hook up. Remember: this was in the middle of the NBA season, and I was constantly on the road. We finally got together again in Chicago, I don't remember exactly when, but I'm thinking it was the middle of February. I picked her up at the airport and took her to the little brick ranch house I had in Northbrook. The place was all right, but a shack by NBA standards—not the kind of house to impress a Hollywood starlet.

"Do you really live here?" Carmen asked.

"Yep," I said.

We went to eat sushi, came home and just lay there in bed and looked at each other and talked, talked, talked. She was there four or five days, sleeping at my house—in my bed—and we never made love.

Unreal.

When people ask me when things really got going with Carmen, I always say, "In Chicago." That was when the Dennis/Carmen thing went places Dennis Rodman had never been before. We had some strange kind of spiritual connection. What I now know was a real relationship was developing. This wasn't just about flesh and bone. I'm looking at her, and I'm not seeing her beauty. I'm not seeing Carmen Electra, the *Baywatch* babe, the *Playboy* pin-up. I'm seeing the heart of Tara Leigh Patrick, the feisty gal from White Oak, Ohio. I was falling in love—not that I knew it. I'd figure that out months later. However, this wouldn't play out like some white-bread fairy tale. No, no, no. After all, this *was* Dennis Rodman and Carmen Electra, and our particular fairy tale was destined to be twisted—and, of course, X-rated.

✦ ✦ ✦ ✦ ✦

Toronto, February 19, 1998. The Bulls came to town, and after kicking Raptor butt 123-86, Carmen and I jump-started our evening by teaming up to corrupt this young trainer for the Bulls. We hired this pro to put on a live sex show in the kid's room. The girl came in, did this strip tease and the rest for me, Carmen, the kid, George, and a couple of Bulls teammates. Everybody was taking all this in, having a good time, and when Carmen and I had been sufficiently "entertained," we decided to break out and ended up in my bedroom at the suite.

George, as always, was right outside.

I don't know if it was the booze, the sex show, or the brisk Canadian climate, but there wouldn't be any talking, talking, talking that night. I turned on the television, cranked it up very loud, and we began making love.

It took a while, but the television was so loud that there were complaints, and hotel security came calling. George tiptoed into the bedroom to turn off the television, and his timing was really bad—or good—depending on your point of view. Carmen was getting close, and right about then, she got a little carried away.

"This is yours! Yours!" she shouted.

Then came the "good" stuff.

"Take it, nigger! Go ahead, take it!"

I cleaned that up a little bit, but you get the idea. Well, George couldn't get his ass out of there fast enough. Me? All I heard was someone shout, "Nigger!" and my ass was up in bed.

"What the hell?" It was déjà vu Southeastern Oklahoma State—"Who's-that-fucking-my-white-daughter?" shit. Then I realized it was Carmen doing the shouting.

The next morning we went downstairs to breakfast, and Carmen, George, and I were sitting in a booth. George held off as long as he could, and then in mid-bite, he said, "So Carmen, what's with the racial slur?"

Carmen turned bright red and I started laughing.

"You heard that?" I said. "Man, she called me 'nigger,' and I jumped up to see if there was somebody else in the room."

Now Carmen hadn't meant anything by it. She's not like that, you know? She was just trying to heat things up, milk the moment for all it was worth. George knew that. He was just giving her a little shit. We all ended up laughing about it.

So that was our first time—just another romantic evening with Dennis Rodman.

After that, we made up for lost time and had sex like seven days straight, ate Chicago up behind closed doors. There was a ton of pent-up energy to release, and we were like two tigers going at each other. We'd throw each other here, throw each other there. She'd slap me here. I'd slap her there. I would do this to her. She would do that to me. We were bouncing off the walls, throwing lamps, breaking tables. I mean, I don't know how many hotel rooms we destroyed having sex. Anybody who heard it must have thought we were fighting, or trying to kill each other.

When we tired of hotel rooms, the Berto Center, the Bulls' practice facility, became our domain. We had sex in the training room, the weight room, this, that. We did everything under the sun at the Berto Center, everything that you could name. We didn't care where we had sex. All the guys are going to read this book and go, "Damn!" It was intense. It was crazy, but it worked for me and her. It worked. Sexually, she made me feel like I was different.

After Toronto, even though there were always other girls lurking around in the background, Carmen took center stage in my life. She was always the lady of choice whether it was coming to games, clubbing, charity events—whatever—and every chance I had, I'd either fly to see her or fly her to see me. Still it wasn't unusual for me to put Carmen on the plane in the afternoon and meet another girl for dinner that night.

We kept hanging out and hanging out and she eventually confessed that she had always wanted to meet me, that she'd told her girlfriends, "That's the guy I'm going to marry—that guy." And I looked at her like, "Wow! You want to marry a guy like me? I don't know about that, girl. I don't know about you and me getting married."

I wanted to, and I didn't want to. One day "yes." The next day "no."

◆ ◆ ◆ ◆ ◆

After the 1997-1998 season was over (the Bulls won a third straight championship beating the Utah Jazz in the finals), I flew to France to make a movie called *Simon Sez*. In my first starring role, I would play a secret agent trying to rescue the kidnapped daughter of a close friend. It had a happy ending. During the filming, I flew Carmen over to join me. One day, we ended up shopping for watches in the city of Nice on the French Riviera.

I have had a thing about watches ever since the bone-headed stunt I pulled when I was a 19-year-old janitor/master criminal working at the Dallas-Fort Worth airport. I stole 15 watches, was caught—on video no less—and ended up in jail. This was like grand larceny, and they could have locked my ass up for years. You might think I lifted the watches to supplement my pitiful $6.50-per-hour paycheck. Nope, I was playing the big shot. I gave the watches away to my mother, sisters, and friends—didn't sell one—and the cops were able to recover all of them. That saved my ass, and they let me go, but not before I had spent a scary-as-hell night in jail. An angel was looking over my shoulder in those days. So now, one of my trademark moves is to buy people close to me a watch. Like George—he still wears a Rolex I gave him as a "thank you" after my first year with the Bulls.

Anyway, we were wandering around in this French jewelry store looking for something nice for Carmen. Turned out she didn't need any help. The girl felt perfectly at home in a jewelry store. While she didn't get a watch, she did pick out these nice diamond earrings, this nice diamond necklace, this nice diamond ankle bracelet, and this nice diamond toe ring. The prices were marked in francs so at first I didn't know what the hell I was getting into. Then they brought me the American Express thing to sign, the total translated into good old American dollars. My hands started shaking. I started to hyperventilate. I went outside and sat on the steps, and George joined me, placing his hand on my shoulder.

"You okay?" he asked.

I shook my head.

"You know, if this relationship with Carmen doesn't work out, you have to get all this shit back."

My three-year run with the Bulls was over, I wasn't sure I'd even have a job the next year, and this wasn't some $10,000 outfit at Versace or even a $50,000 Mercedes. I was about to sign for $250,000 worth of jewelry.

Carmen took off for L.A. with her bling, and a few weeks later, the film wrapped. The night I got home, George and I took the Bentley into L.A to have dinner with Carmen and some friends, and afterwards we went clubbing, hitting every joint in town. When it came time to leave, George was driving, Floyd "Mr. Social" Ragland was in the passenger seat, and Carmen and I were in the back. Within 10 or 15 minutes, Floyd was passed out, slumped against the passenger side door, and Carmen and I were naked in the back seat.

George was like, "I'm over this shit," and he's flying down the road at 80 miles per hour trying to get us back to my house in Newport Beach. Yet, for George, this backseat coupling turned out to be more than the usual heels-to-the-back-of-the-driver's-head routine, turning into what almost amounted to a three-way.

At the beginning, Carmen was facing me, sitting straight up in my lap. Then she started to bend over backwards. First, her hand was on George's shoulder, then on the dash, and, before it was over, her torso was arched like a bridge over the front seat—all but lying on top of Floyd, who had chosen a very bad time to pass out. As for George, if he had turned his head, he would have gotten a nipple up the nose. Now Carmen, she's not what you'd call a shy, retiring flower, and she really didn't give a shit. After a while, she even struck up this running conversation with George.

"George, would you tell Dennis to stop? I'm getting tired."

"Sweetheart," said George, trying to keep his eyes glued to the road, "all you have to do is get off him."

Then she gave up on George and went directly to the source.

"Honey," she said to me, "I'm getting tired."

I laid off. I'd like to think that I laid off for good—George says that's not how it happened.

"It was like a *Three Stooges* skit," George recalled. "Dennis would wait like 30 seconds, then he'd say, 'Are you okay?' Then he'd start up again. Then she'd be like, 'George, I'm tired. Dennis?' He'd stop for 30 seconds, start up again, all the way to Newport Beach."

Now George denies ever slowing down to prolong the show, but the evidence is stacked against him. For while it may have been very late and very dark, this was a busy California freeway, and there was always oncoming traffic, headlights flashing across Carmen's naked body. Then there was the up close and personal *Debbie-Does-Dallas* soundtrack. What we're talking about here is a live sex show featuring one of America's leading sex symbols being witnessed by a man who confesses to having had a hard-on that he "could have chopped a tree down with."

Didn't slow down?

Shit, I would have.

About this time, word got out that Carmen and I were seeing each other. Now there truly was a threesome: Carmen, me, and the media.

CHAPTER SEVEN

THE MARRYING KIND

One night Carmen and I were out drinking in Newport Beach, my hometown, and we decided to fly to Vegas. Then we decided since we were going to be in Vegas anyway, we might as well get married. Made perfect sense to a couple of drunk people. So Carmen called her best friend and a couple of other folks to be witnesses, somebody thought to bring roses, and we were on the way to the airport in the Bentley—George Triantafillo at the wheel.

So far, so good.

Carmen and I had been talking about marriage off and on, seriously and not so seriously, drunk and sober ever since Toronto. Today if someone asks me who was hottest on the idea, I'd have to say that tilts in favor of Carmen. She was the girl—no big news there. Not that I wasn't for it. I was just waiting for the right moment. So were my handlers.

George, my then agent, Dwight Manley, and my lawyer didn't want to see me lose everything I had to some gold-digging scumbag. Long before Carmen came along, they had a contingency plan in place. At any serious mention of marriage, George was to call Manley and then stall until somebody got there with the papers.

Anybody who wanted to marry Dennis Rodman had to sign a pre-nup agreement. Once the girl signed, I could do whatever I wanted.

No signature, no marriage.

So George woke up Dwight Manley.

"Dennis wants to get married," he said.

"Not until she signs," said Dwight, as he dispatched my lawyer to the airport.

When we pulled up on the tarmac at the Orange County Airport, the plane was all gassed up, ready to go. George pulled the pilot aside.

"We can't go yet," he said. "We're waiting for somebody."

"Bullshit!" I said. Pre-nup or no pre-nup, I wasn't going to wait. "We're leaving now," I said, and everyone got on the plane.

The pilot shrugged. "He's paying the bills," he said to George. "We're leaving."

Clearly, this was a guy who didn't know George Triantafillo.

"No way," George said. "If you start that son of a bitch, I'll blow a hole in the engine."

The pilot was bug-eyed. I don't know what he was more worried about—the plane or George packing heat.

"That's a million dollars," the pilot said.

"Dennis can afford it," said George.

Then the pilot, co-pilot, and ground crew gathered around and started yapping about George's threat, and if they could get past that, whether it was legal for George to get on the plane with a gun. I tried to get them back on track.

"Come on, let's go, fuck it! I don't need no stinking pre-nup. She doesn't want my money. She loves me."

The pilot came out of the confab and informed us that he wasn't flying anywhere with all the hassle. That was when I fired George for the millionth time.

"Cool," said George, "but since you owe me a shit-load of money, I'll be taking the Bentley."

"Fine," I said. "Go fuck yourself."

By this time, Carmen had started crying. I couldn't handle that.

"Fuck the plane," I said. "We'll drive to Vegas. George, give me the keys."

"Don't you remember, you gave me the car," said George.

"Okay, whatever. Drive us to Vegas."

"You fired me. I'm not driving your ass anywhere."

"Okay, you're rehired. Drive."

"It's not that easy."

"I'll double your salary."

Done. So we were off to Vegas—I thought. Before we could get back in the car, George put in another call to Manley.

"Just drive them around in circles until they pass out," said Manley. "I'll meet you at Dennis's beach house."

About an hour later, I woke up just as we pulled into my garage at Newport Beach. "What the fuck is this?" I said. "We were supposed to go to Vegas."

"Vegas is closed," said George.

Motherfucker.

After that miscue, Carmen and I were even more determined. We kept trying to get married, trying to get married. Would you call that stupid? Would you call that idiotic? Would you call that downright immature? I don't know what it was, but we wanted to get married so badly. It was something within us that wanted us to be together—almost as if it was out of our control. It's amazing we didn't get married sooner than we did.

✦ ✦ ✦ ✦ ✦

Las Vegas, November 14, 1998. It was five o'clock in the morning and my right-hand man Thaer Mustafa and I were playing blackjack, winning for a change, at the Hard Rock. We had been up all night, of course, and I was pretty much wasted. Carmen had gone to bed hours before.

"Go get Carmen," I suddenly said to Thaer. "I want to talk to her."

Thaer knew better. Wake Carmen up, and you have a hornet's nest. She's throwing shit—yelling and screaming. There has to be a fire in the building to get her out of bed.

"You nuts?" answered Thaer. "I'm not doing shit."

I went to my backup, this goofy security guard we had hired for the trip. This guy thought he was James Bond, but was really more like Barney Fife. So I called the clueless one over, whispered something in his ear, and he was gone. Thaer shook his head, expecting we had a 911 call in our future.

About an hour later, Deputy Fife and Carmen showed up, and Thaer couldn't believe it. Carmen's make-up alone usually took that long, but there she stood. Thaer asked me how Fife got her moving.

"I told him to tell her, 'Get up. Dennis wants to get married.'"

Thaer was like, "Holy shit!" He even seemed happy for me for about a minute. Then he started worrying. "You're wasted, I'm wasted," he said. "How you going to get married right now?"

"Fuck it," I said. "I love her. I want to get married."

And this time, it wasn't even faintly her idea. The four of us borrowed this Range Rover and headed over to city hall to get a license. It was maybe 7:00 a.m., and there was already a line. We paid our $35, and, license in hand, took off for this chapel that I knew about because it is right next to Olympic Gardens—my favorite strip club. The chapel was named "The Little Chapel of the Flowers."

We woke up the reverend, opted for the basic $185 wedding package, which included "the groom's boutonnière," according to the *New York Post*, and Barney Fife went to work. He practically frisked the reverend before beginning a search for cameras and microphones. He was looking behind pictures, shining a flashlight into air vents, crawling around on the floor, looking under benches. Thaer and Carmen were making fun of the guy. Finally I said, "Dude, come on. That's enough. Let's get on with it."

We were standing there at the altar, Carmen wearing "a dark colored pants suit and a black leather jacket," and me "a baseball cap and khaki shirt," according to the *Post*, and the reverend wanted to know if there was a ring.

Yes and no.

Carmen was wearing this, like, $80,000 ring that I'd bought her. It wasn't a wedding ring, but it would pass. The reverend took the ring and started talking about unity, what the ring symbolized. He was going on and on and on because it was Dennis Rodman and Carmen Electra. He was putting on a show, really getting into it.

Finally, I'd had enough.

"Listen, dude," I said. "Get on with this bullshit before I change my mind."

That set Thaer off, and he fell on the floor laughing. Carmen? Most women would go, "What'd you say?" and stomp out. Carmen didn't blink an eye. She just looked at me and smiled. The reverend was shocked. I turned around to tell Thaer to chill, and then I started laughing.

Somehow, we made it through our vows, and, the deed done, the question was what to do for a reception.

"Why don't we go to a strip bar?" I suggested.

Carmen was like, "I can't. I have to get back to L.A."

Some work thing. A *Hyperion Bay* shoot, I think. I had a car drop her off at the airport and ended up spending my wedding night, morning, whatever, partying with Thaer and Barney Fife.

Years later Carmen told a reporter for a website called FemaleFirst.co.uk that she knew the marriage was a mistake from the first, and she "... had a feeling of dread as soon as she got on the plane."

"When I married Dennis, deep down I knew it was stupid," she said.

Bullshit. She's just trying to rewrite history. If ever there was a couple in love, it was us. I'll go to my grave believing that.

The wedding was all over the news within an hour of us leaving the chapel.

Enter the spin doctors.

"From what I can determine, it's not legal. It sounds like he was deeply intoxicated," my agent at the time, Dwight Manley, told the *New York Post* two days after the wedding. "Obviously, anyone that would marry someone that was intoxicated to the point that they couldn't speak or stand had ulterior motives of some sort." The word "leeches" made it into print.

Manley's spin was that this shameless gold digger named Carmen Electra had tricked a shit-faced Dennis Rodman into getting married. Carmen's publicist was quick to deny it, "Inaccurate and untrue," she said.

But Manley's version stuck. Even today, the average person you ask on the street will tell you the same thing: Carmen scammed Dennis.

What a crock.

I heard Manley's spin, and I was like "What the fuck?" My publicist sent a handwritten note to Carmen's publicist, which appeared in print the next day.

"I love Carmen and am proud to be married to her," the note read. "I apologize for any false statements given on my behalf regarding my marriage to Carmen Electra."

I don't remember this, but later Carmen would tell the *Post* that she "... drove out to see me to try and figure out what was going on. We watched it [the Manley statement] together on every news channel."

Carmen was way pissed, of course. We ended up fighting, fighting, fighting—trying to figure out what to do about it.

She's like, "End it! End it! End it!" meaning the marriage, so the public wouldn't think she was some kind of conniving bitch. So we came up with this idea for an annulment. At that point, I was willing do anything to make her happy—so I'm like, "Where do I sign?"

What came next made it seem like I was schizo, listening to my Carmen-loving heart one day, my Carmen-hating handlers the next—but that's not the way it went down. I was just trying to get the annulment done as fast as possible so Carmen and I could start fresh.

My lawyer filed the papers on November 23, 1998. The marriage was nine days old. In California, there is a form for just such sad occasions, the "FL-100," which offers six—and only six—grounds for annulment. If you're going for a divorce or separation, you have the nice, vague "irreconcilable differences." But for an annulment, the only categories are: "petitioner's age at time of marriage," "prior existing marriage," "unsound mind," "fraud," "force," and "physical incapacity." That's it. Me? I don't give a shit. Just get it done. So my handlers huddle, and they go with what they got. Since nothing else even remotely applies, they check the boxes marked:

☑ Unsound mind (as in plastered)

☑ Fraud

In other words, we were back where we started.

"IT WAS LIQUOR AFTER ALL," screamed the *New York Post*, reporting on what they called a "bizarre flip-flop."

Instead of clearing Carmen of charges of being a conniving bitch, the annulment papers reinforced the notion. The whole thing had backfired—and my signature is right there on the goddamn form. Did I read what I was signing? Nope. Did I ever tell anyone I was too drunk to know what I was doing? Nope. I'm not sure my lawyer understood the nuances of the situation.

"Dennis alleges he was so inebriated at the nuptials that he didn't know which end was up, what he was doing," he told the media.

Carmen's publicist countered, but it was too late. The damage was re-done. "Carmen and Dennis mutually agreed upon the termination of this marriage several days ago," the publicist said, "due to all the events that occurred."

What-fucking-ever.

Meanwhile an enterprising reporter for the *Post* talked to folks at the Clark County Marriage License Bureau and the Little Chapel of Flowers in Vegas.

Both denied I was drunk. "We don't issue a license if they are intoxicated, no matter who they are," said a license bureau supervisor.

The clerk who actually sold us the license said, "He was fine as far as I could tell."

"He was not intoxicated," said somebody from the wedding chapel. "He said so himself, and you should take his word for it."

Even Carmen waded in. "I've seen Dennis drunk before,"—no shit?—"and he didn't seem drunk," she told *People* Magazine.

"I asked him, 'Dennis, is this really something you want to do?' He said, 'Yes,' and he asked me the same question, and I said, 'Yes.'"

Drunk, not drunk, it doesn't matter. I knew exactly what I was doing.

The act may have been impulsive, but the sentiment was not. Carmen and I were crazy in love, and we were going to get married sooner or later, one way or another. It was inevitable. Now staying married—that was something altogether different.

By the way, the annulment didn't take.

Why? I don't know.

Despite all the uproar, Carmen and I were still married and looking to the future. Anyone trying to keep up with what was going on with us, need only have read the *Post*:

New York Post—December 8, 1998: "She's a very classy woman, no matter what my manager or anyone said about that she conned me," Rodman says, "You don't have to be drunk to want to marry a woman like that. That decision I made was my decision and hopefully stays."

New York Post—December 11, 1998: "I am still in love with him," Electra says. "There is possibly a future for my relationship."

Chicago Tribune—January 20, 1999: "As of Tuesday, [Dwight Manley] was Rodman's former agent."

New York Post—January 23, 1999: "Electra appeared on the Howard Stern show ... [and] said the marriage is solid despite reports her hubby is two-timing her with Scores dancer Stacey Yarborough."

New York Post—February 6, 1999: "After only three episodes starring Carmen Electra-the former *Baywatch* babe who married NBA star Dennis Rodman—the WB is pulling her struggling drama *Hyperion Bay* off the air."

New York Post—February 23, 1999: "Rodman signed with the Lakers and the couple were 'lovey-dovey,' as the *New York Post* would report later, Rodman claiming he and Electra 'were happily married, but living in separate homes.'"

✦ ✦ ✦ ✦ ✦

After I signed with the Lakers, Carmen played the dutiful NBA wife, coming to games and all that shit. Of course, she never made it until halftime, and my right-hand man, Thaer Mustafa, was pissed from having to wait for her to get her shit together. I understood that. She was now a big-time celebrity, thanks to me, and the spotlight was going to be on her so she was feeling the pressure to look good. All I was saying was, "Start earlier." Coming in late shows disrespect.

Anyway, when she finally arrived, it was more of the same. She was signing autographs, not paying attention to what's going on.

Thaer was like, "This is your husband—watch the fucking ball game."

Come a television timeout, she was dancing, and people in the stands were going crazy. Now I'll admit the girl can dance, but this ain't her show. This is a fucking basketball game. So I'm the frustrated husband, signaling "Sit her ass down! Get her to stop!" to Thaer. Not much chance of that—she was a whore for attention.

But I have to admit: the girl looked fine, and she was mine.

Looking back now, I realize that those early months were about as good as it would get for Carmen and me. Of course, I managed to fuck it up. I don't know what I was thinking. There I was, 37 years old, and it had finally happened. I had met the love of my life and married her. It should have been a done deal. But three months into a marriage where I was supposed to be "forsaking all others," I was still partying my ass off.

Same old Dennis.

Comes the inevitable in late March of 1999. I was still with the Lakers, Carmen was out of pocket somewhere, and, following a 99-91 win over the New York Knicks, I was holed up with female company at the Four Seasons Hotel in Beverly Hills. Another one of those enterprising reporters, this one from the London *Times*, would report I was in Room 821. Whatever the room, I was having a large time.

Then Carmen showed up.

I had come close to being caught red-handed before we were married. I was having a beach party at my Newport Beach house, 300-400 people, and the "adult industry" showed up. One of the girls took a liking to me, and we did what we did. Somehow, Carmen got wind of the party. She walked in the door, looking like the Bulls' logo—smoke pouring out her nose. First, she cornered the girl, and then she turned on me.

"Did you screw her?" she asked. "Did you screw that porn star?"

"Yes," I said. "As a matter of fact, I did."

World War III.

It's one thing to suspect somebody might be fooling around on you—it's quite another to stand there face to face with the slut-ho competition.

But that was nothing compared to what was about to happen at the Beverly Hills Hotel. This dumb ass, who to this day bills himself as a super bodyguard, let five-foot-four Carmen Electra bully her way into the bedroom, where I was in bed with not one, but two girls—a buck naked ex-girlfriend who happened to be a masseuse and a *Playboy/Penthouse* model wearing one of *my* T-shirts. As for me, I had my earrings on.

It was like the *Jerry Springer Show*.

"Carmen went ballistic. She yanked the covers off the bed and started screaming at us," the *Playboy* model told the London *Times*. "The whole thing was a nightmare. She was jumping up and down on the bed, screaming and cursing at the three of us."

"The other woman and I were cowering in bed, while Dennis was lying back as though he hadn't a care in the world," the woman continued. "He said he had never seen me before, as if I just dropped through the ceiling and happened to land on his bed."

After about 15 minutes of this, Carmen left—but she wasn't done with my ass.

No, No, No. …

Later she was like, "Fuck you! Fuck you! Fuck You! I'm going to be with somebody that's going to treat me right."

Who could blame her? You can't fuck with a girl's emotions like that—not that I meant to. I was just doing what I did, just being

Dennis. And the *Playboy/Penthouse* woman had gone on and on and on in the *Times*, saying the "sex was fabulous," and "we probably did just about everything two women and a man can do in bed."

Now I had not only cheated on Carmen, but, with a little help from the media, I had embarrassed her in front of the world. I loved her, but I guess I didn't show it.

We broke up, and I tried and tried and tried to get her back, but when you fuck up like that—get caught with another woman, make that two women—that's probably the last straw. Still, I did everything I could to get her back, to get the magic back: flowers, gifts, crying jags, the whole deal.

Nothing worked. Nothing new.

No matter whom I've dated, it has always come down to that fateful day where she's sitting here, I'm sitting there, and she's asking, "Did you sleep with this girl? Did you sleep with that girl? Are you going sleep with that girl?"

Being straight up, real, I say, "Yep, yep, yep."

You want Dennis Rodman? You have to accept the whole package. I don't want to be your boyfriend if you'll feel degraded when I sleep around. Don't want that. We'll just be friends. Carmen and I decided together that, since being married to me was hurting her so badly, we'd get divorced and try to date again, which seemed logical—so that's what we did.

New York Post—April 7, 1999: "'Carmen Electra and Dennis Rodman have announced they have mutually agreed to end their six-month-old marriage under amiable circumstances,' said the couple's spokesman. 'Miss Electra and Mr. Rodman are and will remain friends.'"

Turned out I was dead right about one thing: when we got divorced, Carmen didn't want anything—not a penny.

Nothing, zilch, zero.

About a week after Carmen filed, the Lakers let my ass go after only 23 games. The grounds?

"Irreconcilable differences."

Carmen started dating other people—rock stars Tommy Lee and Fred Durst—and we went for weeks without seeing each other or talking or connecting at all. I went nuts, trying to get her on the phone, driving by her house in the middle of the night, this and that. At my worst, I was curled in a ball moaning, repeatedly screaming, "I fucked up! I fucked up! I fucked up!" I was punishing myself for not being with her.

Most of the time, when I want to get over somebody, I go out and have sex with other girls.

Sleep with this girl.

Sleep with that girl.

But even that didn't stop the pain.

Carmen must have been feeling the same way, because we got back together for a little bit, but because of the things I'd done and the things she'd done, it was never quite the same. I even stripped for her—she loved that—did this, did that.

All kinds of crazy shit.

Nothing. There was no turning back. Still, we continued to date off and on, going nowhere, until the fall of 1999 and the beginning of the end in South Bee-itch—Miami, baby—playground of the stars.

CHAPTER EIGHT

THE PASTA THING

Miami, Friday, November 5, 1999. According to police reports, she—Patrick, Tara Leigh, "alias Carmen Electra"—and I—Rodman, Dennis Keith, "alias 'The Worm,'"—had very different versions of what exactly led to the late-night brawl. About all we agreed on was that we had been clubbing and drinking the night away in South Beach before returning to Room 302—my suite at the swanky Bentley Hotel—around 4:30 a.m.

I was in town to work on a movie called *Cutaway*, starring me, Tom Berenger and Stephen Baldwin. The script involved a skydiving cop putting the hurt on skydiving drug dealers or something like that. Carmen had come down to visit, and we were all staying at the Miccosukee Resort and Convention Center, a Miccosukee-Indian-run hotel in the Everglades National Park near our shooting location. I soon decided that was too far from the action, and I booked us another set of rooms at the Bentley in South Beach. That's where we were when the brouhaha began.

In Carmen's version, we were "watching MTV together when Co-Defendant [me] became agitated when Defendant's [Carmen's] ex-boyfriend appeared in a video."

I was supposed to have said, "You fucking whore! Get the fuck out! Go with Fred!"

(That would be Fred Durst of the rock band Limp Bizkit.)

This was all total horseshit—pure fiction—not that I did any better.

I told the cops that the "Defendant" (that would be me) was asleep—passed out actually—when "Co-Defendant (Carmen) began poking Defendant with a rose stem."

That too was horseshit.

Here was when what we told the cops and the truth began to converge.

Big picture: For whatever reason, a knockdown, drag-out fight ensued that went up one side that hotel and down the other. I really don't remember much of this, a fleeting detail here and there—forget the sequence of events—since I was, you guessed it, "shit-faced."

Here's a blow-by-blow pieced together using media accounts, the statements Carmen and I gave to the cops, and Thaer Mustafa's recollections.

First, after the opening blow-up, Carmen claimed that I "forcibly escorted" her out of my room onto a "concrete walkway," where she cut her toe. I then "slammed the door." She came storming back inside, "punching Co-Defendant about his body [yelling], 'How could you do this to me?'" as my statement put it.

We then "began to wrestle on the bed." Carmen claimed she got "hit on the left side of her head"—could have happened, but it wasn't on purpose—and "in fear for her safety, fled the hotel room and went upstairs to Witness #1's [that would be Thaer's] room."

Now, anyone who believes Carmen Electra was "in fear for her safety," wasn't there and obviously doesn't know the girl. This 110-pound hellion jumped my 230-pound ass, and it was all I could do to keep her off me.

That I remember.

So Carmen "fled" to Thaer's room, by her account, telling the cops she wanted him to help her get the hell out of there. I stomped in.

"'You want your fucking purse?'" I supposedly yelled.

I "threw her black purse at her, hitting her in the face." That resulted in a "fat lip" as the *New York Post* phrased it. Then Carmen "fled to the lobby and waited for her limousine."

I was right behind her.

"Look in your purse," I yelled. "You're not going anywhere." I had hidden her identification, passport, and credit cards. Somewhere in the report, Carmen claims that I "tore a silver chain off her neck." Anyway, I didn't want her to go, so I asked the desk clerk to call the cops. That was likely redundant. This was around seven o'clock in the morning, and by then, we'd been raising hell for a couple of hours. Anyway, Thaer was like, "Bad idea on the cop-calling thing," and he was trying to get Carmen out of there before they arrived to keep her from being arrested. Still under the influence, I was thinking, "If the cops come, she'll have to stay, and we can work this thing out."

Stupid.

Meanwhile Thaer finds Carmen's identication and stuff where I hid it—in the bottom of one of those big cylindrical ashtrays with sand in the top—and loads Carmen into a limo for her ride to the Miccosukee Hotel.

The cops arrived at Room 302 to find me "lying on the floor behind the door." Why? Only Herr Jägermeister knows. They reported that "the room was in disarray."

I'll say. The place was trashed. It was so bad that it looked like we had been having sex in there. Officer Paul Acosta took my statement, the cops talked the limo driver into bringing Carmen back, and Officer Christi Tanner took her statement. Officer Tanner then moved on to Thaer and took his statement.

"I told her the whole story—almost," Thaer recalled. "I left out a couple of things, like the pasta thing. I told her everything else."

"The pasta thing." Now we're getting somewhere. Let's start over.

Flashback to 4:30 a.m. in Room 302, the Bentley Luxury Suites Hotel: I was passed out face down on the bed. Carmen undressed me, and for reasons unknown, decided to give me a sponge bath.

When she was done, she was telling Thaer—why he was there I don't know—that as wonderfully nasty and kinky as I was in bed, you'd think I would grant her this one little indulgence. Then she told him what she planned on doing.

Thaer was like, "I wouldn't do that if I were you."

She was like, "He's not going to do anything, he's passed out."

Thaer says she started looking around in the kitchen for something suitable. She found this box of pasta—penne pasta—in this gift basket that had probably been there for years.

Thaer was still saying, "No, you're not—this is a really bad idea."

But she was saying, "Yes, I am; he never lets me do this to him."

Now all of us have things we will and won't do, like and don't like in bed. And sometimes you and your partner just have to agree to disagree. That's the way it was with Carmen and me—until then.

The woman is on record as saying I have "a nice butt."

A little too nice apparently.

For whatever twisted reason, Carmen would occasionally ask me to let her—"Won't hurt a bit!"—shove things up my "nice butt." But I was like, "No. No. No. Homey don't play dat."

My life-long policy has been, if you're going to be inserting anything in Dennis Rodman's butt, it best be in a hospital setting, and involve a fistful of K-Y jelly and a board-certified proctologist.

Carmen was like, "Whatever."

So the woman takes this piece of penne pasta—this uncooked, hard edged, penne pasta, a couple of inches long—and sticks it where the sun don't shine. Well now, I felt that sharp edge in my tender parts, and I came out of that bed flailing.

"What the fuck?"

I accidentally sent Carmen's tiny little ass flying. Thaer says she actually went airborne. I was trying to wake up, didn't even know I hit her. She landed on both feet and came back at me like a wounded wolverine, freaking out, hitting and slapping, trying to get at my face, yelling and screaming. I was wide awake by now, standing, buck naked, just trying to keep this whirling dervish off my ass. She was pissed because I hit her, and I was pissed—well you know why I was pissed. After a few minutes, Thaer waded in, broke it up, and took her upstairs to his room to calm her down. Then he came to check on me, and she was right behind him, still screaming. Thaer took her back up to his room and gets her calmed down again. Then I showed up in his room doing a little screaming of my own. That was when I must have thrown the purse.

"You shouldn't have hit me!" she screamed.

"You shouldn't have—you know!" I replied.

Back and forth.

Back and forth.

Her room.

Thaer's room.

My room.

The halls.

The balconies.

The lobby.

Somewhere in here, the $25,000 Rolex I had given her sailed over a balcony railing, and Thaer was out there in the bushes trying to find it. Somebody called the cops (could have been anybody, we woke up the whole hotel) about the "domestic disturbance" (wasn't anything "domesticated" about it).

Finally, after a couple of hours of this shit, things were on an even keel, and we were waiting in the lobby for the limo to take Carmen back to the Miccosukee. The hotel security guard was standing around, and Carmen started telling her story.

"Dennis hit me," she said. "He did this, he did that."

The guard looked at me, looked Carmen up and down, and said, "You probably deserved it."

Oh shit!

That did it. Looking back, I'm thinking the security guard was right. She probably did deserve it. I mean, a man's butt is his castle, but that wasn't something anybody needed to be saying aloud—not to a crazy woman. Carmen went absolutely nuts, ratcheting up to an entirely new level of full-throttle, fucking berserk.

When the limo finally arrived, Thaer literally had to pick the woman up and carry her to the car. She made her getaway, driving right by the arriving cops.

As I said, the cops talked to me, then they got on the phone with Carmen's limo driver. First, the driver claimed he didn't know where she was. Thaer had told him to keep driving, no matter what, determined to keep Carmen and me apart. But the cops were saying, "You don't bring her back, you're going to jail too." So they talked to Carmen.

All the cops knew was that two people were fighting, one a six-foot-eight man, the other a tiny woman. They didn't care who was at fault or the extent of the injuries—the cops told CNN there was "very minor facial scratching, very minor"—domestic violence was domestic violence. So when they finished listening, the cops decided they had a genuine case of "domestic battery" on their hands. They handcuffed Carmen and me and hauled us off to the Miami-Dade County Jail where we had our pictures taken.

These mug shots are far from "Nick Noltes," but they are memorable. I was wearing this shit-eating grin, looking like I'm really happy to be there. Carmen looks like she could be coaxed into a smile. If her lip was swollen, it didn't show. The only good thing to come out of this phase of our little adventure was the "note" that Officer Christi Tanner wrote to close out my official police statement.

NOTE: *After being brought to the Miami-Dade County Jail's holding facility, Defendant stated to please tell the Co-Def that he was sorry, that he overreacted, and that he loved her.*

◆ ◆ ◆ ◆ ◆

Two nights before this run-in with the law, I had met attorney Roy Black at a Miami club. Black is the guy who saved William Kennedy Smith's ass following rape charges in West Palm Beach a few years ago. He has also represented actor Kelsey Grammer, artist Peter Max, and sportscaster Marv Albert.

He gave me his card and said, "One of these days you're going to need me. Hang onto that card."

So it was Roy Black to the rescue. He sprung us for $25,000 apiece with an agreement to stay at least 500 yards from each other for 30 days.

"Charging them with this is an overreaction," he told the media. "Both of them are upset; they've been charged, and Dennis is more upset that she's been charged.

"They both told me that this was a misunderstanding between the two of them," continued Black.

I'll say—a misunderstanding about my butt.

They let us loose that afternoon.

"I'm sorry. It was just one of those situations," I told the media before leaving in a "white Mercedes," while Carmen took off in a "Chevy Blazer."

Thaer and I went back to the Miccosukee, and all I wanted to do was see Carmen, talk to Carmen—but her publicist booked her on a flight out of there. After that, we were talking every day, pushing Roy Black to get the separation order lifted. That was all we wanted. We wanted to be together. About three weeks later, prosecutors dropped the charges.

"There simply wasn't a crime," said Black, "But because of their celebrity, everyone took notice.

"[It's] typical of what happens between a married couple," Black continued.

What a fucking night.

Reality Check: Never pass out lying on your stomach.

In the battle of Miami, there were tons of fireworks, tons of light and noise, but no real damage was done—just two crazy motherfuckers having at it in a balmy climate. The real battles—the ones with the heavy artillery when the buildings were leveled and lives were lost—were triggered not by unofficial uses of pasta. The real battles, the only battles that ever mattered, were about one thing only: other women.

When I was single, I always had one main girl that I'd kind of cling to, and with the rest of them, I just had sex. The main girl usually wouldn't be sleeping with anybody else, but I would be. She would know I was fooling around, but she didn't care—or at least she wasn't telling me if she did. Some girls even seemed turned on by my philandering.

When I hooked up with Carmen, she became the main girl, and I just kept on doing what I had always been doing—didn't see any reason to change. Same thing after we were married. Carmen wasn't cool with that. Back in January of 1999, reported the *New York Post*, she told Howard Stern, "If I found out he was cheating on me, I'd leave him. I'm not going to put up with that."

Still, the entire time that I was with Carmen, I couldn't—wouldn't—stop sleeping with other women. So a couple of things came down, and Carmen was like, "You're going to have to change your ways."

I'm trying to make her believe "It'll never happen again, it'll never happen again." Meanwhile, in the back of my mind, I'm thinking, "It'll never stop happening. That's who I am."

Sometimes I wish I could actually be with one person. I've had the opportunity many, many times, but that isn't my lifestyle. Carmen wanted me to live with her, but I never did. If I had, if we had gotten a feel for each other that way, I think we'd still be married. But my lifestyle isn't to settle down with one woman, you know? My lifestyle is to go out there and be Dennis Rodman—be who I am. In my line of work, Dennis Rodman is expected to do this, this, this; but now I know that in a personal atmosphere, it doesn't work that way.

Not in the real world.

My fantasy woman would appreciate me for all the things I have done. She'd understand I might have some difficulties in life, but she would be there to support me no matter what's going on. At the same time, she'd understand that a man is a man. You can't change a leopard's spots. She'd understand that I might have a fling or two.

Yeah, right. Not going to happen.

A woman will never open her arms, and say, "You know, I'm here. Come, no matter what happens." There's always fine print, escape clauses, disclaimers, and shit. Maybe I expect too much.

✦ ✦ ✦ ✦ ✦

It wasn't meant to be with Carmen, but our love was magic while it lasted, and despite all the pain, I would never take any of it back. If I had an opportunity to have a woman in my life like her again, I would. We had a special connection.

So here's to Carmen Electra—Tara Leigh Patrick—she was a true-blue girl to me, and I have nothing but respect for her. She'll always be in my heart. If I wasn't married, if she wasn't married, who knows?

We've now come to the end of my bad-boy-meets-bad-girl, lives-noisily-ever, up-yours, can't-you-see-that-we're-busy, heartbreaking Carmen Electra love story.

What went wrong? When all was said and done, she couldn't tame the wild man—and neither could I. Our divorce became final in late 1999.

Reality Check: Like the song says, "Once you have found her, never let her go."

CHAPTER NINE

THE BATTLE OF NEWPORT BEACH

"Newport Beach was probably his downfall," Thaer Mustafa told a reporter.

"In terms of?"

"Everything. That's what screwed him up," Thaer said. "His partying. He had an unlimited number of worthless friends who would go drink with him."

"Parties every night?"

"Oh, yeah. Any time he went out, he'd bring a party home."

"What was a typical day like?"

"Drinkin'. Drinkin' every single fucking day. Every single fucking day," Thaer said. "Not one day off. If he was awake, the guy was drinking."

"He even stopped going to the gym, which is strange for him," Thaer continued. "He wasn't going to the gym at all. All he was doing was drinking."

◆ ◆ ◆ ◆ ◆

I was still playing for the Bulls when I bought the Newport Beach duplex in 1996 for $800,000 and change. It was a long way from the Dallas projects. The pink stucco, 3,500 square-foot house

79

faced what the Visitor's Bureau likes to call "pristine beaches," had a patio jutting out into the sand, and royal blue awnings shading windows upstairs and down. Nothing but sunshine and surf.

Why California? Why Newport Beach? My agent at the time, Dwight Manley, had both his office and home in Orange County. At first I thought of the duplex as a vacation home, a place to hang out and party when I was in California. I lived in the upstairs unit and converted the whole downstairs into a full-blown night club, even incorporated the garage. I added a full bar just like you'd find in a commercial club, a dance floor complete with one of those rotating mirrored balls, tables and chairs, and hung up a couple of signs: "Club 4809," on the gate out back, as in "4809 Seashore Drive," and a neon "OPEN," sign on the beach-side, second-floor balcony. The only difference between my house and an actual club was that everything was free, courtesy of the owner, one Dennis Rodman. That and the zoning. The house was in a residential area.

Early on, there weren't that many problems because I was on the road playing basketball most of the time. The real trouble began after I signed on with the Lakers in 1999 and decided to settle in Newport Beach permanently. Before that I really didn't have a home. I was basically a hotel person—a hotel junkie.

Newport Beach, the home of John Wayne until his death in 1979, was a traditional town with a bunch of old money, and in the early days I was seen as a breath of fresh air. That shit didn't last. Within months I was on a first-name basis with half the cops in town. Before I moved to Newport Beach, I had been a moving target: drunk in Vegas one day, L.A. the next. The cops would give me a break here, give me a break there, because I was "Dennis Rodman." But now I was in one place with one police force and way, way, way too much time on my hands. During my playing days, whenever I had a break I would be partying full time. Now I was on one continuous break with one continuous party. Women, sex, rock 'n' roll, you name it. When you showed up at Club 4809, better count on an all-night party. It was all good, or at least I thought so at the time.

Soon the cops started getting noise complaints from my neighbors. So the cops would show up, ask me to hold it down, and I was like, "Fuck you!"

They let it slide for as long as they could, then they went, "You know, Dennis, we can't take this anymore. Keep it up, and we're gonna have to do something."

"Have at it!" I said.

So we had this world-class pissing contest going on. "The Battle of Newport Beach," I called it. It was mostly skirmishes. We'd crank up a party, the cops would arrive and issue some kind of citation. That happened a lot—about 80 times in the eight years I lived there, if you believe the newspapers.

"Somebody is calling us," a police spokesman told the Associated Press. "We're not just going out there and finding it. People are complaining."

Then the cops started shadowing my ass. It was like, "You see that car? He drives that car. Watch him. Watch him." It got to the point where I was watched all the time.

I got my first DUI on December 22, 1999. I was hard to miss in what the AP described as a "bright yellow Volkswagen with blue flames shaped like naked women."

"We know his vehicle, and we can't just let him go," a cop told the wire service. "He's not above the law."

I pleaded guilty to that one, telling the AP, "the police were just doing their job." They fined me around $2,000 and suspended my license.

From the tone of some of the newspaper stories written at the time, you would think there was some kind of one-man crime wave going on. But actual arrests were rare. They hauled me in a couple of times for public drunkenness, once in L.A., once at the local Hooters, where I sprayed the patrons with a fire extinguisher. But with all the drinking I was doing, the real issue was never public drunkenness or driving under the influence, but noise, noise, and more noise.

In early 2001, the AP quoted from a letter one of my neighbors sent to the cops.

"I have a right to peace and quiet," the letter said. "And I would hope that the city as well as the police department can accommodate its loyal tenants, rather than appease a disgraced athlete who has nothing better to do than throw parties."

So the cops drag me into court on all these noise complaints. Sometimes I won. Sometimes they won. But all in all, nobody won. Meanwhile, my parties grew bigger and bigger, and the neighbors got madder and madder. The Newport Beach City Council took up the challenge, trying to toughen up the noise ordinances. I threatened to run for city council. *The Guardian*, a British newspaper, would report sightings of "Let Dennis Have Fun!" T-shirts. Turned out I couldn't run because I wasn't a registered voter.

The height of the Battle of Newport Beach came with the "in-your-face party" I threw to celebrate my 40th birthday. It was the biggest spectacle seen in Newport harbor since 1917, when they filmed silent film star Theda Bara in the barge scene for *Cleopatra*.

As for the birthday party, I was thinking, "You want noise? I'll give you fucking noise!" So I hired not one, but two rock bands, and at two in the afternoon on May 13, 2001, I made my grand entrance to the "B-DAY BASH," as the invitation billed it, in a helicopter that circled a a few times before landing on the beach. I was greeted by 200-300 people. Party time!

I hopped off dressed in a "red baseball cap, white shirt with orange sleeves, and baggy yellow velvet shorts," according to the *Los Angeles Times*. So did I get to enjoy my party? Nope. A couple of dozen cops showed up, some in riot gear, responding to "50 complaints from irate neighbors," as a police spokesman told the *Times*.

"They have to have permits to have live music," the spokesman told the newspaper, adding they weren't real thrilled with the helicopter landing, either. So I jawed with the cops off and on for what seemed like hours.

"We were trying to get him to obey the law without an unfortunate confrontation," Lieutenant Rich Long told the *Times*.

After the cops threatened to arrest my ass and charged me with some shit (the *Times* reported it was "three counts of disturbing the peace and one count of playing live music without a permit"), I agreed to move the party to my restaurant, Josh Slocum's, which was only a couple of miles away.

If you believe the media, up to that point the cops had been to my house more than four dozen times in the previous six years. They would make 20 more visits in the next eight months. Not for anything as spectacular as the B-DAY BASH, but enough to keep the pot boiling.

Reality Check: If you're spending more time with the cops than your kids, there could be a problem.

Lieutenant Rich Long from the police department talked to me a couple of times about my antics. "Dennis," he said, "you have to quit doing these things, because it's gonna get you in trouble and mess your life up." He was right. Nobody's going to get a life sentence for cranking up some window-rattling rock 'n' roll at two o'clock in the morning. But when you're partying so hard you absolutely don't give a fuck, shit can happen. Stuff comes up missing. People get into fights. Druggies appear. Trouble can come from even the most unexpected places.

Take the "librarian."

I was sleeping with this girl, this nice clean girl, and she wasn't really a librarian, she just looked like one. She kept coming around, coming around, and after a while she wanted more than I was willing to give.

So I was in my bedroom at the beach house one night doing what I do, and a couple of my friends spot her coming up the stairs armed with this huge steak knife. They tackled her and took the knife away. I came out to see what all the ruckus was about, and they were like, "Dennis, stop sleeping with this girl, you're making her crazy." I don't know about that, but something was making her ass crazy. Booze likely. Whatever.

That's the kind of stuff that happens when everybody is fucked up all the time. Crazy shit. I was lucky to walk away from that one unscathed and, like Lieutenant Long said, without getting in trouble and messing up my life. I mean, what if the librarian stabs me, gets stabbed herself, kills one of my friends? Life can turn on a dime.

◆ ◆ ◆ ◆ ◆

In early 2000, I was not just having trouble with the law in Newport Beach. It was more widespread than that. I had seven lawsuits pending in Las Vegas alone and three more in Los Angeles. In Vegas, four of the incidents happened at the Hilton Hotel, two on the same hell-raising night, April 19, 1998. In the first, I was said to have "sexually assaulted" this "adult entertainer" by "grabbing her breast and shaking it," according to court records quoted in the *Las Vegas Review-Journal.* In the second, I was accused of getting way too friendly with a Hilton cocktail waitress.

"He came up behind me with a bear hug and picked me up," the waitress told the *Review-Journal.* That caused her to spill the tray of drinks she was carrying. While picking her up, I was said to have placed my "hands on the sides of both her breasts."

As for the five other Vegas suits: two more women claimed I grabbed their breasts, and a third said I attacked her after she tried to take my picture in the lobby of the MGM Grand. Then there was the cashier at Caesar's Palace who claimed I "pushed-punched him," and a craps dealer at The Mirage who accused me of rubbing my dice on his bald head and privates for luck.

In L.A., two of the three lawsuits resulted from a single stay at the Argyle Hotel in October of 1998. In the first, according to court records, I was accused of "jamming a hundred-dollar bill and [my] hand down the front of [a cocktail waitress's] blouse." The second, according to the Associated Press, involved some kind of "sexual assault" on a woman who came to my hotel room expecting a party and found me alone. In the third L.A. lawsuit, also according to AP, I was accused of chest-butting this 23-year-old guy at the Fat Burger.

While these three incidents and all but one of the seven in Vegas had happened two, sometimes even three years before, they were still keeping my lawyers busy in 2000 sorting out who did what, when. Was I guilty? With a few exceptions, who knows? Since I was usually drunk, I simply didn't remember. That made it hard to come up with any kind of defense. It was their word against whomever we could round up who was sober on the night in question. Meanwhile the meter was running.

So I ended up reaching "confidential" settlements for most of the lawsuits, meaning I cut a large check that opposing lawyers couldn't talk about other than to say their client was "very pleased," "very happy" as the *Las Vegas Review-Journal* phrased it for a couple of cases. I made the whole thing worse one night when I decided to get cute on the *Tonight Show*.

"Me and my accountant decided we're gonna have, like, a $50,000 rule," I told Jay Leno.

And he was like, "What's that?"

"That's when basically if I screw up with a girl or they think I'm screwin' up, then rather than going to court, I'll just give 'em $50,000," I said.

Bad move. I figure that one cost me about $200,000. Even so, it was not a bad idea. Just one I shouldn't have been announcing on national television. It's almost always better to settle. I learned that lesson from a cheerleader.

In 1995, this NBA cheerleader I had slept with here and there for several years sued me for infecting her with herpes. Wanted me to pay her a million and a half dollars. There was just one little problem. I don't have herpes. End of story, right? Wrong. I did win the first round. My lawyers managed to convince the jury the case had nothing to do with herpes (or money, for that matter) and had everything to do with a woman being scorned. In her mind there had been some kind of serious relationship going on. Not. So the jury sided with me. Her lawyers appealed, arguing in court documents that "evidence of her prior sexual history, employment as a nude dancer, and breast augmentation surgery should have been excluded under Rule 412," whatever the fuck that is. It took several years, but I finally walked away with a victory, if you'd call it that. Legal fees for my "win" added up to about a quarter of a million dollars.

When dealing with lawsuits, it's hard to sort out the people who have good reason to be pissed at Dennis Rodman from the leeches who are just looking for a paycheck. But at the end of the day, it doesn't matter. Unless they really, really, really piss me off, I just cut their ass a check and get on with my life.

I'm not going to say how much I've pissed away on lawsuits over the years, but let's just say if I'd thrown that money into the stock market, my early retirement prospects would be greatly improved. Just another price to pay for partying, partying, partying, booze, booze, and more booze.

✦ ✦ ✦ ✦ ✦

When I first moved to Newport Beach, I thought one of the great things about having a permanent home, living in one place, would be the opportunity to make real friends, people who would always be around. It didn't work out that way. The good and bad news about me is I don't discriminate. Everybody's welcome: rich, poor; gay, straight; scumbag and model citizen. And when the big neon "Open" sign hissed on at Club 4809, that could make for an interesting collection of folk.

"The hardest thing about working with Dennis Rodman is not working with Dennis Rodman. It's dealing with the entourage," my bodyguard, Wendell, told a reporter. "Dennis himself is laid back. It's dealing with the knuckleheads that he had chosen at that time to surround himself with."

Looking back, I can see there were several categories of people always in generous supply on a given night in Newport Beach:

"Drunks," who were happy to start drinking with me at ten in the morning and stay steady at it until dawn the next day or the day after, for that matter;

"Hangers-on," whose job was to get drunk with me, laugh at my jokes, and sleep with as many women as possible, while making sure I paid for everything;

Dennis with his agent, Darren Prince.

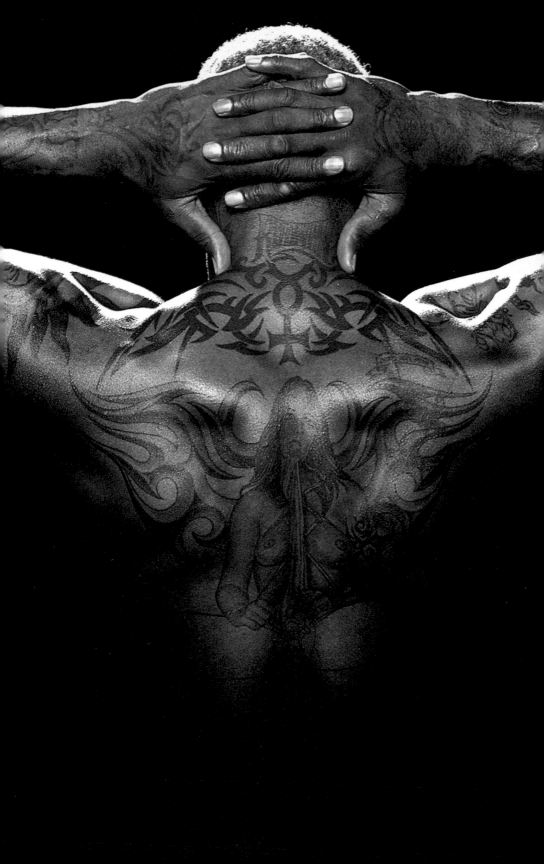

Reality Check

YOU CAN'T BE BOTH FREE AND FAMOUS

"Strays," who would hop on the Dennis Rodman party train on a given night of carousing and ride it for all it was worth;

"Sluts," who you know about.

"I can't tell you, man, how many times we came in the house at five, six o'clock in the morning, totally wasted, me having to carry him upstairs," Wendell told a reporter. "We have to stop at the Fat Burger and get a Fat Burger, him and his buddies, knocked out, with food all over them. Just food all over the place, just totally fucking wasted."

Then there were the women.

"The lifestyle he was living, that's an empty life, man," Wendell continued. "I walk in his bedroom and literally have to pick some chick up and take her home, who he didn't even know. And she didn't even know him. But then when he woke up, he'd be alone again."

Somebody once asked me, "How did partying affect your personal life in those days?"

I replied, "Bro, partying was my personal life."

And what was personal would soon start spilling over into my professional life.

Now I admit there were times when I was playing ball when partying would get in the way: I'd be hung over at practice or go missing, this, that. But in those days there was never any question about what came first. But after I moved to Newport Beach, the work-party balance flip-flopped. It was like, "We now interrupt this party for work," and not even Magic Johnson could change that.

CHAPTER TEN

MAGIC MOMENTS

Magic Johnson first tried to save my ass in 2002. He and his agent cooked up this idea for a charity event in the Hamptons, the playground of rich New Yorkers. They knew I had thrown a party or two up there, and so the agent called, and I agreed to co-host a celebrity basketball tournament. While we were talking, I told the agent that I was toying with the idea of returning to the NBA. He later mentioned it to Magic, and Magic said he'd like to help. That was huge. Magic's got a lot of credibility with GMs all over the league, and they knew, as the agent said, "He's not gonna go to bat for a guy he doesn't truly believe in." So the agent says to Magic, "Let's go down to Newport Beach and surprise Dennis with the news."

So they called ahead to my handler in Newport Beach and said they were coming at such and such a time, make sure Dennis is at Josh Slocum's. Whatever you do, don't let him leave. This was when I was binge drinking, and you just never knew. So the two of them showed up unannounced. I'd had a couple of cocktails, of course, and that made me even happier to see Magic. I was like, "Holy shit! Holy shit! Magic Johnson is here."

Magic and I hugged on each other, did a bit of catching up, and then got down to business. Magic said he could help me get on with the Knicks. He was like, "I've got a lot of pull there. If you start working out, coming up to UCLA two, three times a week, we can make this happen. But you have to cool it on the partying. The body's not gonna respond at 40 like it did at 30."

"No problem," I said.

Right before he left, Magic said, "Listen, I'm having a grand opening tomorrow for this 24-hour fitness center up in Sherman Oaks. I would love for you to come and be one of my guests."

I'm in.

All during the meeting, I'd been sizing up Magic's agent, this guy named Darren Prince. Then in his early thirties, Darren was New Jersey born and bred, and had the accent and attitude to go with it, but with a lot of heart and warmth just beneath the surface. He's not that tall, under six feet, has dark hair and is attractive enough—you should see his fiancée—but the bottom line was I liked the guy. And we had a bit of a track record. When my old agent, Dwight Manley, and I split up back in 1999, I called Darren, drunk, to see if he might be interested in representing me. He was cool with it, and he called Dwight to make sure he wasn't stepping on any toes. Dwight gave him a "thumbs up" and told him to get hold of my sister, Debra, who was then my business manager. Darren left her a ton of messages, but Debra never returned his calls. So I ended up with an agent named Steve Chasman for a couple of years.

By the time Darren and Magic came to Josh Slocum's, I was again in the market for an agent, and I was thinking, "If he's good enough for Magic Johnson. ..."

So when he was on the way out, I handed Darren this huge box of shit out of the backseat of my pickup truck, all these business proposals that had been sitting around collecting dust while I attended to the only business I really was interested in—partying. "You're now my agent," I told him. "Go through all this crap and see if we can make some money together."

I'm not sure when I actually signed with Darren, but it wasn't long after that. Why Darren took me on, I'll never know. I think maybe it had something to do with this boyish enthusiasm for sports he had developed as a kid collecting baseball cards back in New Jersey. As an adult, Darren had turned his childhood hobby into a successful sports memorabilia company before parlaying that into Prince Marketing Group, where he serves as agent and marketing guru for a long list of clients including me, Joe Frazier, and his first client, one Magic Johnson. What I really like about the guy is that when it comes to his clients, Darren is a fan first, a businessman second, and I'm thinking it was the fan in Darren that made him take on the hard case known as "Dennis Rodman."

When I arrived at the grand opening of the fitness center in Sherman Oaks the next day, around 200 people were waiting in line to get Magic's autograph. Magic had a reason for inviting me. He knew I had been roughed up a bit by the NBA since leaving the Bulls, and he wanted to boost my confidence, show me the public hadn't forgotten about Dennis Rodman. It worked. The fans spotted me, and they started screaming, "Dennis! Dennis!" The media came running over and then, in Darren's version, "Magic's line little by little started moving into the direction of Dennis."

I couldn't believe it. We're talking Magic Johnson, bro. The main man. But like Magic said, "When Dennis Rodman walks into a room, it's like everyone else becomes invisible."

I wish things had gone as well with the workouts at UCLA. I blew the first one off. Just didn't go. Second one, I got so hammered the night before, I couldn't make it. I missed the third one because of a little booze-inspired ego flare-up. I was like, "I don't need this, I can get back in the league without workouts, without Magic." So I blew a real chance to get back in the league, thanks to my drinking. It wouldn't be the last time.

There would be another little NBA nibble in 2002 courtesy of Magic. Magic was business partners with a guy named Howard Schultz, who owned the Seattle SuperSonics. He told Schultz, "You should sit down with Dennis. I think he could help your team."

So when we were in New York, Darren and I drove over to Schultz's house in the Hamptons, and he was like, "Can you help this team?"

"I can help fill the stands," I said. "I can get 11 or 12 rebounds a game, no problem. I can help young players."

A lot of these kids today are like, "I got my $50 million guaranteed, what else is there to prove?

Everything, baby. You can spend every fucking nickel of that cash, and it won't buy your ass one rebound, one basket—much less a championship. No matter how much you're making, you still have to play. That's the kind of shit I could have laid on the young players in Seattle. Shultz wasn't interested.

"Your reputation is so bad," he said, "I don't know if the city will embrace you or hate me for making a move like this."

I'm thinking, "Whatever." Some people hate me. Some people love me. But no matter where they fall, they're all buying tickets.

Then Schultz's wife came out of the house with their two sons. She was gawking, the kids holding balls they wanted autographed. She was like, "I'm sorry for interrupting, but you're my idol. I just had to come out and get an autograph and a picture."

So I was signing autographs, posing for snapshots with Schultz's family, and I leaned over and whispered in Darren's ear, "This is a guy who obviously doesn't talk things over with his wife."

I mean, the wife may not have known a damn thing about basketball, but she knew star power when she saw it. And that's what I can bring along with those dozen rebounds a game. That's what fills seats. That's what makes money. And next to winning championships, that's what the business is all about.

As for that bad-boy reputation Howard Schultz was so worried about, it was soon destined to get a hell of a lot worse.

CHAPTER ELEVEN

T.V. GUIDE

Newport Beach, September 23, 2002. It was one thing for me to get falling-down drunk and show my ass in the relative privacy of Club 4809 or Josh Slocum's. It was quite another to do it on national television. But that was the next logical step in the downward spiral of Dennis Rodman.

The *Best Damn Sports Show Period* interview was supposed to take place in L.A., and Thaer couldn't find me. Then somebody ratted, and Thaer located me and a couple of drinking buddies at a bar in Irvine.

"We gotta go," he said.

"I'm not going," I said. "Call Darren."

Darren had promised John Salley, an old Detroit teammate, I would do the interview, and they had promoted the hell out of it.

"You gotta do it," Darren told me. "If you don't, they're never gonna listen to me again. I'll lose all credibility. All my other clients will be screwed, because no one is going to take me seriously anymore."

"I'm not fucking going," I said.

Darren didn't give up. "What if I talk them into coming to your house in Newport Beach?"

Whatever.

So Thaer corralled me, gave the slip to my drinking buddies, and we went back to the beach house. Meanwhile my buddies were calling, calling, trying to get reconnected. Thaer put a stop to that.

"I grab Dennis's cell when he's not looking, turn it off," recalled Thaer. "In a minute, he's like, 'Where's my phone?' 'I dunno,' I said. 'You probably left it somewhere.'"

That's the kind of shit you can get away with when you're dealing with a drunk.

At the house, Thaer helped me clean up and get dressed. I was still drunk, but starting to level off, when the camera crew arrived and started setting up. Meanwhile I was getting thirsty.

"I'm starving," I said, for Thaer's benefit.

He wasn't buying it. "You stay here. I'll go get the food," he said, determined to keep me away from the booze until the interview was over.

But then he made the mistake of turning his back, and I was out of there. I hooked up with the girl across the street, hopped on her moped—all elbows and knees—and we disappeared. We got back a few minutes before air time, and I handed out tacos to the crew. It was like, "See, I really was hungry after all."

Thaer was shaking his head. "You're fucked up worse than you were an hour ago," he said.

I was opening my mouth to deny it when the dumb-ass moped girl said, "Yeah, we went and did shots." I'll say. Five or six in maybe half an hour. But it was too late to turn back.

The producers of the *Best Damn Sports Show Period* had done us a huge favor, scrambled together a crew at the last minute and spent like $5,000 on a helicopter to get their asses to Newport Beach on time.

So the red light comes on and things were looking good for about two seconds. Thaer had me decked out in a nice outfit, complete with shades, baseball cap, the usual. Then I opened my mouth, and it was pure liquor talking.

"John Salley! I love you, John Salley! Oh, I love you so bad. I love you so bad, John Salley!"

Thaer's like, "Oh my God!"

Then I did this scream I do when I'm drunk. Think Tarzan with a chest cold. It was a total disaster. All this live on national television.

Thaer called Darren with the news. "Your client just ruined any shot of an NBA comeback and made a complete idiot of himself," he said. "He just did an entire interview drunk."

So I ended up embarrassing myself, Darren, John Salley, and the *Best Damn Sports Show Period* and added to my rep as an unreliable flake on a downward spiral to oblivion. All in a day's work.

Reality Check: Don't drink and go live.

I had been up drinking all night before a meeting Darren had scheduled with a couple of producers from *Celebrity Mole*.

"They're coming down to find out if they want to hire you," Thaer reminded me. "You don't just have this job. Nobody wants to give you a job because you're drunk all the time."

Nobody trusted me. Nobody wanted anything to do with me because I would commit to something and then just blow it off, like I did for the ESPYs one year, or I'd show up drunk like I did for the *Best Damn Sports Show Period* fiasco. So this *Celebrity Mole* thing was a chance to redeem myself while collecting an easy $50,000. And, like Darren said, a weekly hour in primetime on a major network for a couple of months wouldn't hurt—you can't buy that kind of exposure. So he was like, "Don't blow this interview."

Me, I was thinking it was not so much the exposure or even the money I needed as the work, something to keep me busy. I knew I did better with the partying, did a better job of keeping things in balance, when I had something to do. Not that you could tell the afternoon of the interview.

I showed up drunk, Michelle by my side, and we sat around drinking wine at Josh Slocum's as Thaer prepped me on *Celebrity Mole.*

"Act like you've seen it," he said.

Whatever. I flagged down a busboy and asked him to bring us some beers out on the dock. I had decided to hold the meeting out there, because it was such a beautiful setting. Sunshine on blue water. Sleek white yachts in their slips. So it would be a business meeting with beer on the side for the boys, a bottle of wine for Michelle. Life was good.

Thaer met the two producers in the parking lot out front. They were driving what he would later describe as a "piece of shit" rental car and were wearing shorts (one in denim cut-offs), T-shirts, and sneakers. They didn't look like people anybody would take seriously. We all sat down, I offered them a beer, they accepted, and then they began this long, boring song and dance about *Celebrity Mole.* It was going to be shot in Yucatan. The idea was to identify the traitor, the mole, who was "sabotaging" everything. There were games. Quizzes. Stephen Baldwin, my old co-star from *Cutaway,* was one of the nine celebrities in the cast. Blah. Blah. Blah.

I was about to nod off when I heard a plane fly over. I looked up. "That's a G-5," I said. Then I started reeling off imaginary specs for the plane. The two guys looked at each other.

Thaer jumped in and steered me back into *Celebrity Mole* mode. The producers started yapping again. I heard a boat, looked over, made up a name for it, and ad-libbed some more imaginary specs.

"I mean he was talking out his ass to these guys," Thaer recalled. "Complete gibberish."

Finally one of the producers tires of all the chatter about boats and planes and cuts to the chase.

"Dennis, have you ever seen the show?" he asked.

"Fuck the show!" I said.

Thaer was thinking, "Oh shit!"

"What he means is the particular show doesn't matter," Thaer said. "He could do any show."

Nice try. I figured we were fucked. Not that I really gave a shit. Now Darren, that's a different story. He'd been trying to put this gig together for months, and he wasn't about to let it go.

"We gotta fix this," Darren told Thaer.

So after talking to Thaer, Darren called the casting agent. The plan was to get to her before the two producers could tell her, "This guy's a flake," he's this, he's that.

"I just talked to Dennis," Darren told the woman. "What's with these two guys you sent down here? Dennis thought they were pulling some kind of joke on him."

She was like, "What?"

Then he told her how these two dudes showed up in a crummy car wearing shorts and T-shirts, were drinking beer during a business meeting, and how I thought I was being punked.

She was like, "Are you kidding?"

"No. No, I'm not," said Darren.

Fifteen minutes later, Thaer calls her with the same story. The guys were dressed like bums, Dennis thought they were a joke, this and that.

So when the two producers got back and said, this guy's bad news, this guy's a drunk, whatever, she had a ready explanation. It was all a big misunderstanding. Dennis wasn't wasted, he was just playing with you.

Yada, yada, yada.

It worked. Darren and the casting agent sealed the deal, she said she liked my "Who-gives-a-shit?" attitude, and soon Michelle and I were enjoying an all-expenses-paid trip to Mexico, which we turned into a working honeymoon.

For real.

Michelle made an honest man out of me at the Orange County Court House on my birthday, May 13, 2003, and we left the next day for the *Celebrity Mole* shoot in Mexico with Darren and Thaer in tow. At that time, Michelle and I had been together for about four years and had two kids. So it wasn't like we needed a honeymoon to get the sex life up to speed or anything.

We spent two weeks south of the border and, while I did get drunk a couple of times, it was nothing major. I was working, so I didn't drink as much. Off set, anyway.

In what would end up being in Episode 4, *Mole* host Ahmad Rashad gave four of us, me and these three girls, the chance to make some easy money if we would eat the worm from the bottom of a bottle of Tequila. The girls were grossed out. So I went, "Fuck it. I'll eat the worm. I'll eat everybody's worm," like I was doing them a big favor, you know? So I downed, I think it was, four Tequila shooters with worms, we made $6,000 on the deal, and the girls made me out to be this big hero. "Oh, thank you, Dennis. Thank you. Thank you."

Me, I was just taking advantage of an opportunity to have a couple of drinks.

When the Mexican part of the shoot wrapped in late May, the production moved back to L.A. for the big finale. I holed up in Newport Beach for a few days and soon was back to my bad habits. Come the day of the finale shoot, I was upstairs in the beach-house duplex sleeping one off with the doors locked, not answering any calls. The way the house was laid out you had to go through two locked doors to get to my unit. Thaer had been through all this before—me not answering the door, hiding out, refusing to do what I was supposed to do. So he had gotten with the cleaning crew and had a couple of keys made without me knowing about it. So I was lying in bed, and I heard the key turning in the lock. No problem. I had latched the door. That didn't stop Thaer. He knocked the fucking door down and came barreling in the room under a full head of steam.

"Get up! Get in the fucking shower!" he shouted. "You're going to do this show!"

"Fuck it! I ain't going," I said, and jumped up like I wanted to fight. He pushed me back down on the bed.

"He knew by the tone of my voice I wasn't fucking with him," Thaer recalled. "I was gonna whip his ass, or he was gonna go to the show."

I don't think there was much chance of him whipping my ass, but I went along anyway. At that point, there were only two contestants left in the *Celebrity Mole* competition, and I had a chance to win a whole lot of money. Not that I would make it easy for Thaer or the producers.

About three hours after Thaer dropped me off at the hotel in L.A., the producers were calling him. "Where's Dennis? Do you know where Dennis is?" Thaer called some of his spies and they got me back in time.

It was never easy with Dennis Rodman.

Long story short, I ended up winning the damn thing. I figured out who the mole was and got more right answers on the final quiz. Sound like silly horseshit? Maybe so. But the payday was good. I made $220,000. Not bad for a drunk who *Mole* fans slammed for not taking note one during the competition.

We wrapped the show in late spring, and the only thing left was to keep my big mouth shut until the series aired in January. Now I'm a guy who can't keep a secret sober—forget drunk. But if I had let on who the mole was, who won the game, it would have cost me millions, or at least that's what the contract said. So I just kept on doing what I did on the show. You know how everybody went around saying "I'm the mole, I'm the mole"? Well, I just kept that shit up for however long it was.

"I'm the mole," I said.

"No, Dennis, really come on."

"Yeah, I'm the mole."

It was like that was the last leg of the competition. To really win, you had to keep your mouth shut. And I'm nothing if not a competitor. So I walk away with it all. Advantage Rodman.

For me, television has always been a crap shoot. Win some. Lose some. The *Best Damn Sports Show Period* interview had been a total disaster, *Celebrity Mole* a major triumph that proved that, partying or not, I could still focus when I had to, just like when I was in the NBA. And, to outsiders at least, it looked like I had really turned my life around. Nope.

Reality Check: Television giveth and television taketh away.

CHAPTER TWELVE

SPORTS SINNER

Newport Beach, September 6, 2003. It's amazing it took them as long as it did. Like Michelle told them, "The last three years for Dennis have been a party. Nothing but drinkin' and drinkin' and drinkin'."

But we were about midway through the five-month shoot for a two-part reality show called *Rodman on the Rebound,* and ESPN still hadn't caught me drunk on camera. They had missed a big opportunity on the afternoon of September 2, when the cops cited me for "public drunkenness" after spotting me, literally, falling-down drunk on the dock outside of Josh Slocum's. ESPN would make up for it four days later.

On that balmy evening in early September, I was in the parking lot welcoming people to Josh Slocum's, which, as the sign says, offers "seafood, fine meals, and libations." Lots of libations. Decked out in a black T-shirt, blue baseball cap, and jeans, I tried to usher three girls inside as the ESPN camera rolled.

I give one of the girls a half-hug.

"We heard this place was fun," she said.

"Oh, honey, it *is* fun," I replied, slurring my words. And on this particular night, it was going to be a real fucking barrel of laughs.

Cut to dancing inside.

"Right now, what Dennis cares about is drinking," said my wife Michelle on camera.

To prove it, ESPN would soon follow Michelle's sound bite with video of the raving-drunk, "Mr. Entertainment," Dennis Rodman. By the time this tape was shot, it was after legal drinking hours, sometime after 2:00 a.m., and the joint was empty. Just me, Thaer, Darren, and Michelle hanging out in the back, me holding court.

I sat in the middle in a blue easy chair, Darren on the right in an identical chair. Michelle was seated to his right, Thaer standing off to the left. As I raved, a lazy blue strobe light swept over the dimly lit scene, at times being picked up by the mirrors on the back wall. First, I dissed Darren.

"I don't need you," I said. "Seriously, I'm gonna tell you right now, I don't need you for nothing."

Darren was smiling, but that wouldn't last.

Then I moved on to Thaer. "You know what, Thaer? I don't need you. I don't need you at all," I said, raising my voice. "I made my career without your ass. Hello!" I gestured wildly, huge hands clawing the air.

Cut to Darren. He wasn't smiling anymore. His client was showing his ass on videotape that would be seen by a gazillion viewers on ESPN.

"You swore to me you'd be on the court," Thaer said, bringing up my NBA ambitions. "I think you will be on the court, but not if you keep drinkin' like this."

That called for a little historical perspective, and I jogged his memory, saying I had partied a lot harder in Chicago and still pulled down umpteen rebounds a game. Thaer pointed out I had been a lot younger. Then Michelle weighed in, my favorite bad girl sounding like she was auditioning for a shot on Oprah.

I sat there playing with my fingers, biting my lip, looking like an eight-year-old boy being chewed out by a grouchy school marm as my favorite drinking, smoking, tattooed, beautiful, blonde delivered a mini-lecture on "family values," reminding me that I had a wife and kids now and needed to clean up my act.

From Michelle, ESPN cut back to me and I was crying. What brought it on, other than a river of booze, I don't know. Anybody hip to the ways of television knows I actually could have tuned up right after Michelle's lecture or they could have caught me on tape an hour later and put the two together in the editing room. What I'm saying is: I have no idea why I was suddenly crying.

"I know I fucked my life up. I did it," I said, blubbering. "Everybody thinks I'm stupid. I'm not stupid, you know. I made my life what it is."

And apparently I wasn't real happy with the way that life turned out. ESPN closed out this segment with the camera still on me, as I, still crying, mumbled, "It's all love. It's all love. It's all love." Long, long pause. "It's all love."

I didn't look like a guy who would be returning to the NBA anytime soon. I looked like a drunk on his final glide path into oblivion. Commercial break. Thank God.

Ever think you were the life of the party and then see snapshots, video, of yourself and think, "Oh shit! Who is that fool? That drunk?" That's what watching *Rodman on the Rebound* was like for me.

The reality series was supposed to tell a feel-good story about Dennis Rodman's comeback to the NBA. But what ESPN would catch on tape was not my comeback, but my downfall, arriving just in time to see me bottom out, personally and professionally.

So why did I drink?

"He can't stand being famous. He can't stand the fact that he can't go anywhere without people bothering him," Darren told a reporter. "And the only way to feel comfortable with the public is to drink."

"When you're drinking every day, you're suffering inside," Wendell told the same reporter. "Dennis is an extremely introverted person, extremely introverted. Yet he placed himself in an extroverted position, meaning a basketball superstar. So in order to deal with what that comes with, he [turned to] alcohol."

"His image is playboy, wild man–slash–superstar athlete," Thaer told ESPN. "And no matter what he does, he has to keep up that image, whether he wants to or not."

So why do I think I drank? At first, I drank because I enjoyed it. I drank because I loved to have a good time. Then I drank, drank myself silly, so I didn't have to think about all the shit that had happened to me in my career and in life in general. Shit like getting canned by the Lakers and the Mavericks, marrying and divorcing Carmen Electra, parting ways with my longtime agent/friend Dwight Manley, and firing my sister.

I gave my sister Debra the boot in early 1999. This was after she called me at this club called Gate in West Hollywood with the news that the Lakers had let me go. It wasn't a "kill the messenger" kind of thing. She was convinced L.A. fired me because of my partying. So she tried to put her foot down. She was like, "Listen, you gotta stop. The NBA is sending you a message. They're over your wild and crazy crap."

I wasn't hearing her. I was like, "You need to go," and she went back to Dallas. So now there was no one around who had known me before I was a big shot, no one who had loved me when there was nothing in it for them. I was on my own and had no one to answer to. Dennis Rodman had a license to party, and I hung my shingle at Club 4809.

You don't just wake up one day and you're an alcoholic. It takes a lot of work. And by the time the ESPN cameras showed up to tape *Rodman on the Rebound* in the summer of 2003, I had been steady at it for about four years. Now I drank all the time. I drank all the time, every fucking day, 24 hours a day, without a care in the world, not even my kids, not anybody.

I had become a drunk, and that was the reality, the ugly reality documented on video tape by ESPN. *Rodman on the Rebound* had now become "Rodman on the Rehab." If Darren, Wendell, and Thaer didn't know that the show was a catastrophe in the making before that drunken September night, they had to know it then.

ESPN had this "great footage" of a drunken Dennis Rodman losing it on camera, and they had editorial control. They and only they
would decide what was going to be aired on national television.

I was fucked.

Still, on tape at least, Darren soldiered on, trying to negotiate my
way back into the NBA. He was making a list and checking it twice:
Indiana Pacers, Memphis Grizzlies, Miami Heat, Denver Nuggets,
Detroit Pistons. The man gets paid to be optimistic, and he was
earning his money.

Those NBA pitches would come to an abrupt halt in mid-
October, after my sorry, motorcycle-wheelie-attempting ass had a
close encounter with a light pole in the parking lot of the Treasures
Gentleman's Club in Vegas. After that, Darren's attitude toward the
reality show, was like, "Fuck it! Forget damage control, there is no
way to put a happy face on this shit." So he sicced the cameras on
me the day after my motorcycle accident. He was thinking that
while the show was going to be a public relations disaster, something good might come out of it if I "could see myself as others see
me," as the old adage goes. That might wake my ass up, he thought,
get me into rehab.

So at 9:45 a.m. on October 20, 2003, ESPN showed up at my
room at the Hard Rock to get some footage of what was left of
Dennis Rodman. A quick recap. I was coming off a two-day drunk,
and the accident had left me with 70-some stitches in my right shin,
lacerations on my left, and two badly bruised and swollen knees.

I dressed up for the camera, putting on the top half of the lime-
green scrubs the nurses had given me to wear home from the hospital and completed the ensemble by tying a white towel around my
waist, creating what looked like a terrycloth mini-skirt. Close-ups
revealed a puffy face and dark circles under my eyes. My earrings
were still in place, but I was missing my left nose ring. I looked every
bit of my 42 years and then some.

The camera rolled, me grimacing, as my driver swabbed the
stitched-up right shin and the "beef jerky" left shin. It was not the
kind of footage that was going to show up in an authorized biography. It was like, "You've heard the story of the downfall of Dennis

Rodman, now here's the pictures to prove it." As for Darren's hope that the video would wake me up, the show wouldn't air for six weeks. In the meantime, it was the same old Dennis.

A week after the motorcycle accident, I was back in Vegas for the Radio Music Awards, ESPN hot on my trail. That was the night I got shit-faced, pinched P. Diddy on the ass while he was doing a television interview backstage, and capped off my performance by getting kicked out of the place. The good news was that on the tape shot at the awards show you couldn't tell I was drunk. ESPN made up for it later that night after I parked my ass at this bar in the Aladdin Hotel for the second Dennis drunk-on-camera scene.

I was wearing the same outfit I wore to the Radio Music Awards: jeans with an unbuttoned, long sleeve, white shirt over a blue and white Southeastern Oklahoma State basketball jersey—number 10, baby—with "Savages" appliquéd across the chest. I topped the outfit off with a matching blue baseball cap.

Maybe it was the outfit or maybe it was because I was smoking a cigar and throwing down one Grey Goose and cranberry juice after another, getting drunker and drunker and more and more obnoxious by the minute, but I wasn't exactly a chick magnet that night. If the cameras don't lie, I was only able to pull in three women in about two hours.

"You want me?" I asked this blonde wearing an off-the-shoulder white blouse.

ESPN fast-forwarded the tape. "What are you talking about?" she asked.

"That's up to you," I replied.

She gave me a playful, "Oh-you-bad-boy" slap to the thigh. "I'm not going to do anything funny," she said.

The girl left. "She's stupid," I said to the bartender.

Next up, I spotted another girl. "Hello!" I shouted across the room. "Hell-ooo!"

ESPN fast-forwarded to this brunette sitting with me at the bar. It was now 1:15 a.m. She was wearing shades, a red baseball cap, a sleeveless black top, with a silver crucifix around her neck. You could tell this nervous Christian was anxious to leave, but I kept saying, "Stay, stay, stay stay," like 10 or 15 times. She left.

"Phone! Phone!" I shouted, as another brunette joined me, her back to the camera. Guess she didn't want her mama to see her with Dennis Rodman. My bodyguard, Wendell, showed up at 2:45 a.m. Time to go. He escorted me and four girls, including the blonde in the off-the-shoulder blouse and the brunette wearing the crucifix to my 19th floor suite. I didn't allow the camera inside. Bad move.

The blue double doors to the suite closed, and the camera lingered outside where Wendell and Darren had a little chat about my immediate future, and the subject wasn't basketball. Both were dressed in black. It seemed appropriate.

It had been about a week from what was supposed to have been my wake-up call, the motorcycle accident. Not only did I almost kill myself, I had ended any hopes of returning to the NBA for the foreseeable future, and my career as a celebrity whatever was in jeopardy. What's more, everybody who cared about me—Darren, Wendell, Thaer, and Michelle—had been threatening to pull up stakes. Rock bottom, baby. No career. No family. No friends. All because of booze.

So did that stop my drinking?

Nope.

Not that everyone around me wasn't trying to help—like Wendell. He had been my bodyguard for about three years when I first moved to Newport Beach before he quit out of sheer exhaustion.

"Working with Dennis was like getting on a rollercoaster that never stops," he said. "The only way you can get off is you drop off. 'Cause it never stops."

Wendell had come out of retirement to help get me straight. He didn't need the work. One of the 38 straight men in the fashion industry, he had been happily hanging out with his family and managing his business, "Wendell Wade Williams Custom Clothing," before Darren gave him a call—three calls actually. Now, after less than a week, he had already had it as he told Darren in the hallway outside my suite's blue double doors.

"I have no problem sticking around to help him become healthy," he told Darren as the ESPN camera rolled. "But our strategy right now *isn't* working. And if you and I and Thaer don't sit down and put together a new game plan, then we are just as sick as him."

"Uh huh," mumbled Darren, looking like a beaten man. Or maybe he was just worn out. After all, it was coming up on four o'clock in the morning.

"You can't compete with these young kids when you're 42 years old on two hours' sleep and 15 hours of [bleep] Jägermeister," Wendell continued.

The camera loves Wendell, and Wendell loves the camera. Warm, down to earth, a "philosopher from the 'hood," someday he should get his own reality show. In the meantime, he had to settle for hijacking this one.

"Let's have our own little reality show," Wendell said to Darren. "Reality one: Dennis Rodman is an alcoholic. Reality two: if he keeps drinking alcohol, there'll be no NBA."

As of that sound bite, *Rodman on the Rebound* officially stopped being about a "rebounding" basketball player and started being about a "rehabbing" alcoholic.

So to sum up: at around 4:00 a.m. on Tuesday, October 28, 2003, in Las-fucking-Vegas, Nevada, my fate was being decided, on camera, by two very tired men standing in a hotel corridor. In hindsight, I'm thinking it would have been better to invite the camera inside. So exactly what was going on behind my 19th-floor suite's blue double doors? That night, I haven't a clue. The next day? There was a gang bang, baby, as Darren, Thaer, Wendell, and ESPN combined forces to jump my bones in what they called an "intervention."

CHAPTER THIRTEEN

PARDON MY
INTERVENTION

L as Vegas, October 28, 2003, 12:45 p.m. The setting seemed all wrong. The living room of the suite was cheery, bright, light streaming through open drapes. There were yellow walls, facing couches with wide orange and yellow stripes, and a perky green plant. The place looked like a set for one of those local women's shows.

I sat on one couch, my back to the sliding glass doors—Darren and Thaer sat directly across from me on the other. Wendell was camera right in a straight-backed, upholstered blue chair. The camera was set up behind Darren looking over his shoulder at me, occasionally panning right to get Thaer and Wendell.

Cut to a close-up of my "get-on-with-it" right knee, that was bouncing up and down, up and down, working off nervous energy.

Darren set the stage.

"We're in the fourth quarter now with two minutes to go. It's your life on the line. Because if nothing changes, I'm gone," said Darren, "He's [Thaer's] gone. Your wife just called me—this is for real this time. She's got a noon meeting with a divorce lawyer tomorrow."

Why was ESPN there? Again, Darren had invited them in. By then, we really were in full blown, nothing-to-lose mode.

Time to vent.

"I honestly think that this alcohol has got you, brother," said Wendell. "It's got you, man. It's hurting you, bro."

"I don't want to see you go out like Joe Louis," said Darren, "as a casino host for a thousand bucks a week."

Not a good example. Many a black man would gladly swap lives with Joe Louis, casino host or not. He was a god.

Next up, more with Wendell. At this point in the shoot, he knew that ESPN had more footage of me in clubs than on court, more drinking than dribbling. And the little bit they had on court was of me fiddle-fucking around by myself. There was zero footage, not a frame, of me actually playing basketball.

"That's not a rebound tape," said Wendell, pointing at the camera. "That's Dennis Rodman's funeral. No NBA team's gonna go, 'Oh, yeah! Dennis Rodman gets all the [bleep] in the world and goes to the clubs. Let's bring him on board to win a championship.'"

The first upbeat comment came from Darren when he switched into agent mode. "In a matter of a week, this whole thing could be turned around," he said, "but you gotta be committed to it."

Cut to the resolution.

"Talk to me, Dennis, what is our game plan?" asked Wendell. "You're the coach of this whole team. What is our game plan?"

"What's the game plan?" I asked, then looked out window. Luckily there were no airplanes or boats in sight. "You tell me," I said wearily. "What's the game plan?"

"The game plan is to get sober, stay sober, and get your ass on board," said Darren.

Sure, I thought. But don't pretend like it was your idea. "What'd I tell you I was going to do, Thaer?"

"He already told me he was gonna take the pill when we got back from Vegas," said Thaer. "He told me that before we left."

The "pill" was something called "Antabuse," a drug the judge had ordered me to take as a part of the settlement for the public drunkenness charge back in September. According to the rexmed.com website, Antabuse, when combined with "even small amounts of alcohol," can cause, among other things, "nausea," "copious vomiting," "confusion," and in "severe reactions," "unconsciousness, convulsions, and death."

Other than that, it's cool.

ESPN wrapped up the intervention scene with me pacing back and forth in the cheery hotel suite trying to digest what just happened.

"I don't really pay attention to too many people or listen to too many things people say," I said on camera. "So they must care if they came and said something. It's not like I don't realize myself. I mean, I'm not stupid, you know? What they're telling me is what I tell myself all the time."

After briefly mulling it over, I decided to "Try this angle. See how it works."

So the big dramatic scene of the reality series, *Rodman on the Rebound*, was not Dennis Rodman running on the court to a standing ovation or snagging 18 rebounds in the first game after his comeback to the NBA. No. No. No. The big dramatic scene of the *Rodman on the Rebound* was a drunk being confronted by his friends during an intervention.

"Friends are here to support you, lift you up," Wendell had said. "You know you got a problem, we know you got a problem. We're gonna help you. Why? Because we love you."

It made for good T.V., but, truth be told, I had begun to gradually make my way back months before. Like I had said at my press conference announcing my return to the NBA way back in July, I was working out, not enough, but making a stab at it, and my weight was down. And I was partying less, maybe three or four days a week instead of 24/7. What I'm saying is the seed had been planted months before that showdown in Vegas. The intervention was more of a turning point for Darren, Wendell, Thaer, and Michelle than it was for me. I was already on my way.

I'll have to give ESPN credit, the guys did their best to end the reality show on a high note. They show me sober, working out, and "waiting by the phone" for a call from the NBA. They even promoted the show as an "intimate look at Rodman's comeback efforts." And even though this was not a show about a basketball player, but a show about an alcoholic, the closest they came to mentioning my drunken antics was a reference to "off-the-court challenges."

A couple of paybacks before putting the reality show to rest. There were only three people on the show who came off like assholes: me, of course, in my two drunk scenes, NBA commentator Stephen A. Smith, and my old Detroit teammate, Bill Laimbeer.

Smith, the son Howard Cosell never had, said of my playing days, "Dennis Rodman as a person was quite frankly horrific. I don't think he has any place in this league."

Later Laimbeer weighed in.

"You have to assess the strengths and weaknesses that Dennis would bring to your ball club," he said. "And right now the weaknesses probably outweigh strengths tenfold over."

Smith, who makes a living being an ignorant asshole, isn't worth talking about. As for Laimbeer, would it have killed him to either decline to do the interview or just say some horseshit like, "Getting back in the NBA will be an uphill climb, but I wish Dennis the best"? Would that have killed his sorry ass?

Rodman on the Rebound aired at midnight eastern standard time on December 3–4, 2003.

Reality Check: Don't drink and do reality shows.

Following the intervention, ESPN cornered Darren in the back of an Aladdin Hotel limo for a parting comment.

"This is it, there's no turning back at this point," he said. "Either he's gonna make it, or the guy's gonna be dead in a couple of years."

Nah. It never would have gone that far—not that I wasn't out there. But as I said in that raving drunk scene at Josh Slocum's, I knew exactly what I was doing. I always knew when the time came I could reel it back in, bring myself back to what I call my "safe place." I've always been able to do that. I just never wanted to do it before. But it was there waiting. And I've always gone there when I needed to get my shit together.

People have always thought I was just this train wreck, this fucking devil running wild, you know? It was never like that. The partying was something I let happen. I created it. I could have stopped it at any time, but I didn't. I wanted to see how far I could take the roller coaster before it came to a dead end. People thought my dead end was the motorcycle accident at Treasures or my ass-showing antics at the Radio Music Awards. But it was more than that. It was like my whole life culminated into one big foot that hit the brakes. It wasn't just one thing. It was a lot of things.

As for the partying, I was just over it. I was tired of drinking. Tired of women. Tired of setting up my table, getting my troops together. Bored with it. Like on my last birthday, everybody was like, "Hey, let's go party!"

I went, "Well, okay, all right. If I have to. You twist my arm." It was routine, you know?

So I went to my safe place. A place where no one can hurt you. No one can bother you. It's like going to the Garden of Eden. I go there to be peaceful and humble, and think things through. I knew I needed to get my shit together. I needed to do this. I needed to do that. I could see I was partying and drinking to bypass all the heartache and pain I suffered in life. And I realized whether it was problems with my fucked-up family, my kids, my career, or my love life, I had to find a new way of dealing with it. The liquor, the partying, the women weren't working any more.

So I took the pill, the Antabuse, not that it was totally voluntary. There was the court order—or at least that's what they told me.

"I literally, literally, put that thing in his mouth every day for months," said Wendell. "I drove from L.A. to Orange County every day to give him his pill."

I found out while working on this book that Darren, Thaer, Wendell, and my lawyer had conspired against me.

"Because of the Treasures thing, me, Darren, and the lawyer," said Thaer, "we completely lied to him. Told him he was court-ordered to take the Antabuse, which was not true."

And they kept on telling that lie, saying the court order had been extended, and I ended up taking that shit for about a year and a half. Turned out lying was SOP for these guys.

"I lie to him every day," Thaer told a reporter. "I lie to him about what time a meeting is, what time our flight is every time we get on a plane. Because if I tell him what time, he'll wait until the last second."

I guess this would be a good place to thank Thaer for all the fucking meetings I've made and flights I haven't missed, and, oh yeah, for all the Antabuse I've taken and alcohol I didn't drink.

Here's to you, bro.

✦ ✦ ✦ ✦

In one of my favorite scenes from *Rodman on the Rebound*, I was walking to my car behind the beach house when I spotted the ESPN crew.

"What year is it?" I asked. "Two thousand and three?"

They thought I was kidding.

"No, seriously," I said.

"Yes," some woman replied.

I was two days sober then, the fog just beginning to lift, and I soon began taking stock. For the better part of a decade, I had spent nearly all my free time pretending "every day was New Year's Eve." But now New Year's Day had finally arrived. No more booze, no more partying, no more spending every waking hour in search of the next good time.

Wendell, at least, was happy for me, as he would tell a reporter: "Once Dennis became sober, the party was over, because that's not who he is.

"Every day is New Year's Eve?" he continued. "Every day is a Tuesday."

The reporter asked me if Wendell was right, if my ongoing attempt to "live every day like it was New Year's Eve," was over.

"Nah," I replied. "It's never, ever gonna be over."

But it was going to be different. Now it was more of an attitude—a big grin without the party hat, you know?

A state of mind, without the champagne.

Or at least that was the plan.

So on the 30th day of October, 2003, in Newport Beach, California, I had my life back. Now what? This really was the first— make that the second—day of the rest of my life. I could see there were many things that would need cleaning up during the long string of New Year's Days just ahead. Both my careers, the one as a basketball player and the other as a celebrity spokesman, were on the downswing. My personal life was in a shambles, my marriage to Michelle hanging by a thread. I had been a lousy father, a stranger to my two youngest kids, a distant memory to my two oldest and their mothers. I had even split with my family down in Dallas. As for my neighbors, the people in Newport Beach thought I was a freak and a flake. It was time to show them I was a normal person. Or at least as normal as a six-foot-eight, pierced, tattooed, blond-haired black man can be. All in all, there was a ton of work to be done.

CHAPTER FOURTEEN

YOU'RE NOT IN CHICAGO ANYMORE

As I was lying in University Hospital in Vegas after my motorcycle accident, Darren was looking back, considering how very close we came.

"I spoke to Phil Jackson no more than 48 hours after the accident," Darren later told a reporter. "He didn't make any promises, but said he'd be willing to sit down and talk. 'Phil,' I said, 'he's being flown into Denver this Wednesday for a workout.' And Phil was like, 'If there's anything I can do to get him signed with Denver, let me know. Otherwise call me towards the end of the week, and by the way, I'm glad to hear that Dennis has been slowing down on his partying.'

"Well, two days later we've got headlines in every friggin' newspaper in America," Darren continued. "'Dennis Rodman Crashes Motorcycle,' 'Dennis Rodman Cited for DUI,' 'Dennis Rodman Gets 75 Stitches.' So in two seconds in a strip club parking lot, we go from having Phil Jackson's ear and a guaranteed workout with the Denver Nuggets to nothing. Zilch. Back to square one."

After that, Darren would give it a rest. Then when I had been sober for like two months, we decided to try to bring my NBA career back from the dead. During the next year, I had close encounters of the frustrating kind with the Lakers, Knicks, Nuggets, and Cavaliers, and logged a little playing time for Fuerza Regia in Mexico and the Long Beach Jam in California. Along the way, I had a little fun as corporate spokesman for a line of "herbal sexual enhancement" products and posed nude for a billboard that would generate major buzz in Hollywood and New York City.

The NBA comeback trail began less than a month after my accident when I appeared on the *Tonight Show*. This was part of a public-relations campaign Darren cooked up to let the world know I was through partying and was now serious about playing ball again. I didn't want to go on. I don't like talking about personal shit, especially when it looks like I'm feeling sorry for myself. But they ganged up on my ass, and Thaer, Wendell, Michelle, the kids, and I all went down to the studio.

Jay introduced me as "The new and improved Dennis Rodman," and we were off and running. I told him about the motorcycle accident while I was partying in Vegas.

"More than two beers on this one?" Jay asked.

"Oh, there was *way* more than that," I said. "*Way* more."

That got a laugh. Then things turned serious.

"I haven't had a drink in three-and-a-half weeks," I said. Today that sounds like nothing, but at the time, it was a big deal—for me at least.

The *Tonight Show* thing turned out great. Thaer and Wendell both said it was my best interview ever, and thanks to Jay, I got my message out without sounding sappy.

Once we got the P.R. ball rolling, Darren called up Magic, again—this was in December of 2003—and told him I was sober for real this time and looking for an opportunity. So Magic hooked us up with Phil Jackson—again.

Phil told me there were three things that had to happen if I were going to have any chance to play for the Lakers that season. First, I needed to hook up with a minor league team in the ABA (American Basketball Association) to prove I could still play. Second, I needed to start scrimmaging with Magic's bunch at UCLA to get team owner Jerry Buss's attention. Third, somebody on the Lakers' team would have to get injured to create an opening.

Darren got busy. He called Magic, told him what Phil said, and asked if he would help out. "No problem," Magic said. Then I swallowed my pride and signed with the Long Beach Jam on December 22, 2003.

"I look forward to suiting up with the Jam and playing basketball again," I said in the press release, "My ultimate goal is to get back to the NBA."

Like I told the *Chicago Sun-Times*, my agreement with the Jam would allow me to accept high-paying (as much as $100,000 a crack) "exhibition engagements and an NBA contract at any time."

Then fate gave me a nod. The day before I signed with the Jam, Karl Malone took a jump shot and got tangled up with Scott Williams, this six-foot-10, 260-pound power forward from the Phoenix Suns. Malone came up lame: sprained medial collateral ligament. The X-rays were normal, according to the *Los Angeles Times*, and at first, they were optimistic. But 10 days later, it was clear Malone was going where he had never gone before: the injured list.

"Missing seven, eight, nine games in one spell when I haven't missed that many in 18 years is frustrating," Malone told the *Times*. "I feel like I let a lot of people down."

The prospects were not good for the 40-year-old Malone.

"A lot of these injuries can last four to six weeks," Coach Jackson said.

What's more, Malone's replacement, Rick Fox, was coming off foot surgery and was less than 100 percent—which made things easier for me to slide into the lineup.

So I was thinking, "Holy shit! Hell froze over, pigs fly—this could really happen."

I waited. A week passed. Then another week. Nothing. I made my debut with the Long Beach Jam on January 16, 2004, snagging 14 rebounds in a 130-110 win against the Fresno Heat Wave. A sellout crowd of 4,373 came to the Long Beach Pyramid to see me play my first game since I had been shit-canned by the Mavericks two years earlier. Tex Winter, Phil Jackson's right-hand man and the guy who invented the triangle offense, was in the stands.

Meanwhile I was hungry to get with Magic, hungry to scrimmage with his guys up at UCLA, and I was calling Darren three or four times a day. "Have you heard from Magic? Do you have a time? When do I need to be there?"

Nothing.

By this time, I'd been sober for about three months.

After my second game with the Jam, I realized I was nowhere near being in basketball shape. So we told the media I strained a calf, and I sat out nine games.

A month passed. Malone was still down. I, on the other hand, was healthy again, and said goodbye to the Jam in February, "with hopes of making it back to the NBA," as the team press release put it.

Nothing.

On March 9, I returned to the Jam for the ABA title game against the Kansas City Knights. I pulled down 14 rebounds in 23 minutes in a 126-123 win before scouts from the Lakers, New York Knicks, and Toronto Raptors.

"I was a little more aggressive, had my hops, my deer legs back," I told the *San Diego Union-Tribune*. "If I'd played 30, 35 minutes, I'd have gotten 20 [rebounds] easy."

The payoff for the title win wasn't big. The owner gave the team "a $5,000 bonus to disperse among themselves," as the Jam press release put it. Whatever. I now had a sixth championship under my belt.

"I think the Lakers should get me at least as an insurance policy," I told the *San Diego Union Tribune*, "All the [players] are falling like flies. They know I know the offense, know the system, know the guys."

Nothing.

Meanwhile I was still trying to hook up with Magic.

Nothing.

Finally, on March 12, Malone returned to the Lakers, and my NBA hopes for the 2003-2004 season were over. Malone would reinjure his knee in the second game of the playoff finals on June 9, and the Lakers would go on to lose the series to Detroit 4-1.

I'm still wondering if I could have made a difference.

I don't know why Phil Jackson never pulled the trigger. He had every opportunity to do so. Maybe he got cold feet because of all the drama going on with Shaq and Kobe that season, not to mention Gary Payton, who never quite jelled in L.A. As for Magic, he knew I was sober, serious this time, but with his crazy schedule, with all his business interests, personal appearances, this, and that, we just never hooked up.

◆ ◆ ◆ ◆

On April 19, 2004, I pled guilty to DUI for the Treasures motorcycle crash, and a couple of hours later, I was pulled over on Santa Monica Boulevard in L.A. A reporter ran me down, and here's how they told the story on celebrities411.com:

"The cop said, 'Where's your license?'

'My friend has it,' I said.

'You mean your friend carries your license?'

'Yes.'"

So Thaer pulls up beside us, and the cop asks, still quoting celebrities411.com, "'Why do you have his license?'

"'Because he loses it all the time.'"

It ain't easy being me.

That same spring, at about the same time the Lakers were dragging their feet, I put a call in to Isiah Thomas, my old Detroit teammate and current Knicks GM, to see if I could get on their playoff roster. Isiah was like, "Not right now, but let's talk about your joining our summer league team."

The way it worked, the Knicks were going to have a mini training camp that summer up in Westchester for about a week, then they were going to fly out to Long Beach to play against some other summer league teams. If I did well, they would sign me for the coming season.

So Isiah ran this by the powers that be, got an okay, and the Knicks booked my flights, reserved me a room at the Westchester

Marriott, the whole nine yards. All I had to do between then and mini-camp was lie low, not say a word to the media about anything to do with the Knicks.

After that, "We just kind of sat back," recalled Darren. "I didn't need to call anybody else. I knew this deal was going down. There was no doubt in my mind."

Then about a week before the summer league started, I flew into New York City to make the talk-show rounds. I was then the corporate spokesman for a line of "herbal sexual enhancement products," EnjoyRX for women, and EnduranceRX for men, "available in pill form or as a taffy chew." The company thought I could "reach a target demographic" that they were "extremely interested in."

Cool.

So I flew to New York to promote this stuff on a bunch of talk shows including *The View* on ABC. I was sitting there with Barbara Walters, Star Jones, and the rest of them, and they were yapping, yapping, yapping—I couldn't get a word in edgewise. So finally, I said something like, "Y'know, I came here to make an announcement, and nobody's letting me talk." Well that didn't *even* slow their asses down.

They were talking, talking, talking until out of nowhere, Star Jones went like, "We're not being fair to Dennis. He's got a big announcement." Now Star had on this New York Knicks jersey, number 10, insinuating I was going to say something about signing with the Knicks and getting my old number back. But I was cool, remembering what Isiah said: "No media."

So I changed the subject, told them I was there to make a special announcement. "I'm gay," I said, and we all started laughing. "No, I'm kidding. I'm kidding." Big joke, y'know? They kept on asking me about the NBA, and I said it looked like I was coming back, but I wasn't going to name the team. "You'll find out soon." Shit like that. Later they gave me a chance to talk up the benefits of EnjoyRX and EnduranceRX, which was my only reason for being there in the first place, and that was it. Just another day in the media factory.

Didn't think a thing of it.

Two days later, Darren got this call from Isiah.

"I could just hear in his voice that something was wrong," Darren recalled.

Isiah was like, "I've got a major problem."

Seems the owner of the Knicks pissed in his pants when he heard I said I was gay on *The View,* and he didn't want me on the team.

Darren goes ballistic, screaming and yelling, and Isiah was giving it right back to him. Then everything settled down, and Isiah was like, "I love Dennis like a brother, but my hands are tied. There are people above me."

And there're people under you too, *brother*—like this guy named Dennis Rodman, who got totally fucked.

✦ ✦ ✦ ✦ ✦

I signed up that July to play in the NBA summer league out in California, but tore a calf muscle the first day of practice and never made it back onto the court. After I got over that injury, I had another go-around with the Denver Nuggets.

This time I made it to the workout—on September 21, 2004— but cut it short because of ingrown toe nails. I got those taken care of, and about a week later, I was back at the Pepsi Center for a two-hour scrimmage.

"I was running, jumping, and doing my thing," I told the *Denver Post.* "I think they freaked out. They couldn't believe I am 43 years old."

According to the *Rocky Mountain News,* General Manager Kiki Vandeweghe "declined to comment."

Coach Jeff Bzdelik said, "He played well."

Darren predicted Denver would "sell out every game."

Partying?

"Rodman says he has been sober for more than a year," the *News* reported.

Kiki told me, "I think you should stay another day."

I declined. I thought they'd seen enough. I knew I had. As I was leaving, former Laker star Michael Cooper, then a Denver assistant coach, said, "I'll see you Monday," which was the first day of the Nuggets training camp.

"I'll call you tomorrow," said Kiki.

"It's a slam dunk," thought Darren.

"I'm looking forward to a phone call," I told the *Rocky Mountain News*.

So it was around six o'clock the next night and still no call. We were freaking out. Darren had left a couple of messages. Reporters were calling. No word. Finally, this sports geek from a radio station called. The training camp roster was out, and my name wasn't on it—another dropkick to the gonads, this time from the Denver-fucking-Nuggets, for God's sake. Kiki made it official when he finally called Darren at like nine o'clock. But there was still hope. NBA rules allowed 20 players in camp, and there were only 19 on the Nuggets' list.

That very same day, I signed to play two exhibition games in the Liga Mexicana de Basquetbol (Mexican Basketball League) for Monterrey's Fuerza Regia—as part of what sperts.net called, "[my] quest to prove to the Denver Nuggets that [I was] committed to returning to the NBA." It also had something to do with my "quest" to make a few bucks: the dudes paid me $50,000, which turned out to be about $1,500 dollars per minute.

I played just six minutes in my first game in Mexico on October 8, 2004, sitting down after I strained a groin muscle. The fans booed the shit out of me. I made it up to them two days later, playing 24 minutes in my second and final Fuerza Regia game, before 11,000 fans in a 107-95 win over Correcaminos of Tamaulipas. I pulled in something like a dozen rebounds.

The Nuggets weren't impressed. So I signed with (but never played for) the Orange County Crush. With a little help from my lawyer, I switched teams after maybe a hundred people showed up on the campus of UC-Irvine for the Crush's first game, signing a two-game deal with the Long Beach Jam.

My debut was delayed by "minor" knee surgery on December 9, 2004, and I played my first game on February 13, 2005, pulling down 12 rebounds in a 108-106 victory against the Ontario Warriors. Then my knee injury flared up, and I wouldn't be able to play in the second game.

In the middle of all this, I posed nude for a billboard for the People for the Ethical Treatment of Animals (PETA). In the picture, I had my chin in my hand like "The Thinker" and sported bright red hair. "Think Ink, Not Mink: Be Comfortable in Your Own Skin and Let Animals Keep Theirs," the copy read. As for the visual, the message was: "Be like Dennis, adorn yourself with tattoos rather than fur." The billboard was part of PETA's "Rather Go Naked Than Wear Fur" series. I was in good company: Pamela Anderson, Kim Basinger, and Christy Turlington also posed. My billboards would get a lot of attention when they debuted in Hollywood and New York in February 2005. It was a nice distraction.

Meanwhile back at the NBA, there was one more slap in the face to endure before I wrapped up the 2004-2005 season.

✦ ✦ ✦ ✦

Cleveland, "The Mistake on the Lake," March 2005.

Rick Mahorn, my old Detroit teammate, called. The new team owner, a guy named Dan Gilbert, wanted to talk to me one on one. He was apparently looking to shake things up, and if the conversation went well, there could be a 10-day contract in it for me. Whatever. We had a nice 30-minute talk; then, you guessed it, I never heard from him again. I don't know what the guy was afraid of. There wasn't shit I could have done that would've made things in Cleveland turn out any worse. After this guy took over, the Cavaliers, a team with superstar Lebron James, went on to lose 16 of its last 27 games, fell from fourth in the division to not even making the playoffs, fired their coach, fired their GM—did everything but set fire to fucking Lake Erie. And you're telling me the man was worried about what kind of havoc Dennis Rodman might wreak on the team? I mean there is your occasional "distraction," then there's your total destruction. The dude took a wrecking ball to the place. Shit. Think Cleveland might have made the playoffs with Lebron James *and* Dennis Rodman in the line-up?

The Cleveland nibble would be my last chance at a NBA comeback during the 2004-2005 season. It wasn't a good year.

Reality Check: Sometimes hard work doesn't pay off.

After being jerked around by my "friends" in the NBA, I was getting a little paranoid. The league had offered me nothing but blind alleys and dead ends, and, all in all, my attempt at a comeback had been a rat fuck of gigantic proportions.

It was like everywhere I went, bringing Dennis Rodman on was okay with this guy, okay with that guy, okay with another guy, and then, at the last minute, all of a sudden, the deal falls through. Somebody up above, I figured, maybe even at the league level, was shutting my ass down. NBA Commissioner David Stern was a likely candidate. I've got no evidence. Just an inkling. Call it intuition. But I'm thinking all these years later, Stern was getting his final sweet revenge on the last of Detroit's "Bad Boys."

Stern became commissioner in 1984, the same year Michael Jordan came into the league. Early on, when Detroit was winning back-to-back titles in 1989 and 1990, Stern loved the "Bad Boys," and had no problem with us living up to the name—kicking people's asses, throwing people down. But when Jordan and the Bulls started coming on, he turned his back on us. All of a sudden he was like, "These guys are dirty."

We weren't dirty. We were men playing basketball—not boys, but *men.* You drive the line, you will pay. Bill Laimbeer was known for putting your ass on the canvas, and Rick Mahorn did the same thing. Back in the day, when somebody knocked you on your ass, you got up and played. Today, somebody knocks you on your ass, and they call a "flagrant foul." What horseshit. Like I told the *Chicago Sun-Times*, "They've watered down the game with zone defenses and calling more contact fouls." Now if you're trying to hurt somebody, that's different. But if a guy goes to the basket, gets hammered, and falls wrong, that's just part of the game—or at least it should be.

When I first came into the league I was one of those boys I was talking about, this herky-jerky kid running up and down the court, jumping around, just glad to be out there.

Isiah Thomas fixed that.

We were playing L.A., and I don't remember exactly what I did wrong, but Isiah was pissed. There were like 18,000 people in the stands and they could tell something was going on, but couldn't really see it. Isiah grabbed a handful of my jersey and then he hit me quick and hard in the chest with his fist—knocked the pure D shit out of me.

"This ain't party time!" he said. "Goddamn it, you need to get your fucking shit together!"

That was the day I learned how to focus on the basketball court—this from a guy who was maybe six-foot-two and didn't weigh shit. But he was a man passing down the word to a boy, y'know? He had gravity. Can you imagine somebody trying that shit today? David Stern would fine the hell out of their ass.

Stern couldn't get away with the crap he gets away with now back when Michael Jordan, Magic Johnson, Larry Bird, and Kareem Abdul-Jabbar ruled the league. All those guys were way bigger than David Stern, and he didn't dare cross their asses. But he's in control now, because nobody has the star power of a Jordan. So he's handcuffed everybody in the NBA: "You can't do this. You can't do that." So you got a game played mostly by young black men controlled by a 60-something white guy. It's time to put the game back in the hands of the players and the coaches.

Oh, and while I'm at it, that offer I made to Stern when I was with Dallas—the one where I challenged him to a boxing match in the nude—that still stands.

Just give Darren a call.

We'll sell the place out.

CHAPTER FIFTEEN

TAKING CARE OF BUSINESS

At the same time my NBA career was tanking, my career as a celebrity rep was picking up. Remember that *Tonight Show* appearance? Viewers may have thought I was just making a fashion statement by wearing the Southeastern Okalahoma State Jersey and the baseball cap sporting a GoldenPalace.com logo. Not. It was all about money, honey. Every time that adidas sells one of those "True School Authentic Vintage Throwback Jerseys," as they call them, I get a cut. As for GoldenPalace.com, I have a substantial contract with the online gambling casino that dates back a couple of years, and being a walking billboard for the company is the least of it.

GoldenPalace.com is known for its "guerilla marketing." These guys will do just about anything to get the company name out there. When Karolyne Smith from Salt Lake City put her forehead up for bid for advertising space on eBay, they took her up on it and paid $10,000 to permanently tattoo "GoldenPalace.com" on her skull. Angel Brammer of Glasgow, Scotland, made the same offer with her ample cleavage, but this time the tattoo would be temporary, lasting only 15 days. So the guys at GoldenPalace.com purchased what their website calls a "Massive Media Opportunity," Brammer's humongous 42-GG breasts, for a bargain-basement $800.

Also on eBay, the online casino bought a partially eaten grilled cheese sandwich said to contain a likeness of the Virgin Mary for $28,000, a 1999 Volkswagen Golf once owned by the Pope for about $250,000, and the naming rights for several children and adults. There are several more "Goldies" running around out there these days. And when an Ottawa radio station put an alleged Britney Spears pregnancy test up for bid, the company snapped it up for $5,000. The GoldenPalace.com logo has also been plastered on a herd of 100 cows in Sarasota, Florida, and on the backs of a long series of boxers—beginning with Bernard "The Executioner" Hopkins for his middleweight title match with Felix Trinidad at Madison Square Garden in 2001. Hopkins reportedly bet the $100,000 rental fee on himself. Good move—underdog Hopkins knocked out the previously undefeated Trinidad in the 12th round.

In 2002, the good folks from the Nevada Athletic Commission took GoldenPalace.com to court, trying to stop them from stenciling their logo on boxers. When the casino won, they claimed it was "a victory for free speech." But the real victory was for "free publicity." Every time GoldenPalace.com "tattooed" a boxer, it generated news coverage, which, of course, was the whole idea. The same goes for each time they pulled some kind of stunt or bought weird shit on eBay. Meanwhile, no matter what kind of off-the-wall thing they were doing, they always seemed to find a way to raise cash for some charity.

It turned out Darren knew one of the guys over at GoldenPalace.com, and when he told me about all their antics, I was like, "This is a match made in heaven." Since I signed with them, I've run with the bulls in Pamplona twice, raising thousands for M.S. research; played host at the 2005 Wife Carrying Championships in Sonkajärvi, Finland; and, also in 2005, I led the eight-day, 3,000-mile Bullrun road rally.

For the rally, several dozen cars (somebody guessed the collection of Ferraris, Lamborghinis, Rolls-Royces, and the like were worth about $13 million) made the trip from Miami to Los Angeles. You probably heard about Bullrun, since we left a trail of speeding tickets, reckless driving charges, and hick-town, "Them-big-city-folk-can't-git-away-with-that-shit-here!" newspaper stories.

"[They] disturbed the peace of our nice little community with just wanton disregard for anybody else," a Colorado State Trooper told the *Summit Daily News*.

They may have had a point. In one 500-mile stretch between Salt Lake City and Reno, we would manage to collect 20 tickets. I did my part, picking up three in my gold Lamborghini. But like Lieutenant Darrell Hinton of the Cortez, Colorado, police department told *The Durango Herald*, "Someone who can afford a $200,000 dollar car isn't going to worry about a speeding ticket."

Now all this was no big deal until the Dennis Rodman crime wave washed over the Tomahawk Auto Truck Plaza in Glenwood Springs, Colorado. After we pulled out, a clerk accused me of stealing a cowboy hat and stiffing them for like $20 worth of gas. What horseshit. To borrow from Lieutenant Hinton, "If a guy can afford a $200,000 car. ..." But because it was Dennis Rodman, the story made headlines.

Reality Check: Live by the media, die by the media.

GoldenPalace.com is the kind of edgy company you would have expected to take on Dennis Rodman, even when I was drinking—they are some wild sons of bitches. But adidas? Nah. That deal proved I had come a long way from the days when Converse cancelled my shoe contract citing a "morals clause." My newfound respectability would even lead to a deal with The Upper Deck Company—an outfit Darren calls "the largest sports licensing and sports memorabilia company in the world."

I signed with them about the same time I was meeting with Phil Jackson in December of 2003. The Upper Deck Company wouldn't touch my ass when I was a basketball mega-star with the Chicago Bulls. Too hot to handle. Now I would be joining the likes of Michael Jordan and Tiger Woods on the company roster. The Rodman basketball cards became available in January 2004.

A final sign that Dennis Rodman was going mainstream was my appearance in a Super Bowl commercial in 2005. The 30-second spot for Silestone quartz countertops featured Chicago sports legends Mike Ditka, William "Refrigerator" Perry, Jim McMahon, and me. I'm the one with the orange hair taking a bubble bath. In the spot, I claim to be "Diana Pearl," which was actually the name of one of the countertop colors. The company paid almost $2.5 million to air the spot, and it was a milestone in my celebrity rep career.

In a little over a year's time, I had gone from video of Dennis Rodman nursing his wounds in a dark Vegas hotel room to video of Dennis Rodman pitching a product in the most high-profile commercial showcase the world has to offer. That was some comeback.

The reason was simple enough. The new Dennis Rodman was marketable. I still had an edge, but I was no longer *over* the edge. As I told the *Chicago Sun-Times*, "I have toned down my personality and my lifestyle.

"A lot of the crazy stuff I did when I was playing—wearing a dress, make-up and playing the tough guy—that's pretty much in the past."

By the middle of 2005, my comeback as a celebrity rep was complete. I had ongoing deals with GoldenPalace.com, adidas, and The Upper Deck Company, among others; had new contracts to launch Dennis Rodman jewelry and furniture lines; was opening a second Rodman's restaurant, this one in Hawaii; had signed up to shoot several reality shows; and was scheduled to play exhibition basketball games in China, Finland, and Sweden.

I was not only back on track, I was doing better than ever.

CHAPTER SIXTEEN

MICHELLE, MY BELLE

I took the phone call in Vegas, and the first thing I thought was, "She's dead." First thing. Any rookie motorcycle rider taking on those winding mountain roads up at Big Bear is just asking for it. Sure, my wife, Michelle, was riding a bike known for its easy handling—a 1992 Harley Davidson Fat Boy—but it's still a lot of motorcycle for a beginner to grapple with, all 650 pounds of it.

And there was another problem. The Fat Boy was one of my old bikes (I had given it to her for a birthday present), and the wingspan of the handlebars was perfect for a six-foot-eight guy with long arms—not so perfect for Michelle.

So the group left Running Spring, California, around noon, and about a mile out of town, Michelle was coming down the mountain, going too fast, trying to keep up with her friends—two guys and two girls. The road curved right, and she drifted across the centerline. She tried to pull the bike around, but couldn't manage the handlebars, and the goddamn thing was headed straight toward oncoming traffic. She over-corrected, hit the shoulder, and that was it. The Harley slid along the guardrail, hit a guardrail post, threw her, then slid another 40 feet. Meanwhile Michelle slammed into the guardrail, and her helmet popped off. If the guardrail isn't there, she goes over the cliff and her ass is dead. Her friends called for help, and she was airlifted by helicopter to the emergency room at Loma Linda University Medical Center.

So I got the call, freaked out, and Thaer and I caught the first flight out of Vegas. At the time, Michelle and I weren't even talking—not at all. It was the usual off and on, hot and cold shit. But she's my wife and the mother of my kids.

We got to the hospital. She had a broken leg, collarbone, and ankle; two cracked vertebrae; assorted bruises; and bumps on her face that looked like cherries. But she was going to survive, make a full recovery. Now I was pissed. What was she thinking?

"Is it that serious?" she asked.

"You're lucky to be alive," the doctor said.

She was so out of it that she didn't even know what had happened and thought she'd been in a car accident with the kids.

About a week later, after having a rod surgically implanted in her left leg, Michelle came home from the hospital in a wheelchair, wearing a neck brace. I knew she was going to be fine when she started bitching. She was all upset because I wasn't "there" for her and the kids after the accident. Said her mother and her friends stepped in and took care of things while she "had no idea what I was doing. No idea."

What I was doing was working to make money to pay her fucking hospital bills. Turned out Michelle had not made it down to our accountant's office to sign some papers, and she didn't have health insurance. I still don't know how much that's going cost me, somewhere around $100,000.

Later, Michelle said the accident was a big turning point for her in our relationship. She was like, "That's it. Done!" Again, because I wasn't "there" for her.

Well who does she think called her mother in Seattle and flew her ass down? As for the kids, I was "there" most every day when Michelle was in the hospital. Not that I had shit to do. The nanny didn't need a lot of help. Anyway, I am always taking care of my kids.

They live in a nice house. They have nice clothes. They've got everything they want in the world.

Of course, if you're a man, you know all that doesn't mean shit. You can talk yourself silly, present evidence, pile up the facts, whatever: she's still right, you're still wrong, get over it. If you ever want to get laid again, you best start groveling. No big deal. For the past few years, it seems like Michelle and I are always in the middle of either breaking up or getting back together. It wasn't that way in the beginning.

◆ ◆ ◆ ◆ ◆

I don't remember any of this, but Michelle claims she first laid eyes on me at the Cheesecake Factory in the Fashion Island Shopping Center in Newport Beach in 1997. She was there with a guy friend, and she says we started talking, something about her tattoos and piercings, me using my usual colorful language, "motherfucker" this and "motherfucker" that.

Then I asked the guy, "This your wife?"

He was like, "No. If she were you wouldn't be disrespecting her like that."

There was a little more jawing back and forth, and that was it.

A couple of years later I was at Margaritaville in Newport Beach with Jeremy Gallagher and a couple of other friends listening to—I think it was the Blue Machine band—and throwing back a few Redheaded Sluts, a concoction made out of Jägermeister, cranberry juice, and peach schnapps. Michelle and her way-hot girlfriend walked by. Everybody was drooling over the girlfriend, but Michelle kept parading back and forth, trying to get our attention.

After a while, I got up to go talk to the girlfriend, but suddenly Michelle was in my face—at least that's the way I remember it. Michelle says I called her over to the table. Whatever. We all ended up drinking Kamakazis, having a good ole time.

Later we left Margaritaville and went down to a club called White House in Laguna Beach. Michelle got lucky. Her husband had left the place five minutes before we got there. Unfortunately, his best friend was still around, and he tried to drag Michelle out of my pick-up truck. She kicked him away and told him to "Fuck off!" Words were exchanged, but the guy was outnumbered, so he disappeared. Shortly thereafter, Michelle started getting phone calls from her husband. She was like, "Screw you. I'm staying with Dennis."

He kept calling.

She kept hanging up on him.

"I felt like I was in high school," recalled Jeremy.

Meanwhile, Michelle's way-hot girlfriend got sick, threw up, and went home. Michelle stayed and ended up going to the beach house with me. She was married. I was still with Carmen Electra.

"We were both being bad," said Michelle.

Some badder than others.

So we were in my bedroom going at it, and her phone rings again. She answers it again. Guess who? She told him not to call back, and we went on about our business. I was thinking, "This is the kind of girl I like. Fucking bold as hell."

This was in December of 1999. We started seeing each other, but then I signed with the Mavericks and was off to Dallas. We kept up a phone relationship, and I called her one day, said, "What's up?" She was like, "My husband beat my ass." She claimed he had broken her nose in two places. I can't vouch for that, never saw her, but at the time, I took her word for it.

"Well, go to my house and stay there, and I'll take care of you," I said.

So I moved her and her 10-year-old daughter into the beach house, and I was a big hero. "My knight in shining armor," she called me. I've met girls like Michelle all my life, seen them leave their husbands because of me. Most of the time, I was like, "Not my problem." I didn't want to be tied down. But for some reason, I felt sorry for Michelle.

After I moved home from Dallas in March, I got Michelle and her kid a place in Mission Viejo. She said she hated her job, so I told her to quit and hang out with me. Normally that would be the last thing I wanted, but there was something about this girl.

Michelle soon got an up close-and-personal look at the Dennis Rodman lifestyle.

Here's a couple of quick stories.

Even though Michelle and I were sleeping together, Carmen was my number-one girl at the time. Michelle was cool with it. How cool? One time when I couldn't drive because my license had been suspended, she actually chauffeured me up to L.A. to see Ms. Electra. Another day when Carmen showed up unannounced at the beach house for a barbeque, Michelle hid next door. Eventually she left, and Carmen stayed. That was the pecking order, and everybody knew it. After hanging with me awhile, Michelle not only knew her place, she knew that when it came to relationships, nothing was sacred, and nothing was permanent.

"She knew exactly what Dennis Rodman was about," Thaer recalled. "She read his books. She saw him every day.

"She got involved in a relationship with her eyes wide open," Thaer continued. "And she knew all these other women couldn't change him. If Carmen Electra couldn't change him, how did she think she was going to change him?"

"Yeah, I knew how he was. I was just praying that things would change," Michelle told a reporter. "Any woman wants to believe that she's gonna be the one that is different for him. And I did, I did believe that.

"I was in denial," she continued. "I didn't want to believe he actually had these other women. And what I didn't see didn't hurt me."

◆ ◆ ◆ ◆

Six months after I got back from Dallas, I was sitting in Josh Slocum's one afternoon, minding my own business, and this girl who had been hanging out with us came in and said, "Congratulations on you guys having a baby."

I was like, "Who you talkin' to? Me? You talkin' to me? I'm not havin' no fuckin' baby."

She said, "Well, Michelle just said she's three months' pregnant."

I was like, "What?"

Michelle was still married, for God's sake. We were nowhere near being an official "couple." I was beyond pissed. Some days I think Michelle got pregnant on purpose. Some days I don't. Every day I'm glad she did. D.J. has always been a joy. In fact, I loved D.J. so much, Michelle and I planned the second baby. The way I looked at it, "We got one; why don't we have another one? Fuck it." So not long after D.J. was born on April 25, 2001, Michelle got pregnant with Trinity.

Then I took it to a whole new level.

While Michelle was still pregnant, I called her on the phone one day and said, "Open your door." Out on her doorstep, she found a Faberge egg and a note. "Will you marry me?" the note read. Inside the egg, an engagement ring. Two years later, already the proud parents of two, we were married at the Orange County Courthouse. A year after that, Michelle filed for divorce.

This was in the spring of 2004, *after* I had stopped drinking. So I asked her, "Why do you want a divorce now that I'm sober?"

"You aren't treating me right," she replied.

I was like, "Well how the fuck you want me to treat you?"

She had a long list of things she wanted me to do to prove to her that I really wanted a wife and family: get rid of the beach house, spend more time with her and the kids, go to church. So I did all that and more.

As Thaer told a reporter, "He does whatever a girl tells him to do when she's leavin' him. He does that over and over again."

"He's changed completely to try to make this work," Michelle said. "He stopped drinking. He sold his crazy beach house. He tried to make a life for us.

"He did everything he could to prove to me that he wanted me back and he wanted a family," Michelle continued. "He went on shows—Howard Stern called me to try to get us back together. He went on television shows with shirts with my face on the front of them that he had made to try to prove to me that he was for real. Pretty cute things."

After I sold the beach house, I was ready for us to buy a house together, but Michelle wanted to rent for a year to see if it was going to work out. So that's how we ended up in the house in Huntington Beach. I also asked my mother for help in saving the marriage. My mother and I had a falling out when she took my sister Debra's side after I fired her as my business manager a few years back. But I swallowed my pride and gave her a phone call for the first time in like five years.

"Could you talk to my wife? Let her know I'm serious," I said. "Explain to her that she's the only person who understands me."

She called and left a message. Michelle didn't call back.

There were two more things I did to get Michelle back. I took her on a belated honeymoon to Hawaii, and then came the capper, something I picked up from an old transvestite friend, and, trust me, bro, it was better than 1,000 empty promises. I went into Michelle's closet and took one shoe out of every shoe box, must have been a hundred of them. I made a Polaroid picture of each shoe and pasted it on the end of the box and surprised her with a super-organized shoe closet when she got back from church.

Home run.

So I got her back, and things were good for about two seconds. Then I started drifting again—back to my old tricks—never at home, ignoring her and the kids, stopped going to church.

"If he's after her, she's running," said Jeremy. "If she's after him, he's not really running, he's just still being Dennis."

By now, you know that "just being Dennis" is code for a lifestyle that includes sleeping around. So Michelle was already pissed before she had the motorcycle accident on May 30, and then came the last straw, when in her mind, I was not "there for her" when she was laid up. She was telling everybody, "He didn't do a damn thing. And that's why we're where we are right now."

Where we were was right back where we started when she filed for divorce in 2004. Michelle still wanted a normal life, and I was not giving it to her. Or at least that's what she said.

"I'm your wife," she said. "You need to include me in your life. I'm a part of you."

I went for the full-court press this time. I asked her to renew our vows in Hawaii, promised to finally get that will taken care of and buy that house together like we'd been talking about. I was willing to do whatever it took to make Michelle see that I was serious about us being together, being a family.

I told her, "I think it's kind of fucked up how we've been living our lives the last five years, and we should plan on just saying 'Fuck it!' and being together forever. Let's just go do it and do it right and make it official, let people know that we're married."

All my friends were telling me I was crazy, that the woman was jerking me around.

"I think Dennis's issue, anytime a woman treats him like shit," Darren told a reporter. "He respects them more, because it reminds him of his relationship with his mom."

Darren wasn't alone. Everybody was saying she treats you bad, that's why you stay with her. Nope. That has nothing to do with it. I stay with her because I love her. She's probably the only girl with whom I've shared a real, clear connection.

And if we ever get our shit together, this could turn out to be a life-long relationship. Michelle is hopeful. "I think that honestly that Dennis and I will always be," she said. "We'll always be. We will be together for good.

"We love each other, love each other to death," she continued. "Everything's good. Everything. Everything."

So despite all the fussing and fighting, coming and going, I love Michelle, and Michelle loves me. This much we know is true.

So we're talking "happily ever after," right?

Wrong.

Reality Check: Just because something is true, doesn't mean it's the "truth."

CHAPTER SEVENTEEN

MR. AND MRS. RODMAN

Here's what my love life is like. I always have this mother ship I call home. That ship is surrounded by lifeboats, which I call "Rodman's Navy." Sometimes I will visit a lifeboat, but I always come back to the mother ship. If the mother ship springs a leak, I hop on a lifeboat to keep me afloat until the mother ship is patched up or another ship comes along. Then I start all over—been doing that all my adult life. Everybody tells me if I want a lasting relationship, I'm going to have to give up those lifeboats, go solo on the mother ship. If I go down, I go down. To me that feels like betting all your money on one roll of the dice.

Did I mention the mother ship sometimes fires on the lifeboats? Swivels her 16-inch guns and fires away, trying to blow them out of the water. A few salvos here, a few salvos there, then the people on the lifeboats break out the UZIs, everybody's blazing away, and boats start going down. The mother ship catches fire. There are secondary explosions. Then the lifeboats start firing on each other, fighter planes appear out of nowhere, and suddenly it's the Battle of fucking Midway—total chaos—or what I like to call, "Just another evening with Michelle."

✦ ✦ ✦ ✦ ✦

I don't know exactly when Michelle's jealousy thing became a full-blown, put-it-in-capital-letters PROBLEM. When we first got together, I was fooling around, she was fooling around, not to mention married, and everything was more or less cool. Maybe it became an issue after the kids came along or after we got married. Whatever. A couple of years into our relationship, Michelle became a living, breathing example of "crazy jealous." Sometimes there was good reason.

"I've had women right in front of me come up to Dennis and say, 'I want to fuck you,'" Michelle told a reporter. "Right in front of me. I'm like, 'Excuse me?'"

Other times, Michelle's jealousy made no sense at all, like in September of 2003, when we were at the Vision Expo West eyewear convention in Las Vegas. I was there to help the Revolution Eyewear company sell frames, sunglasses, whatever. The night before I was to do my "personal appearance," Michelle, Darren, bodyguard William Castleberry and I were at a strip club. I cozied up to one of the strippers and gave her a couple hundred bucks for lap dances.

Suddenly, Michelle goes ape shit. She was like, "What are you doing with your money? You stupid son of a bitch! We have kids. How could you throw away that money?" She grabbed the money from the stripper and put it in her pocketbook. Then she started smacking me—right there in the middle of the club. William hustled our asses out of there before club security got involved.

So we piled in the limo, and Michelle was still ripping me up one side and down the other. She started throwing beer bottles at me, glasses. We're talking really close quarters inside the limo, so it was hard for her to miss. I was dodging, trying to talk her down. No luck. Finally, William got between the two of us. He was like, "Michelle, if you don't stop it, I'm gonna knock your ass out. I'm getting paid to protect this guy." So she backed off, and the first thing I did when we got to Olympic Gardens was buy her a lap dance. That calmed her down. But Michelle wasn't done.

At about 7:00 a.m., we headed back to the Palm, and everybody went to bed except me. I decided to go to the Crazy Horse strip club to meet some friends. Michelle woke up about three hours later and started pounding on Darren's door, freaking out. "Where the fuck is Dennis?" she screamed. Darren was clueless, but after she tore out of there, he called William's cell and told us to get our asses back to the hotel before Michelle had a meltdown. Meanwhile Michelle went downstairs and lit into the hotel security people. "Where's my husband?" this, that. Finally, the president of the Palm called Darren and said, "This woman's out of control. If you don't get her to chill out, we're going to kick her out of here."

There's more.

In December of 2004, I went to Houston to finish shooting the "Diana Pearl" Super Bowl commercial. I stayed over an extra night, and when I got home, Michelle was waiting for me. Darren and his fiancé Symone were there, and they watched as Michelle, as Darren recalled it, "Just winds up and hits him in the face—like as hard as you've ever seen anybody hit somebody."

"You lying son of a bitch," Michelle screamed. "Where the fuck were you last night?"

I lost it.

"If I wasn't who I was, I would knock your fucking teeth out right now," I yelled. "You beat the shit out of me all fuckin' day long. If I lay a hand on you, I go to jail."

Later I asked Darren if he thought Michelle had a jealousy problem. "Oh, a psychotic jealousy problem," he answered.

I've got as many examples of this shit as you'd like. There was the time Michelle was following me and a couple of friends in broad daylight, including this woman I wasn't sleeping with. Michelle jumps out and starts screaming and yelling at her, "Who the hell are you? This is my husband."

"*This is my husband.*"

I don't know how many times I've heard Michelle say that when some woman gets within five yards of my ass—that, and "We have babies." It was like somebody waving a cross in front of Dracula, y'know? Ward off them bitches. She then added another weapon to her arsenal.

We were out drinking one night at this bar, got drunk, naturally, and ended up in the tattoo parlor next door. Michelle started joking around about getting "Rodman" tattooed on her back. And I was like, "Why don't you add a 'Mrs.?'" So the tattoo guy did the drawing, we took a look at it, and said "What the fuck?" Shortly thereafter, Michelle had a "Mrs. Rodman" tattoo on the small of her back, which she would soon begin flashing whenever some threatening "chick" was in my vicinity, as if her saying, "This is my husband. We have babies," wasn't enough. She needed more evidence. Like anybody gave a shit. I know it wouldn't have stopped Michelle. Not even locked doors stopped her ass.

I was upstairs in the beach house one time with some girl. Michelle broke down the first door and then outdid herself on the second one, breaking it in half. By the time she got through the second door, the girl was dressed, and I was hiding behind the door naked. She slapped the shit out of me and screamed, "I'm fucking through with you!" She ran outside. I chased her, and I ended up naked in the street talking to the cops. (These days, Michelle giggles when she tells this story.) By then, the cops were tired of being called to my house in the middle of the night. "One more call," they said, "and we'll haul both of you in. We're sick of this shit with you two."

Then there was the time we were on the way to this Super Bowl party in San Diego. This black girl walks up and wants to get her picture taken with me—standard operating procedure, y'know?

Michelle went nuts. "That's my husband! We have babies," she screamed. She created a fucking scene in the middle of the street—and for what?

"She wants to be part of his life, but every time he makes her part of his life, she goes crazy," Thaer said. "She does something stupid."

"She's so bad that we don't bring her out," Darren told a reporter. "She wants to know why she isn't invited to events—because she would fucking ruin him if we took her.

"It's the truth," Darren continued. "Thaer knows it. Dennis knows it. One girl just walks up to Dennis the wrong way, kisses him on the lips, grabs him or hugs him, and she'll lose her mind."

"Whenever she went on a trip, I wouldn't go," Thaer said. "'Cause I knew there was gonna be drama. So I wouldn't even go. And Darren was like, 'You gotta go.' I'm like, 'I ain't going. Michelle's going with him. I'll get 'em to the airport, and they're on their own.'"

So you've got Michelle, this crazy jealous woman with a bad temper, married to Dennis Rodman, this man who fucks everything that moves.

Gasoline and matches.

No wonder Darren has called it "a psychotic relationship."

"That's the match made in hell, those two," Thaer said. "Mr. and Mrs. Rodman."

CHAPTER EIGHTEEN

FORSAKING ALL OTHERS?

The Newport Beach house was pink with bright-blue awnings. The Huntington Beach house was beige with a red-tile roof. One was party central on a popular beach. The other was a single-family home on a quiet residential street. One was for raising hell—the other for raising a family. So in June of 2004, I said goodbye to a house that had seen more parties than the Playboy mansion, said goodbye to the full bar and rotating mirrored ball at 4809 Seashore Drive, and said hello to the three-car garage and automated sprinkler system at 6621 Horseshoe Lane. It was the end of an era.

The new house was in an upscale cluster development, houses shoulder to shoulder on both sides of the street: stone and stucco, gray, grayer, and beige. On one typical afternoon, kids on bikes, skateboards, and motorized scooters cruised up and down the street in front of the house. My black BMW 745-Li was parked out front, and sitting on a concrete driveway made to look like terra cotta tile, Michelle's white Mercedes S-600. It was "trash night," and up and down the street, plastic garbage cans sat waiting at the curb.

Beginning at 6:15 p.m., hidden sprinklers, little black pipes, rose about three inches out of the ground in front of my house. There was a spitting sound, then a steady hiss. Five minutes later, that first set of sprinklers sunk back into the ground, and a new set rose to water another corner of the lawn. The first time I saw that shit, I was like, "What the fuck? Does Dennis Rodman really live here?" The lawn is tiny, and it's not like you couldn't water it with a garden hose in 15 minutes. The place wasn't me. And neither was the settling down bullshit—no matter what I'd said.

When I was dictating all that mushy stuff that you read a few pages back about Michelle, when I said, "I love her. She's probably the only girl I've ever had a real, clear connection with." At that very moment, there was this other girl I was sleeping with sitting beside me. Right when I was saying it. Then that same night I slept with another girl I hang out with a lot. That doesn't mean what I said about Michelle isn't true. It just means it isn't true in the way an average person would think it's true. I do love Michelle. I do think we have a "real, clear connection." But don't expect me to stop "being Dennis." As for old I-want-a-normal-family Michelle, she's got her own line of bullshit going.

"I'm at a point in my life now," she said, "I'm 38, our kids need a family, I don't want to party anymore. I'm over it."

Yeah, right. Time to can the June Cleaver crap. The very same day I was laying down that "Michelle-4-Ever" rap, she was on the back of a motorcycle headed for the Black Hills Motor Classic in Sturgis, South Dakota—this huge gathering of bike freaks. There wouldn't be any partying going on out there. Lights out at 9:30 for the "Harley Nation."

What I'm trying to get at is: all this lovey-dovey talk coming from both of us doesn't mean what it means with normal people in a normal relationship. When I say I want to "settle down," that doesn't mean I'm willing to give up my lifeboats. When she says she wants a normal family … actually, I have no idea what she means by that. But it doesn't mean what most people would think it means. Normal for Michelle ain't "normal."

So it's time to knock off the bullshit and tell the truth rather than what our family, friends, and Oprah might want to hear. Time to talk about what we really want.

People are always asking me if I am ready to settle down. Wrong question. The question is whether I want Michelle in my life forever. The answer is "yes." What will I do to keep her there? Whatever she wants—for a while. And I mean it when I say that. Then I walk out on the beach, and the harbor is full of lifeboats.

You know that phrase in the wedding vows about "forsaking all others?" I'm Dennis Rodman. That just ain't gonna happen. Never was gonna happen. Never will happen. Meanwhile, I want Michelle to be true to me.

So if you take all this and throw it in a pot, is it possible for us to cook up something permanent, some kind of fucked-up family? So far, we haven't been able to make it work. Like I said, we're always either breaking up or making up: Michelle going postal, me saying anything, doing anything, buying anything, to get her back. This go-around, I bought her a 10-carat diamond ring. She said, "I don't want that. I want *you*."

Well, she's already got as much of me as she's going to get, as much as anybody is going to get. Is it enough? Can it ever really work?

Who the fuck knows?

"He'll always be out there in the limelight," Michelle told an interviewer. "He'll never be able to just be my husband, my kids' father. There's always something more to it."

She's got that right. Cue the violins.

"And I don't know if I can do that anymore," Michelle said to a reporter. "It's taken a lot of strength to get through as much as we've gone through. And I knew it going in.

"Eventually you have to grow up. We have children. They need to be taken care of. They need a father."

Not to mention a mother.

And what about her jealousy problem? "I've changed a lot. I don't fight anymore," Michelle said. "It's not worth it. I've got children, and I'm just not gonna go through that anymore over some skanky chick."

The jury is still out on that one.

Then, as if our real problems are not enough, Michelle is forever finding bullshit problems (she probably picks them up reading those fucking women's magazines) that she says are threatening our marriage. I'm going to run through them one at a time.

Not Even A Problem Number One: I show my love by buying her things.

"He's got a heart of gold. He really does. He's very generous. And not knowing how to love me and the children, y'know, his way of loving is to buy me things," Michelle told a reporter. "He tries to give me things to show me that he loves me. And he just doesn't get that I don't want it. I want him to just love me."

Guilty as charged. I'm trying to be more of a touchy-feely kind of guy. Meanwhile Michelle isn't turning down many gifts.

I take that back. That was a cheap shot.

Not Even A Problem Number Two: I'm irresponsible.

"He has no responsibilities. None," Michelle told a reporter. "And for that matter, neither have I.

"Those accountants take care of everything," Michelle continued. "They pay the house payments, they pay for the cable, they pay the phone—you know there's not too much really left to do."

Sounds pretty good to me, but not to Michelle.

"I've been living this kind of fairy tale life, and it sucked," she said. "I want responsibility back, y'know? I want to be normal."

Where do I start?

First, for a guy with "no responsibilities," I sure seem to be paying a lot of bills—like that cable bill and house payment. In the divorce papers she filed in 2004, Michelle claimed monthly expenses for her and the kids ran to $17,000, including about $2,000 for Michelle's personal trainer and $500 and change for "hair, nails, tanning, and Botox." Take all that and the $15,000 per month in child support I was paying for Alexis and Chance, and the $4,000 I send my mother, and you have a man who feels like he has a shitload of responsibilities.

Not Even A Problem Number Three: Religion.

"I'm a Christian and I need for him to be as well. That's another thing we're kind of struggling with."

I'm not going to touch that one.

Not Even A Problem Number Four: Dennis is a slut for attention.

"He needs to know from people that he still has it," Michelle said. "And he needs to know that from the public and other women, other people saying, 'Oh wow! Dennis Rodman,' instead of me and just his kids being enough. That's what I'm looking for—one day for us to be enough for him."

I'm a celebrity. Getting attention is what I do. It's how I make a living. And like Michelle said, with a laugh, "He's gotta keep doin' that. Got too many kids."

Could Be a Little Bit of a Problem Number One: We're both guarded.

Michelle says her dad pulled out when she was 14, and then her brother passed away.

"I've been through some things with men. So in this relationship with Dennis, I'm pretty guarded," Michelle told a reporter.

And since both of us are guarded, "It's really hard to get close, because I think I'm afraid that he's going to hurt me. He's afraid I'm going to hurt him.

"The one thing we do know," continued Michelle, "is that we love each other."

Could Be a Little Bit of a Problem Number Two: I don't know how to live together.

"He doesn't know how to do it. He just doesn't know."

Like she does. This is a woman who pulled out of a relationship of 11 years to chase my sorry ass, a woman who had a kid with her "first love" when she was 22 and couldn't parlay that into a marriage—much less something that lasted. And here she sits: a couple of decades into her adult life, making up one half of the most fucked-up relationship since Adam chomped down on the apple, trying to play the "girl card" on me?

Bullshit. She's no better at this than I am.

As for all her crap about wanting us to be normal—Girl, have you checked me out lately? Are the nose studs and lip rings a clue? Do you know what I do for a living? Do you know what a 10-carat diamond ring costs?

Normal ain't an option.

Now I don't pretend to be a marriage counselor, but I can tell you one thing: our real problems don't have shit to do with how I show love, whether or not I need attention, who pays the cable bill, takes out the fucking garbage, or leaves the toilet seat up. Our real problems are my lifeboats and her insane jealousy. Throw in our backburner issues, my drinking, and her temper, and you have a melodrama in the making.

There is one woman's-magazine upside to all this: Michelle is *really* good at expressing her emotions.

◆ ◆ ◆ ◆ ◆

As of right now, Michelle and I are still hanging in there. Last I heard, she has decided not to file because "it's not over." Me, I'm hanging in because Michelle is Michelle.

As many problems as we've had, I still put her right up there with Carmen. But Carmen was a shooting star. You can say anything you want about Michelle, but the girl does have staying power.

"I've been by his side. I've stayed there. I've been through a lot of crap with him, and I haven't left," she told a reporter.

"How long have you been together?" the reporter asked.

"Five and a half years—it'll be six years."

"So you're his longest relationship."

"Uh huh—and his closest."

And as far as my friends are concerned, "the most fucked-up." These days, it's hard to find Michelle fans in my posse. "That's his last infection that he needs to cure himself of," said one. So what's the general drift?

She's a gold digger.

"She left her husband and went for the bigger, better deal," a friend said.

She's jealous.

"That's a jealous girl. She's very, very jealous," said a friend.

"That would be the understatement of the century," seconded another friend. "That's like saying Dennis can *kind of rebound.*"

She trapped me by getting pregnant.

"Michelle knew what she was doing when she had those kids. Ka-ching! Let's forget the pill today, and let's cash the fuck in," said a friend. "I don't have any respect for a woman that uses kids as a meal ticket."

All this is pretty much bullshit. Take the money thing. Hello. One of the kids was planned. And if Michelle was just in it for the dough, she could have cashed in a long time ago. As for the jealousy, I give her good reason for that, and it's understandable right up until the point her hand meets my jaw or she coughs up that "He's my husband, we have babies," bullshit and creates an ugly scene.

While my friends are hammering Michelle, they're usually giving me a free ride, saying, "Oh that's just Dennis being Dennis," and she knew what she was getting into before she married him. Hey, that's what friends are for—but the truth is, I ain't exactly a Fat Burger with homemade onion rings myself. The philandering, the drinking—Michelle has put up with her share of crap, and we are still together, much to the amazement of my friends.

"Those two don't belong together. They should have called it quits a long time ago," one friend told a reporter. "Neither one of 'em is going to get out of it alive.

"They do have a dysfunctional relationship," he continued. "If you can call it a relationship. It's just pure dysfunction."

"It's nuts," said another friend. "Their relationship is completely fucking nuts."

I know my friends just want what's best for me, but sometimes I get tired of people who think they know what I want and need better than I do. I know my body. I know my mind. I know my soul better than anybody else. And when someone sits there and says, "I know you, Dennis." I'm like, "Oh, great. You know me? Great."

Reality Check: *You don't know me.*

If you did, you'd know I love Michelle more than anything in the world.

Over the past five or so years, Darren and Thaer have come to understand this. They know how I feel about Michelle and that, as the mother of my children, she will always be in our lives. So I can honestly say that, at the end of the day, Darren and Thaer really do care about Michelle and the kids, and all of us on "Team Rodman" are pulling together, trying to make it work—up to a point. There comes a time when the best thing to do, even for our closest friends, is just to get out of the way and let the two of us work it out.

For even if Michelle and I do have a fucked-up relationship, it's *our* fucked-up relationship. It may be psychotic, dysfunctional, this, that. But as Michelle said, the one thing you can't say is, "It's over."

So just let us be. And I promise that if it ever does fall completely apart, you guys will be the first to hear. Just listen for breaking glass, a thunderous slap, and one last cry of "He's my husband, we have babies."

CHAPTER NINETEEN
MEDIA SLIGHTINGS

Huntington Beach, California, June 11, 2005. The black Cadillac Escalade pulled up in front of my house around 6:00 p.m., and Thaer and the reporter he had just picked up at the Orange County Airport hopped out. Despite past experience, I had agreed to let the reporter follow me around for a couple of days. I never learn. Later he would write that, when he arrived at the house, I "never really said hello, made eye contact, or offered my hand." He didn't take offense—just mentioned it. Whatever. I never do that bullshit with strangers.

I tossed a pair of autographed basketball shoes into the back of the Escalade, and then I led the reporter inside to meet Michelle. D.J. and Trinity met me at the door—that lasted about two seconds—and then went tearing down the hall. Michelle shuffle-stepped into the foyer, moving slowly on her wheeled walker, a white, plastic neck brace propping up her chin. This was only 11 days after her motorcycle accident up at Big Bear, but if you ignored the medical hardware, she looked none the worse for wear—blond and beautiful as ever in jeans and a T-shirt. Miraculously, her face didn't have a mark on it. There *were* a couple of small bandages on her left foot, and if you made the effort, you could see it was swollen.

"This is my wife, Michelle," I said, and she and the reporter started making small talk.

Later the reporter would write that, when introducing Michelle, my "shy, gentle, self-effacing manner," reminded him of "a young Jimmy Stewart."

Mr. Stewart would be rolling over in his grave.

Michelle told the reporter that her shoulder was giving her the most trouble at the moment. Said when she got to the emergency room up in Loma Linda, there was a bone sticking out of her leg. That's the left leg, the one in which they inserted the rod. She had a picture somewhere.

Trinity ran through as the nanny watched from the shadows of an adjoining room. D.J. collared the reporter and showed him this toy motorcycle ramp sitting on the floor—start 'em early, I say—then took off again.

"You have beautiful children," the reporter said.

I gave Michelle all the props and then said my goodbyes to the kids. We were headed to L.A. for an overnighter—a Cedars-Sinai benefit where Thaer had said they would be auctioning off the autographed shoes. Back outside, we hopped in the Escalade, Thaer at the wheel, the reporter in back, already jotting down a bunch of shit in his notebook. At the time, it gave me the creeps. I mean, what kind of pissy little detail had this guy spotted in the last 15 minutes that was worth writing down? It was another reminder that letting a reporter into your life is not always a good thing.

◆ ◆ ◆ ◆

In the spring of 2003, Stephen Rodrick, this reporter from *The New York Times,* came down to Newport Beach to catch up on Dennis Rodman. At the time, I was partying my ass off—pretty much 24 hours a day—but I'd agreed to let him follow me around.

Bad move. The title of the story alone, "No Rebound," gives you an idea of how it went.

In the very first paragraph of a piece that appeared in *The New York Times Magazine* on June 1, 2003, Rodrick described me as "giddy and a little incoherent." Translation: I was drunk. So why didn't the guy just say, "Fuck it! We'll try it another day"? He had a deadline and an agenda.

The gist: Dennis Rodman is finished.

"Like an aging sitcom that keeps getting moved to a worse and worse time slot," he wrote, "Dennis Rodman's celebrity is near cancellation.

"[He] has no endorsements, no public appearances, and few prospects," he continued. "Rodman's collapse is classic American overexposure."

I won't go through my entire 2003 schedule, but at the time this article was written, I had just finished shooting *Celebrity Mole*; had a nice, fat contract with GoldenPalace.com; and ESPN was poised to shoot *Rodman on the Rebound*. So news of my "collapse" was greatly exaggerated. But as they say in the newsroom, "Never let the facts get in the way of a good story."

To prove his point about my failing career, Rodrick talked to my former agent, Dwight Manley. Well Manley hadn't represented my ass in like four and a half years and didn't know jack shit about what was happening in my life. Of course, that didn't stop Dwight from offering an opinion—anything to get a little ink in *The New York Times*.

"Dennis could earn $200,000 a year just being Dennis Rodman, making personal appearances and doing events," said Manley. "He could have a nice life."

I'm not saying what I made that year, but it was a hell of a lot more than that. If he had called Darren, who had been representing me for about two years at that point, he could have found out how my career was really going.

After declaring my career had tanked, *The New York Times* guy moved on. He seemed determined not only to prove I was a loser in the celebrity sweepstakes, but a loser in life as well. I helped him out on that one. I was drunk and obnoxious, putting myself in a position to be fucked, and I paid the price. Not that it was fair—the guy was holding his nose the whole time he was there, but he didn't just come out and say that up front. Didn't say, "I don't like this guy. I don't like his lifestyle." Instead, he piled up one cheap-shot detail after another.

For example, the *Times* reporter didn't approve of these two stray guys who had washed up on the patio at the beach house, their "ample white guts basting in the spring sun." He wasn't any easier on me, writing, "His chiseled body has gone a bit to seed; a tiny pot-belly pokes out ..." and "... a hangdog smile [spread] across his chapped lips."

What an asshole.

After we left the beach house and went to Josh Slocum's, the *Times* reporter hung out with me until the wee hours. Watching me get drunker and drunker. (This is the guy who quit counting after I had 19 shots.) He made note of all the stupid shit I did: cranking up the stereo to "ear-bleeding levels," and "wildly dancing, kicking his massive legs into the air within just a yard or so from middle-aged patrons" causing "more than a dozen guests [to] abandon dinner and leave the restaurant." I showed my ass, and the reporter used it to "prove" that I was an over-the-hill loser.

Cue Mr. Manley.

"He's just a shadow of what he was," Dwight told the reporter. "It breaks my heart."

Oh, please.

About a month later, ESPN came to town to begin shooting *Rodman on the Rebound*. Working from the same Rodman-partying-his-ass-off set of facts, ESPN produced very different results. Like the reporter from the *Times*, they had an angle: theirs was Rodman's NBA comeback. But unlike the *Times*, there were no cheap shots. Not that they didn't have the opportunity—they caught me drunk on camera twice. The difference is, they didn't seem happy about it.

There was many a time that Thaer drove the ESPN crew around from bar to bar looking for my drunken ass. When they couldn't find me, they'd interview Thaer, and in the finished show, Thaer was on camera so much that we took to calling it *Mustafa on the Rebound*.

In the ESPN case, having an angle, an agenda, worked in my favor in a couple of ways. First, they were totally committed to documenting my comeback, because that's how they sold the story to the boss—got him to agree to spend six months and a lot of bucks following me around. So that made the drunk-on-the-rampage angle a subplot. Secondly, once they were on the ground, they were so set on telling that comeback story, I'm guessing that they genuinely couldn't see that the story was making a U-turn and heading in a whole new drunken direction. And while the final product would showcase my drinking problem, the program was still built around the comeback angle with these "supers"—superimposed headlines—used throughout to track my progress toward that goal. Sometimes it seemed a little silly. For example, over video showing me licking my wounds in a room at the Hard Rock after my motorcycle accident, they supered, "10 Days to NBA Tip-Off," although at that point my comeback was beyond dead. If they had been true to what was really going on, there would have been an entirely different set of supers: "Seven Days to the Intervention" maybe, or "20 Days to Sobriety," because what they had on tape was not a comeback, but a downfall.

While *The New York Times* and ESPN had the same basic "downfall" raw material to work with, they shaped it in different ways. Rodrick took a "holier than thou" slant; ESPN a more "This is just the facts, ma'am" approach. There was an undercurrent of preaching in the *Times* story. ESPN was more straightforward, telling the story with less spin. While I didn't like either story, I had to admit that ESPN was at least fair. And when it comes to the media, that's about the best you can hope for. I guess I should be thankful. If ESPN had come in with the same "Let's-fuck-Rodman" attitude as the *Times*, they could have absolutely buried my ass.

About a year later, FOX Sports Net came to town to shoot *Beyond the Glory: Dennis Rodman*. By then I was sober, and they produced a positive, straightforward biography. You could hardly wish for a better coverage, even though Michelle wasn't happy with all the file footage of me and a series of big-breasted blondes.

The point: you never know what you're going to get when you let the media through your door.

If you're talking a reality show or some shit like that, an entertainment program, sometimes Darren can negotiate a little leeway—leave this in, take that out. But when somebody calling himself a "journalist," whether newspaper, magazine, television, or radio, crosses your threshold, it's a total crapshoot. And even if they get it all wrong, there's not much you can do about it. Legally, a celebrity is something called a "public figure," and as long as the news dudes don't just totally make shit up, they can get away with murder. Not that *The New York Times* went that far. The article was far subtler than that.

Take this quote from me that the *Times* dropped into the second paragraph of his story: "Just please don't say I'm an idiot," I said. Not to worry, he never does *say* that—doesn't have the balls—he just throws in enough bullshit to leave that impression, reporting that I "rhapsodiz[ed] at great length and graphic detail about the sexual prowess of [Michelle]" right in front of her. Then he described a little scene with a patronizing chef at Josh Slocum's, who upon seeing one of my drunken, spur-of-the-moment culinary creations, said, "somewhat unconvincingly," that "Dennis helps me with a lot of things. He is so creative."

To be fair to Rodrick, there was one thing he did get exactly right. On that lovely spring day in 2003, I *was* headed toward oblivion. But not because I had "… hit the celeb tipping point," as he put it, but because I was a fucking drunk. The guy couldn't see the alcoholic forest for the I-have-an-agenda trees. So it will be a while before I talk to anybody from *The New York Times* again—not that it makes any difference. Whenever you let anybody from the media inside, it's like having a mountain lion as a family pet. One minute, the damn thing is purring—the next minute the son of a bitch is trying to eat the baby.

And there's no predicting which way it will go.

CHAPTER TWENTY

A "DENNIS RODMAN STORY"

When it came to being a Detroit "Bad Boy," I played second fiddle to Isiah Thomas, Bill Laimbeer, and Rick Mahorn. While I had my crazy moments, mostly surrounding the breakup with my first wife and separation from daughter Alexis, I didn't really begin racking up my own bad-boy credentials until my first season with the San Antonio Spurs in 1993-94. Off-court, the rainbow hair and the fling with Madonna got the media's attention. On-court, in the space of about two months, I head-butted Stacey King of the Chicago Bulls and John Stockton of the Utah Jazz, and before the year was over, I had been fined over $30,000, suspended three times by the NBA, and ejected from six games. "Dennis the Menace" had arrived.

After my move to Chicago, my on-court and off-court images would become one. While I kept up my on-court antics during the 1996-97 season—head-butting a referee, receiving a nice collection of suspensions, fines, and technicals—I picked up the pace off-court with my gender-bender book signings in New York and Chicago and the non-stop partying. Dennis Rodman was now a bad boy 24/7. For every head-butted referee there was a fondled cocktail waitress. Final evidence that I had crossed over to off-court, mainstream celebrity came in 1997, when I headed Mr. Blackwell's "37th Annual Worst-Dressed Women's List." Yeah, that's women's list. Now what I did off-court was as likely—if not more likely—to make news as anything I did on court. The dress-wearing, rainbow-haired, never-saw-a-boob-he-didn't-want-to-fondle, bad-boy stereotype was born, and with it the stock, fill-in-the-blanks "Dennis Rodman Story." A reporter with a set of facts now had a guidebook on what to leave in and what to leave out.

Rodman is drunk and showing his ass? Leave it in.

Rodman gives a wad of cash to a homeless man?—which insiders will tell you I'm known for doing. Leave it out.

Rodman is speeding through Colorado in a $250,000-plus Lamborghini? In.

Rodman's obeying the Colorado speed limit in a used, pastel minivan sporting a "What Would Jesus Do?" bumper sticker? Out.

It's not like I'm the first guy to get pigeon-holed by the media—happens all the time. Poor old Dan Quayle was hammered when he was vice president. "Remember any stories about him doing something smart?" asked one writer, during a riff on media stereotypes. This is no big scoop. Journalists routinely take a set of facts and pound them into submission, making them fit off-the-rack, stock stories or pre-packaged angles. And it not only happens at *The New York Times* and ESPN, but in your hometown rag as well.

Say a white cop in your city shoots and kills a black bank robber. Once the reporter gets the basic facts, he starts running through the list of stock stories to see if one will match up. Did the cop conform to the local "fleeing felon law" or is this a possible case of "police brutality?" Is racism involved? It goes on and on. But whether the subject is crime, politics, or Dennis Rodman, stock stories are the bread and butter of news organizations everywhere.

And if the facts don't fit? Try another angle.

✦ ✦ ✦ ✦ ✦

Oh, I don't know, why don't we start with the police report filed by "peace officer," James Gunter?

Warning: The following is rated X for violence.

"On June 7, 1998, at approximately 9:00 a.m., the body of a black male, minus the head and right arm, was discovered on Huff Creek Road in Jasper County, Texas."

The missing body parts would turn up in a ditch about a mile away.

"Officers attempted to compare the photograph on [the victim's] identification card to the head located on Huff Creek Road," officer Gunter's affidavit continued. "However, a positive identification could not be made."

A "torx [sic] wrench set inscribed with 'Berry'" was found near the body. The cops soon picked up one Shawn Allen Berry, 23, who confessed, naming two accomplices, James William King, 23, and Lawrence Russell Brewer, 31, in the brutal murder of a 49-year-old black man named James Byrd Jr.

"Three ... riders came straight out of hell," said the prosecutor at the trial, according to *Salon*. "Instead of a rope, they used a chain; and instead of horses, they had a pick-up truck."

After the men beat up Byrd, they took that chain, wrapped it around his ankles, attached it to the bumper of Berry's primer-gray, 1982 Ford pickup, and dragged the man three miles down a paved country road.

King was watching out the back window. "That fucker's bouncing all over the place," he said, according to the police report.

Byrd's ordeal ended when "a culvert ripped his head and shoulders off his body," reported *Salon*.

Byrd's sin? He was black.

The story attracted international attention. Jesse Jackson and Al Sharpton came to town for the funeral, as did a contingent from the KKK. Meanwhile, I stepped up. Now I'm not known as a guy who gets involved in social issues, civil rights or otherwise. Maybe that's why the coverage of my PETA billboard was more about Dennis Rodman being nude than my opposition to people wearing fur. In a standard "Dennis Rodman Story," I'm posing naked, not taking some kind of stand. But the murder of James Byrd Jr. by a trio of racist motherfuckers from hell was beyond sickening. After some of my experiences dating white girls in college, I had a "There-but-for-the-grace-of-God-go-I" feeling. So I stepped up and donated $25,000 to the family to help pay for the funeral and establish a family trust fund. That seed money, along with other donations, would eventually lead to the establishment of the James Byrd Foundation for Racial Healing.

I'm thinking much of this is probably news to you. While it's likely that you've heard about the murder of James Byrd Jr., it's unlikely you've heard about my part in that tragedy. In the lists of Dennis Rodman exploits found in stories over the years, you'll almost always see mentions of me wearing the wedding dress, dying my hair, kicking the photographer, this, that, but not the donation to the Byrd family. The reason? It's simply not a "Dennis Rodman Story." Bad boys aren't supposed to give a shit.

So when I Google "Dennis Rodman," "James Byrd," I get only 65 hits—but when I Google "Dennis Rodman," "Bullrun," I get over 500. The difference, of course, is that Bullrun is your classic "Dennis Rodman Story." My fans would expect the "outrageous," "notorious," "freakish," "hot-tempered" bad boy, as various reporters put it, to break the speed limit, drive recklessly, and run people off the road in my "flashy," "high-class," "exotic," car and to be involved in the kind of shenanigans that Nevada Highway Patrol Lieutenant Paul Hinen described to the Associated Press.

"As they got close to Reno, the reports were about them slowing down and blocking traffic and then speeding up," Hinen said. "Two cars running side by side, someone trying to jump from one car to another, passing beer bottles between cars, and throwing beer bottles at other cars."

I tell you, officer, I am shocked by such antics, not that I actually saw any of it. But if it did happen, I'll have to admit it does sound just like something "Dennis Rodman" might do.

The story angle from the Bullrun road rally that got the most play, of course, was my "stealing" the cowboy hat and not paying for gas at the Tomahawk Auto Truck Plaza in Glenwood Springs. What you probably didn't hear was that a week or so later, some mystery woman walked in off the street and paid my gas bill. At about the same time, my Bullrun sponsor, GoldenPalace.com, offered to give $1,000 to the truck-stop owner's favorite children's charity. You didn't hear about it, because these aren't "Dennis Rodman Stories." They sound more like something to do with Tiger Woods. He's a good guy. I'm a bad boy. Of course, he's just as trapped and stereotyped as I am, but that's a story for another day.

The media doesn't know what to do with a Dennis Rodman who donates money to the family of James Byrd Jr., takes a stand against wearing fur, gives money to charity—wears a white hat. A stock, Dennis Rodman bad-boy story writes itself.

Dennis Rodman—good guy? Too much work.

Thank God. If word ever gets out that I'm a soft-hearted, sushi-eating, gentle giant, I'll never work again. People only want to hear the bad news about the bad boy. Of course, there is a line that you can't cross if you want to be marketable.

Take Charles Manson, Jeffrey Dahmer, and that B.T.K. guy: you're not going to see them on a cereal box anytime soon. That's pure make-the-devil-look-like-a-sissy shit. Michael Jackson and O.J. are probably finished forever, at least in the U.S. Get back to me in a few years on Robert Blake. On the other hand, Tonya Harding, the Olympic skater who was involved in the cover-up of an idiotic attack on rival Nancy Kerrigan in 1994, ended up getting a contract with No Excuses jeans and is still getting work—*Celebrity Boxing*, skating gigs, this, that—because of her bad-girl image. The same goes for Monica Lewinsky, the woman Bill Clinton didn't have sex with. They are examples of how far you can take it and still be asked to host your own reality show. I've got a lot of catching up to do.

I've had a lot of hits and misses with the news dudes over the years. That's to be expected with all the thousands and thousands of media contacts I've had. I still average more than a dozen appearances a week—talk shows, reality shows, newscasts, radio, TV, newspapers. I mean the media are always around—always, always, always—and you win some, you lose some. The New York book signing in the wedding dress was a home run, *Rodman on the Rebound* an embarrassment. PETA was a winner, but the brawl with

Carmen in Miami was a real low point. The Stephen Rodrick *New York Times Magazine* article sucked.

So why do I keep putting myself at risk? Why not just tell the media to fuck off?

It's all in the numbers.

◆ ◆ ◆ ◆

Say you were invited to appear at Super Bowl 2005 at ALLTEL Stadium in Jacksonville. You've done something cool, and they want to walk you out to midfield during the pregame ceremony for a nice pat on the ass. They announce your name over the public address system, and 73,000 cheer. That's a ton of people, right?

That's nothing.

Remember that Super Bowl commercial I appeared in that year, which ran right before halftime? It was seen by about 86 million people—that's over twice the population of California. So if you make a living as a celebrity, you've got to get in front of those TV cameras.

On a much smaller scale, remember that grand opening I attended for Magic's fitness center in Sherman Oaks? I don't know how many people were there, several hundred. Who cares? Whether it's a political rally, an opening—whatever—all you need are enough people to be a nice backdrop, what looks like a "good crowd." After that, the real question is whether the TV cameras and newspaper reporters show up. If they do, suddenly your exposure changes from several hundred people to several hundred thousand. And it's the media that delivers that crowd, at first creating and then maintaining your celebrity.

It was the media in New York that took a book signing for *Bad As I Wanna Be* attended by several thousand people and made it into a media event seen and read about by millions. And in the A-list celebrity business, it's the millions that count. The media delivers those millions, and after you've become an established celebrity, you deliver the media—hand in glove. That's how the celebrity-rep business works.

So today, I'm hired precisely because the reporters and cameras are willing to follow me around. That coverage will get the commercial message I am delivering out to the masses free of charge, and the message is more believable than advertising because it's coming from what's supposed to be a reliable source—the news media. The bottom line is: I can't make a living without the media. Without them there is no "Dennis Rodman."

So on a given day, I park myself between the bassinette and the mountain lion and pet like hell, hoping to keep the damn thing away from the baby. It's a scene much like the one Stephen Rodrick described in the opening paragraphs of his story in *The New York Times Magazine*.

"Welcome to Rodman's Reef," I shouted to him. "Welcome to my crazy world. Put your tape recorder away, have a beer, and write anything you want."

I paused and then added seriously, "Just please don't say I'm an idiot."

Reality Check: Sometimes you have to feed the hand that bites you.

CHAPTER TWENTY-ONE

THE INTERVIEW

Thaer bore right, steering the Escalade up the on-ramp of Interstate 405, headed for L.A. As soon as we got up to cruising speed, the reporter in back pulled this palm-sized tape recorder out of a black canvas satchel and slapped on a set of silly-looking headphones. He said he wanted to monitor the sound quality of the interview as it was being recorded. Wouldn't want to miss any of the nuggets of wisdom soon to be tumbling out of my mouth.

I can't remember how many of these "in-depth" interviews I've done—dozens and dozens. They're different from the usual slapdash, hit-and-run, gotta-get-a-quote, sound-bite, newspaper and television interviews I normally do with reporters on deadline. Different because for one, they go on forever; and two, no matter what the angle of the story they're working on, a big part of the interview is usually spent plowing the same old ground. I don't know why the media don't trust each other to accurately report that I was born in Trenton, New Jersey; my father was a no-account son of a bitch; and how I came to be called "Worm."

(When I was a kid, I wiggled like a worm when I played pin-ball machines.)

After the reporter got everything rigged up, he scooted to the front edge of the bench seat in back, then leaned in between the bucket seats up front, almost shoulder-to-shoulder with Thaer and me, sticking the recorder in my face.

"Tape's rolling," he said, and I kick-started my brain into upbeat, "Hey, bro, you're-talking-to-the-world" mode. And that's how we started a series of interviews that spread over the next four days. I was "on my game," and while at times we may have been plowing old ground, the furrows were anything but straight.

❖ ❖ ❖ ❖

(When you showed up in Detroit in 1986, you were green as grass.)

I was just so happy being there, being anywhere in the NBA. Making the pros is the only real goal I've ever had in life, and once I was there, it was like, "I can't believe this. I'm getting to guard Dr. J., Magic, Larry Bird—the best in the world." And I soon changed from a player who had been scoring 30 points and averaging 15 rebounds in college to a specialist in rebounding and defense. I was like, "If I don't have the tools to be a superstar on offense, maybe I can do something else to help the team." It worked out for me.

(What was it like playing for Chuck Daly?)

Great. Coach Daly hated to practice. He said, "Give me all you got for one hour every day. That's it." So every practice was a war—a fucking war, almost every day a fistfight. Bad boys hammered bad boys. We practiced so hard that the games seemed easy.

On court, Coach Daly had a mean streak as far as being competitive—but he had a soft side, too. Off court, he took me in, treated me like a son; he had me over to his house for Thanksgiving, this and that. I was a naïve kid who came out of a small college and just wanted to survive in the NBA. I just wanted to play. I just wanted to get the energy out. He embraced that. He was like, "I've never seen a kid this happy." And even though I didn't know shit about the game of basketball, he loved my energy, and in time, he figured out how to use it. I've got nothing but good things to say about Chuck Daly.

(Do you keep up with Isiah and Laimbeer and the rest of the bad boys?)

I really don't stay in touch with anybody. If I see 'em, we talk about the old days, but other than that, I really don't stay in touch.

(You came of age in Detroit—won a couple of championships, had a child, got married. Then Daly left, the team fell apart, you got divorced. It kind of ended on a bad note.)

Yeah, but I turned a bad thing into a good thing. And for me to do what I did, go and change my image, put the gun to my head, and say, "Okay, I want to shoot—kill—this imposter," that's when everything changed for me individually.

(Then you reinvented yourself in San Antonio.)

I'd say, "revealed," not "reinvented." I just let out what was already inside. Whatever. Everything that I've done since I left Detroit happened for a reason. It has a place. I had a coming-out party in San Antonio. It started with me hanging out with gays, having a good time. Some people seem surprised there was an active gay community down there in white-ass, conservative Texas. Hello. There's an active gay community everywhere. Get over it.

(Your NBA career peaked in Chicago.)

Not just my career. The three years I was in Chicago were probably the most incredible three years that I've had as a human being. I don't ever think I was loved as much as I was loved all over the place in Chicago—the city, the team. The love of Michael Jordan and Scottie Pippen and all those guys, I was like, "I can't believe this shit." I mean the city of Chicago embraced me, gave me the opportunity to be myself and do what I do—give a rock-star performance on the court, give a rock-star performance off the court. I did everything in the book while I was playing with Chicago. They let me be myself—an independent, free, black motherfucker. It was just unreal.

(The Bulls road show. What was that like?)

It was like having God, Moses, the Pope, the Beatles, Elvis, the Rolling Stones, and the Grateful Dead all in one. It was scary. Huge crowds, media chased you everywhere. When we were playing Utah in the Finals one year, we stayed at a hotel across the street from the

Delta Center in Salt Lake. When it came time to head over to the arena, we hopped on the bus, and it took like a half-hour or 45 minutes to get across the fucking street—maybe 100 feet. People were blocking the bus to take pictures, yelling, screaming. Crazy shit.

The first year we played the Jazz in the playoffs was just the opposite. Phil Jackson wanted to get us away from all the craziness and put us up in a hotel in a little town called Park City—population like 7,000—about a half-hour outside Salt Lake. Nothing to do. It was so quiet I was going fucking crazy. So I chartered a jet, flew to Vegas, gambled all night, got back on the jet and arrived at the Delta Center about a half-hour before the team bus arrived. Phil Jackson cornered my bodyguard, George Triantafillo.

"Tell me you haven't been out all night," he said.

"Oh, no, boss," said George.

Phil knew he was lying, but he let it go. That's the great thing about Phil. As long as you're delivering on court, he doesn't give a shit.

Michael Jordan, a man who has been known to gamble a bit himself, came over to George, and asked, "How'd our boy do?"

"He kicked ass," said George.

Later Phil was like, "What are you guys doing after practice?"

"I dunno," George said. "Maybe go get something to eat."

True.

"Make sure the plane's ready," I told George when Phil was out of earshot.

We'd be getting "something to eat" all right … in Las-fucking-Vegas, Nevada. Oh, and we won both games down there—didn't miss a beat.

(Partying the night before a game doesn't sound like a good idea. Don't you think you would have played better without all the partying?)

Nope. I learned that lesson in Seattle in 1996. We were leading in the finals three games to none, on the verge of a sweep, and suddenly I decided to pull a David Robinson. I stopped partying, got a good night's sleep three days running, and we lost two in a row. Major fuck-up. So the night before Game 6 in Chicago, I started the evening with Sake Bombers at my favorite sushi restaurant, and then

spent a little time at Crobar's with a lesbian deejay who billed herself as "Psychobitch," before ending my evening with breakfast at
the Third Coast. So how'd we do? We kicked Sonic ass. I got 19
rebounds, nine points, five assists, and drove Shawn Kemp nuts on
defense. At least one reporter said I was the MVP of the game, and
Sonics coach George Karl gave me credit for the win. The final
score was 87–75, giving us the championship in six.

(Was it all downhill after Chicago?)

I think I got spoiled in Chicago. Phil Jackson knew where I was
coming from. Phil had a sense of me, knew he had a guy who would
go out there and do the dirty work. I was the missing piece on that
team. He was like, "Y'know, Dennis, you're gonna play for me no
matter what. I like your style. I like your dedication. I love what you
do. I love how you care." He knew I wasn't a crazy motherfucker,
that there was a method to my madness, y'know? He liked my pas-
sion, whether it was on the court putting my balls on the line for
the team or partying my ass off 'til dawn.

(You have anything to say about your short stays in L.A. and Dallas?)

If I had to do it over, I wouldn't do it over. L.A. was just a bad
fit. When you get past all my antics, I'm all about team and winning.
There was no team in L.A.; there were the Hatfields and the
McCoys. In Dallas, Mark Cuban used me to put fannies in seats. We
didn't win, and I got a little bad ink—seems like nobody wanted to
see David Stern naked—and my ass was gone. That's the way it goes.

The NBA is a business, and the minute you start thinking somebody gives a shit about you as a human being as opposed to how
you're going to impact the bottom line, you're headed for a fall. It's
a lesson that I'm still trying to learn. Just as in any other business,
you're pretty much a number. They use you. You serve a purpose for
a period of time. As long as you can deliver, you're cool. When the
day comes that you can't play, nobody will return your phone calls.

*(Speaking of David Stern, when you were in Dallas, and the whole
time you were in the league for that matter, you had this ongoing battle with
the commissioner. Have any parting shots?)*

Well, with that guy, you win some, and you lose some. But the
last time out, you might say he outsmarted himself. When Stern

heard that ESPN was producing *Rodman on the Rebound*, he got his panties in a wad and started knocking the show in the newspapers, saying it wasn't one of ESPN's "strongest moments," or some shit like that. Not that he'd seen the show, you understand. Well, the guys at ESPN freaked out—Stern is a powerful dude—and rescheduled the series so it wouldn't run in primetime. It ended up airing at like 1:00 a.m. in New York and 11:00 p.m. in L.A., next to nobody saw it. On the record, we were jumping Stern's ass for censorship and shit, but when the cameras were off, we were secretly whoopin' it up. I mean, Stern himself couldn't have produced a show that made me look any worse than *Rodman on the Rebound*—my ass hits rock bottom *on* camera—and, thanks to him, nobody sees it. Had it been up to us, the son of bitch would have aired at like 3:00 a.m. on Al Jazeera.

So here's a first: thanks, Dave, for covering my ass.

(Since Stern became commissioner 20 years ago, there's been this prolif-eration of guaranteed, long-term, megamillion-dollar contracts. What's that doing to the league?)

Pretty much fucking it up.

The game is not like it used to be. Back in the day, every time you played, every time you went to practice, you had to fight for your position; you had to fight for your job. Today you ain't gotta fight for shit because they're paying players millions no matter what. In the game today, you don't have to do a damn thing.

(So there's no incentive.)

They are killing incentive. Say a player has a guaranteed contract in his pocket: $50 million for six years. What is there left for him to prove? What is there left for him to do? Nothing. He's got the Rolls, the private jet, all the beautiful women he wants, the big house for his momma. He's thinking his ass has arrived. Wrong. To really make it in the NBA, you've got to win basketball games, championships. Nobody gives a fuck how much money you make when you're out there on the court.

(Do you know a player who got the big contract and nothing ever hap-pened?)

I'm not naming any names, but many players have got "the big contract" and nothing ever happened. Teams are paying millions and millions of dollars to guys who can't play—they're hurt or whatever. Still you can't get rid of them: nobody else wants them or maybe nobody can afford them, and so you are stuck with the big contracts. Meanwhile, there's a ton of players who would give up their $50 million—well, maybe not all of it—to win a championship. A ton of players. That's the ultimate goal, and it's not easy. Ask Karl Malone and Charles Barkley, who leapfrogged from one team to another, taking major pay cuts, trying to get a ring. These are great players, future Hall of Famers, but they couldn't get it done.

(How would you fix the contract problem?)

Performance incentives. Pay guys some kind of reasonable base salary, and then make 'em earn the rest of it. "You get this many rebounds, and I give you this many dollars. You score so many points, and I give you so many dollars." At the end of the year, you say, "Let's see what kind of level you're playing at. Maybe we don't want to lose you, so we'll up that base salary and the incentive pay a bit." The way it is now, play good, play bad, don't matter—it all pays the same.

(What advice do you have for young kids coming into the NBA today?)

Long term, it's about the game. Ten years down the road, nobody will give a shit how much money Michael Jordan, Dennis Rodman, or *you* made playing basketball. They'll care about what we did for the game. Aside from that, realize you're blessed to be a part of it and that you're not just here to make some fat cat a lot of money. So do it to the best of your ability, do it to where you feel satisfied. *You*, nobody else.

(What would you tell kids about how to handle themselves off court? You've certainly had your moments.)

I'd tell them to stay in control of what you're doing; don't stray away from what you believe. Don't let anybody, the team, the NBA, your agent, your relatives, or your friends steer you in the wrong direction. They may pay you this, pay you that, but they've got no right to tell you how to think and act when you're not on the court, whether you're partying your ass off or teaching Sunday school. I mean, you get paid to play. You get paid to play. You don't get paid to be nice. You don't get paid to do a fucking thing but play basketball. All the other shit is up to you—deal with it how you want. If you want to be a nice guy and do community service, go do that. Don't do it so people will like you. Don't play that game. If your heart ain't in it, don't do it. The NBA shouldn't control your life, shouldn't say you have to go do this, do that. That's your choice, not theirs. They have no right to tell you who the fuck you're gonna be.

(Is there life after basketball?)

Guys like Magic, he's into so much shit, it's unbelievable—business stuff going on all over the place. He even used to own a piece of Fat Burger, and still may, I dunno. He could make a living just making occasional personal appearances if he wanted to. It's harder for other guys, guys who weren't superstars. They don't know what to do with themselves. They're not gonna sit behind a desk. They're not gonna sit around the house all day. There are only so many rounds of golf you can play. Most of 'em, after a couple of years, you don't hear their name any more. It's like, "You're out of the game, bye, done, you're over. Sit home and count your money."

I'm lucky. I transcended the game. My fame goes beyond basketball, beyond the borders. I was in China a couple of weeks ago, got mobbed everywhere I went, people shouting—do your own Chinese accent—"Dennis Rodman! NBA! Dennis Rodman! NBA!" How the fuck do people in China know about Dennis Rodman? "Dennis Rodman" has become like a worldwide brand name. I stand for something beyond basketball. Freedom, I'd say. Others might call it license.

(Anything you'd like to add?)

Yeah. If I could, I'd take those young players—high school, college, the NBA—wherever they're lacing up, grab hold of their jerseys just like Isiah did to me, punch the pure-D shit out of them just like Isiah, and tell them, "Feel it! Smell it! Taste it! Enjoy every bite! 'Cause the motherfucker only lasts a short period of time, a blink of an eye."

A blink of a fucking eye.

CHAPTER TWENTY-TWO

FAMOUS AS
I WANNA BE

C entury Plaza Hotel, Los Angeles, June 12, 2005. I was running late. Not the first time. The changeover from Dennis into "Dennis Rodman" was taking a little longer than usual. This time, it was a footwear problem. So everybody was waiting around in the suite: Darren, his fiancé Symone, and Thaer in the bedroom, and the reporter in the living room peeking through the door. I had put on this new pair of black "Wellington boots," I guess you'd call them, with these hideous straps across the instep. I looked at them this way, that way, thought about changing shoes, then ended up cutting the straps off. Crisis averted—but I still wasn't satisfied.

In the elevator going downstairs, I kept messing with my shirt-tails. When the door opened to the lobby, I asked Darren what he thought of my one-shirttail-in, one-shirttail-out look; and he glanced over his shoulder, gave his usual "whatever" shrug, and kept walking. Symone waded in. Then, as I stood there with my ass propping the elevator door open, she tucked in the right shirttail so it matched the left, bloused the bottom of the shirt over my belt, stepped back, and pronounced me, "Done." Meanwhile, I'm thinking there are worse things in life than having a beautiful woman dress you.

After over an hour in the making, the ensemble was complete. Showtime. We strolled through the lobby, and I could see the outfit was working, heads turning as we took a hard left and went down the stairs to navigate the red carpet, the first phase of Sports Spectacular 2005—the 20th annual benefit for the Cedars-Sinai Medical Center.

If you see me on the street on a typical day, I'll be wearing drawstring pants, a long-sleeve T-shirt, baseball cap, and basketball shoes, which I'll shed the first chance I get and be walking around in socks. That's like my uniform—the real Dennis. But when I'm making an appearance as "Dennis Rodman," that's a whole 'nother deal. I've got to look the part. My fans, my sponsors, have certain expectations and I meet them—like on this night.

I had on an extra-long, five-button, navy blue "suit" jacket that hit me about mid-thigh and looked kind of like a riding jacket; an open-neck, patterned, satiny white shirt; jeans; and the Wellington boots. I had tied a red bandana around my head and topped it off with a chocolate-colored, felt fedora with a blue headband. I accessorized with shades, about five pounds of multicolored necklace—turquoise, orange, yellow, blue—and the usual collection of piercing hardware.

Normally I turn my head into a human pincushion with hoops in my ears, nose studs, a lip ring. On more festive occasions, I have dressier earrings and this stud about an inch-and-a-half long that replaces the ring in my lower lip. Son of a bitch sets off metal detectors at the airport—anything for fashion. Almost. You'll be happy to hear I no longer wear any hardware in my nether regions.

So how's my fashion sense?

"When it's time to make a statement, he knows how to make a statement," said Wendell, who is currently a fashion designer. "He doesn't have a fashion consultant or a stylist or anything like that. He does it all himself."

So you can blame it all on me—and my tailors.

"He gets mostly everything made. Mostly at Lords or Von Dutch," Thaer told the reporter.

That's not a luxury—it's a necessity. As Wendell said: "You're not gonna find anything off the rack in his size."

The way it works is: I'll go up to maybe, Lords in L.A., pick out a fabric, and then, if it's a shirt, we'll talk about the cut, what we want to do with the collar, cuffs—pick out the buttons, this, that. Then they make it for me. Some stores give me the stuff for the free PR. Others charge me a lot of money.

A lot of money.

When I'm headed out of town to some event, I'll pack a bunch of different stuff—shirts, jackets, hats, shoes—and when it comes time to get dressed, I'll try this, try that, and put an outfit together depending on how I'm feeling at the moment. Sometimes that takes a while.

"It takes him forever to put on a pair of sweats," said Wendell.

"Like a woman?" asked the reporter.

"Like two women," said Wendell.

But when I'm done, even fashion hotshot Wendell admits I have the knack.

"He knows how to make a bunch of avant-garde items look like an outfit," Wendell said. "He knows how to do it, man. And like I say, he's doing it all himself. It's all him."

And unless I'm headed for the Academy Awards or something like that, it's all pretty much spontaneous.

"If he's going to a major, major event, then the outfit is thought out," said Wendell. "If he's gonna be on television, like he's going to the Jay Leno show or something like that, then the outfit is thought out."

The Cedars-Sinai outfit was not thought out. It was a spur-of-the-moment creation. Still I felt good about it as I turned the corner onto the red carpet and was blinded by lights from around 10 television cameras. These guys who looked like secret service agents—black suits, wires trailing out of their ears—herded the Rodman entourage in the right direction. One television reporter yelled, and I stepped up to the red-velvet rope separating me from the media and started yapping.

Normally, you would expect the red carpet to be outside. But inside or outside, it serves the same purpose. Fans think the red carpet is a way of making celebrity guests feel special. Actually, it's a way to accommodate the media without asking much of the stars or, for that matter, the PR people. For a big, celebrity-studded event, there would be no way to accommodate the hundreds of interview requests. So the PR people strike a bargain, line the photographers and reporters up behind a velvet rope and say, "You stay here, and we'll troop the celebrities by." So instead of having reporters and photographers swarming all over the place, pushing and shoving, creating havoc, you have a nice, controlled environment: the red carpet. The media get a sound bite, quote, video, or photo without too much work, and it's easy for the celebs, too. They breeze through, stop to talk to whoever they want to, ignore the rest, and get on with it.

Since I was late, there wasn't exactly a traffic jam on the red carpet, and I was like a one-man show, although I did see San Francisco Forty-Niner great Jerry Rice—one of the night's honorees—down at the other end of the line about 50 yards away. He looked shorter than I remembered.

As I was talking to, I think it was the *Best Damn Sports Show Period*, the still photographers at the next "media station" were just hanging out, waiting for me to come their way. Then they spotted Symone in the shadows behind me. They were like, "Damn! Who's the blonde?" Now Symone always looks good, but on that night, she was the pride of her home country, Australia, looking particularly take-your-breath-away spectacular in this low-cut, pink, corset-looking thing and fitted white pants.

Now most photographers are men, and at first, they were like, "Is that *somebody*?" Then they were like, "Who the fuck cares!" So they started waving her over, like, "Come on down! Come on down!"

Symone has done a lot of spokesmodel work, and so she knew the drill. She walked over and started posing for maybe a dozen

photographers, and there was an explosion of flashbulbs like fireworks on the Fourth of July, enough to make you see orange spots
for a week. She was smiling, just eating it up. The woman is photo-
genic, like me, but for entirely different reasons. She's beautiful.

Me? A photographer once told me, "If you've got a choice
between shooting 50 guys in pinstripe suits and a six-foot-eight
black man wearing a feather boa, who are you going to photograph?
Who do you think is going to make the more eye-grabbing picture?"

I moved on through the media gauntlet to the next reporter, a
camera-mounted light blinding me. A pretty woman from FOX
Sports Net stuck a wireless mike in my face—looked like a black
vibrator—and a guy from Xtra Sports 570 AM, "Southern
California's Sports Superstation" followed suit. I was wearing my
lips out talking. Way in the back, behind the media, several rows of
"civilian" gawkers looked on, trying to get a glimpse of me.

Other celebs walked by on the red carpet as I was talking, and
I recognized faces, but I couldn't tell you their names. Must have
been the same deal for the media, which showed no interest whatever and just let those faces cruise on through. It has been a long
time since I could get away with that. So long ago that I think of it
as the "good old days," days when Dennis Rodman could be anony-
mous, y'know, walk the street, work out, take my daughter Alexis to
the park without feeling like I was center stage.

Reality Check: Fame is a bitch.

If you've been paying attention, you've probably already figured
out that I have this love-hate relationship with fame. If not, you can
sure tell it by listening to the people who know me best.

"He needs to be out there," Michelle told a reporter. "He needs
to be seen."

"He does not want to be famous, but yet that's how he feeds himself," said Wendell. "That's how he lives his extraordinary life."

"He eats it up. I watch him," said Michelle.

"He loves the attention?" the reporter asked.

"Oh, yeah. … He plays like he doesn't," said Michelle. "But I know he loves it. And how can you not?"

"There were points where he cried to me about killing himself," said Darren. "He just didn't want to live anymore. And the last thing he wanted was the fame. He hated the fame."

So who's right?

Everybody.

Where I rank in the celebrity pecking order is something that matters to me. I'm proud that, while other basketball players of my era have mostly disappeared, I'm still a household name. I have staying power. I still matter to people. If I were not so important to society, they wouldn't still be talking about me. I see fame as one way to measure that importance.

When I first became famous in the late 1990s, it didn't mean shit. I was just having a good time, living the life of a rock star. I wasn't saying, "Oh, I gotta go make this move, I gotta do this, I gotta do that." It was more like, "I'm gonna play the game, go to practice, then go out and have a good time." That was my whole thing right there.

Famous or not famous? I didn't care.

Things are different now. Now fame does mean something to me. Now it's a part of who I am, and I don't want to lose it. Michelle hit it right on the nose.

"If you've been used to that for so long, if it were to go away," she said. "I mean, it would be hard. I couldn't even imagine to be so big and then to not have anyone care. I'm sure that's what he holds onto."

People have asked me if I see fame as a "measuring stick" of my worth. Yeah, I'm proud of my fame because of why I'm famous. I'm not famous because of some corporate image-making machine. "Dennis Rodman" wasn't dreamed up in the bowels of some ad

agency. I'm famous, one because I'm one of the best basketball players who ever played the game; and two, because as I went about living my life—"just being Dennis"—I struck a nerve with the people outside of basketball, people who don't know a basketball from
a billiard ball. I've lasted because my fame has meaning, substance, I
stand for something rock solid. As I said before, I've freed people up,
made it okay to say, "Fuck it!" and be your freaky self. I'm proud of
that. I'm not somebody like Paris Hilton who is famous for being
famous. So yeah, I do see my fame as a "measuring stick." It shows
I still matter to people. But being proud of my fame, even needing
it, and *living* with it are two different things.

Fame is cool for about the first five minutes that you're out in
public. I'm like, "They still care. I still matter," and then I wish I
could be left alone to just go about my business. But you're either
famous, or you're not. If you are, you get the whole package—the
good, the bad, the ugly. Here's some "good, bad, and ugly," all in the
same package.

For the past two years, I've run with the bulls in Pamplona,
Spain for GoldenPalace.com. The "Running of the Bulls" is this
centuries-old, coming-of-age ritual that Ernest Hemingway made
famous in his 1926 novel *The Sun Also Rises.* The run is a part of the
Fiesta of San Fermin, which honors the city's patron saint.
Beginning at 8:00 a.m. every day for a week in July, hundreds of
mostly young men run ahead of six, bred-to-be-nasty bulls, that
weigh in at about 1,000 pounds each, leading them from their pens
through narrow cobblestone streets to the bullring about a half-mile
away.

That's the plan anyway. I don't really get to do much running
because people won't let me. I get rushed by fans who want to get
a piece of Dennis Rodman. Five feet away, runners are falling down,
getting trampled, gored, run over—in the past people have even
been killed—and these fools are like, "Fuck the bulls! We want a picture with Dennis Rodman." This year, when it was over—it takes
about three minutes—Thaer was like, "What the hell is wrong with
these people? You got a pissed off, half-ton bull with these huge

horns chasing your ass, and you're trying to get a fucking autograph from Dennis Rodman? It's nuts." So I ended up running from the people, not the bulls. But still, it's a really cool thing—a "Dennis Rodman" thing. Too bad I can't enjoy it the way other people do. But the fans won't let me. They won't let me. Like Thaer says, when you're famous, "You can't do shit."

Meanwhile that same fame means the wire services are beaming a picture of Dennis Rodman in a white T-shirt with a foot-high, red GoldenPalace.com logo on the chest all over the world. The same fame that made it impossible for me to enjoy the event like a normal person is what made it possible for me to be there in the first place, what makes it possible for me to make a living. So you can see why when it comes to fame, I have mixed emotions.

Love it, hate it, can't get away from it. No wonder I'm nuts.

❖ ❖ ❖ ❖

Remember that reality check from earlier: "Fame warps everything?" Well, that's no exaggeration, and it goes far beyond my ability to enjoy simple human pleasures that "nobodies" take for granted. Fame warps every human relationship—*every* human relationship.

Ever since I became famous, my relationships with my mother, my sisters, my friends, my wives, my girlfriends, even my children have all been warped. People I do business with, people on the street, total strangers treat me differently than they treat you.

Michelle summed it up for a reporter. "He can't possibly trust or know that anyone loves him for him," she said. "Since he became famous, [the love] has always been because he's 'Dennis Rodman.' I don't think it's ever been because of who he is as a person."

That same poison spreads to the people around me.

"Do you get people sucking up to you because you're Dennis Rodman's wife?" a reporter asked Michelle.

"Hell, yes! Yeah. It's amazing," she said. "Are you trying to be my friend, or are you friends with me because I'm Dennis Rodman's wife? It happens all the time."

Everything a famous person does begins and ends with fame. Nothing a normal person does is like what I do. The whole context is different. I am literally living in a different world, a parallel universe. We could be walking side by side through the same restaurant, and an entirely different set of rules apply. I'm always being watched. I'm always accountable. I can't have a bad day, make some smartass remark, raise an eyebrow. If I do, it's a huge deal.

If I offend some guy, he won't just let it go, say, "What-fucking-ever," and move on. It's a turning point in his life. How did he react when dissed by the bad boy, when Dennis Rodman challenged his manhood? I'm just trying to eat my sushi in peace, and this guy has shifted into holy war mode. In the past, wild-boy Rodman, most likely drunk, reacted like a normal human being, and got his ass sued. Today's sober "Dennis Rodman" acts like a veteran famous guy and backs off, way off, gives Mr. Intifada a wide berth, and serves up a character-defining war story the guy will be telling his grandchildren.

"Yeah, I called the son of a bitch on it, and he hid behind his bodyguard."

These are not lessons you read in some guidebook or learn at your mother's knee. This is stuff you learn the hard way, making it up as you go along. And as the lessons learned pile up, they lead to a set of rules. Rules that say exactly what "a famous person" can and cannot do. Then you wake up one day and realize you're hog-tied by your own rules—that your fame has become a trap.

I made my last stop on the red carpet, autographing this and that for the non-media "civilians" at the end of the line. Then the secret service dudes led me into this adjoining room—or maybe it was a blocked-off hallway, I don't remember—where the Cedars-Sinai folk had me autograph some basketballs. Thaer was by my side checking everybody out. I don't know if they auctioned the balls off, sold them—whatever. A kid about 12 in a blue blazer showed up and had me sign his program. I still hadn't escaped the cameras. Now the reporter was popping flashbulbs in my face. It's a wonder my ass hasn't gone blind.

I signed an official NBA Spalding basketball, with my distinctive, looping, totally illegible scrawl. I didn't know if this guy was a fan or somebody from Cedars-Sinai. Want to know what fame smells like? A Sharpie. The airplane-cement-on-downers smell of those felt-tip pens—corporate sponsorship anyone?—has been a part of my everyday life for decades.

That and the fucking flashbulbs.

✦ ✦ ✦ ✦ ✦

I used to think of myself as an "accidental celebrity." Not anymore. These days there is nothing accidental about it. I go out of my way to get attention. I was at the Cedars-Sinai benefit not only to promote a worthy cause, but to get in front of those cameras and microphones on the red carpet. "Why" is no mystery. Darren and I work at keeping me famous because that's how I make a living.

I started out being totally free, playing basketball with reckless abandon, screwing with my hair, dating Madonna—just being Dennis. That turned out to be newsworthy. I kept on doing what I was doing, dressing up in women's clothes, pulling down rebounds, winning championships, partying, gambling—free as a bird. That led to more coverage, fame, lawsuits, and the first appearance of those rules I was talking about. Now the book of "Rodman's Rules" is so long and involved that it makes the NCAA rulebook look simple; and my days of total freedom are long gone. To put it in Biblical terms: total freedom begat media coverage begat fame begat a list of freedom-sapping "no-nos." I'm caged by my own rules—the rules of fame. How do I fix it? I could drop out of sight, of course, give up my fame; but then how do I make a living? And I don't want to stop being that symbol of freedom, either. It's like anything else: I have to find a way to strike a balance.

Reality Check: You can't be both free and famous.

I can't have all the benefits of fame—the good—without living with the bad and the ugly. The bad and the ugly? Seems like we've been through that. I can't live a normal life. I have no privacy. Everything I do is "news." I'm no longer free. All human relationships are warped. The good? Fame makes me a lot of money, proves to me I still matter, feeds my ego, and, on good days, is a hell of a lot of fun.

A *hell* of a lot of fun.

So just like just about everything else in life, fame has its upside and its downside. It's like having a dog. He gives you all the love, but he's got to be fed and he's got to be walked—he's got to be cared for. Sooner or later, no matter what you do, he's going to crap on the carpet. Count on it. That's part of what having a dog means. Every single time. If you want a dog—I hate to trot this one out, but it fits—you got to take the good with the bad. Same goes with fame. Just as there ain't no dog without dog shit, there ain't no fame without people shit. People are going to disappoint you. Count on it.

So you just learn to live with it.

Here's one final reality check to balance out all my bitching about fame, to put things in perspective. It isn't true, but let's just say Carmen Electra only wanted to sleep with me because I was famous. She was using my ass to advance her career. Is this supposed to be some kind of big problem? I mean, I'm a guy, and Carmen Electra, one of the most beautiful women in the world, wants to sleep with me.

Am I asking, "Why?"

No. No. No. No. ...

Repeat after me, bro: "Who gives a shit?"

Again, "Who gives a shit?"

One last time: "*Who gives a shit?*"

> **Reality Check:** When it comes to the good, bad, and ugly of fame, sometimes even the ugly is good.

Very, very, very good.

CHAPTER TWENTY-THREE

NOT YET UNDERRATED

We were backstage at the Century Plaza Hotel, following the men in black suits down a narrow, institutional hall. No red carpet here. We pass a head-high rack filled with dozens of silver candelabra and arrive at what looks like a kitchen staging area. There was a pause, and then the suits pushed through the door; and we walked out into a huge banquet hall filled with round, linen-draped tables for ten: must've been 100 of them. There was a stage on the right with a backdrop of billboard-sized video screens showing the Cedars-Sinai "Sports Spectacular 2005" logo. The five of us—Darren and Symone, Thaer, the reporter and I—were led single-file through the crowd, weaving our way to a back table.

We got to our table and a bunch of fresh-faced little white boys lined up for autographs. I signed a program, this ugly purple-and-green basketball, another program, another ugly basketball—where did they get these things?—and the boys disappeared. Later, Kareem Abdul-Jabbar stopped by, and I stood up to say hello. We talked a little bit, and then the reporter spotted Kareem. I could tell he was about to piss in his pants. He was trying to get up, I guess to introduce himself, knees hitting the bottom of the table, fumbling around, but before he could get on his feet, Kareem was gone. For the rest of his life, he'll be telling people, "I almost met Kareem Abdul-Jabbar."

John Salley, my old Detroit teammate, swung by. He would be co-hosting this thing with his *Best Damn Sports Show Period* buddy, Tom Arnold. Then Ron Artest, David Stern's latest headache, came over to say hello. He's the guy from the Pacers who waded into the stands during the brawl at Detroit last season. Before it was over he had cold-cocked some fan. Artest ended up sitting out the rest of the season. ESPN.com reported that the suspension cost him about five million big ones.

"We have to make a point that there are boundaries in our games," David Stern told ESPN. "One of our boundaries, that has always been immutable, is the boundary that separates the fans from the court. Players cannot lose control and move into the stands."

Artest's antics have led some people to start mentioning him and Dennis Rodman in the same breath. Nah. Artest's 73-game suspension ranks number one all time. The best I could ever do was 11 games (for kicking the TV photographer), bringing me in at number six. Latrell Sprewell ranks second, suspended for 68 games in 1997 after choking coach P.J. Carlesimo. Let's see, cold-cocking an asshole fan, choking a coach? Add clothes-lining David Stern to the list, and for some folk (not Dennis Rodman, mind you), you'd have three of an NBA player's top-five basketball fantasies.

I spotted Kobe Bryant on the other side of the banquet hall and started to think everybody who was anybody in California sports was at the Cedars-Sinai benefit. And as folks started digging into their salads, I checked out the people at our table. Paul Westphal, an All-Star NBA player from the seventies was sitting a couple of seats to the right with his wife. He grew up in California, was a two-time All-American at USC before being drafted by the Celtics in 1972. Drew Gooden, now with the Cleveland Cavaliers, was on my left, the other side of Thaer, with a beautiful Asian girl—could have been his wife. I don't know. Gooden played his high school ball at El Cerrito, California (near Oakland). Another black guy I didn't recognize and a black girl filled out the table. Gooden probably doesn't know there was a fleeting moment last spring when it looked like we'd be teammates. It was hard to believe this fresh-faced kid was in the league. He looked like a baby to me.

My ass is getting old.

If you counted me, at this one table, there were three generations of the NBA. Westphal played from 1973 to 1984, I played from 1987 to 2000, and Gooden has been in the league since 2002. Add one more guy, say Wilt Chamberlain, and you pretty much have the whole modern history of the league covered. Of course, I am an important part of that history. Not that I've gotten my due.

Not yet.

Charley Rosen of FOXSports.net described me as one of the five most underrated players of all time. Well, it's too soon to call me underrated. Give it a few more years. My fans bitch because I was never on an Olympic Dream Team, didn't make the list of the 50-greatest NBA players of all time back in 1996, and I'm not in the Hall of Fame. There are three reasons for all that: timing, timing, and timing.

When the first two Dream Teams were put together for the 1992 and 1996 Olympics, I was known to be damn good, but I had not yet established myself as a superstar. And for that first Dream Team, players who were not bona fide superstars needed not apply. That was the team with Michael Jordan, Magic Johnson, Larry Bird, Charles Barkley, Karl Malone—it goes on and on. Looking back now, the original Dream Team could have easily have been dubbed the "Legends Team." All but two of the players on that roster would go on to make the list of the NBA's 50 greatest. No wonder they won all eight of their games with an average winning margin of 44 points before taking home the Olympic gold medal in Barcelona.

When the next Olympics rolled around in 1996, I still hadn't peaked, and there was a new issue to deal with: public relations. At the 1994 World Basketball Championship in Toronto, some of the guys on what at the time was billed as a kind of off-year, "Dream Team," showed their collective asses with "taunts, crotch-grabbing, and other demonstrations of boorish behavior," as Phil Taylor put it in *Sports Illustrated*. Suddenly the "Dream Team" was the "Ugly American Team."

"Some of the behavior that might be acceptable when you're playing pickup with your friends," Bible-thumping, 1996 Olympic team member David Robinson told *SI*, "isn't acceptable when you're playing in international competition in front of the world."

So when it came time to pick players for the '96 Olympics, the selection committee went for Tom Sawyer, not Huckleberry Finn.

Sports Illustrated quoted C.M. Newton, then president of U.S.A. Basketball, as saying the U.S. would be selecting a team with "character, not characters."

I'm guessing that, at that point, if anyone in the league qualified as a "character," that would have been me. So I probably would have been odd man out no matter how good I was on the court. While I think I am an outstanding example of what America, freedom, is all about; others aren't so sure. Even my mother, in a sound bite in *Beyond the Glory*, my video bio, said I "went totally ballistic" when I was in San Antonio.

After I peaked in 1997-98, winning that seventh rebounding title, I looked like a possible contender for the 2000 games, but as it turned out, I wouldn't even be in the league. Come Dream Team IV in 2004, I had been out of the NBA two years. Not that they couldn't have used me. That dream turned into a nightmare, as the team only managed a third-place finish in Athens.

As for not being on the list of the 50 Greatest Players in the *NBA at Fifty*, it's the same basic deal: timing. Some of my fans give in to the paranoia, pointing out there is a message and a full-page picture of David Stern peeking out from behind a basketball on the very first page of the damn book, even before the title. Stern, they say, made sure Dennis Rodman was left off the list. I tell them to turn the page to the two-page spread of Michael Jordan, Shawn Kemp, and me going for a rebound—not quite equal billing with Stern, but close. So forget about Stern. The reason I didn't make the top 50 is because the book was published in October of 1996, meaning the voting was done months and months before by what was called a "panel of 50 experts"—coaches, players, team executives, and media guys like Kareem, Marv Albert, Larry Bird, Red Auerbach, and Oscar Robinson. (Players couldn't vote for themselves.) So the voting took place before I had peaked, winning my fifth championship and seventh rebounding title in 1997. It's never too late, though. In April of 2004, Lacy J. Banks, a columnist for the *Chicago Sun-Times* suggested a few revisions for the list. She tossed 12 players out and added 12 new ones including me and Tim Duncan, Kobe Bryant, and Kevin Garnett. Not bad company.

Even before Lacy J. Banks came along to give me a promotion, I liked to think of myself as the 51st greatest. My ass is all over the *NBA at Fifty*. It's kind of like the editor had everything ready to go for a "Dennis Rodman" spread, and I didn't get the votes. I still appear in eight pictures, half of them shot above the basket looking down on me jockeying for a rebound; and there's one, full page, extra close-up of me facing a forest of microphones wearing shades, a red jacket, and a matching shapeless cap that's looks like it was made out of discarded scraps of sofa upholstery. As for mentions, when rebounding comes up, I get mentioned. So while I might not have made the cut for the "50 Greatest Players" list, I sure made the cut for the *NBA at Fifty* book. Again, I am all over that son of a bitch.

Finally, my fans gripe that I'm not in the Hall of Fame. That, too, is premature. I just became eligible, and we have yet to submit the paperwork. So for those who say I've been underrated; again, I say get back to me.

Anything that gets voted on, like the Hall of Fame, is political and, of course, subjective. Not that I did that badly in the popularity contests over the years. Even at my wildest, I made the NBA All-Defensive first team seven times and was named Defensive Player of the Year twice. Of course, I only made the All-NBA team twice in 1990 and 1992, and was actually left out during my peak years at Chicago.

Unreal.

But when you get down to it, the real deal is not votes, but stats. It's like what Bill Russell said in the *NBA at Fifty* about winning and losing: "There are no politics, only numbers ... and there is nothing subjective about that."

Well, Bill Russell piled up some numbers in his day, and so did Dennis Rodman.

Dennis Rodman.

CHAPTER TWENTY-FOUR

A PLACE IN HISTORY

Basic statistics guarantee Dennis Rodman a place in NBA history. Seven straight rebounding titles: best of all time. Better than Wilt. Better than Bill Russell. Better than Wes Unseld. I'm one of only a handful of players to win as many as five championships—six if you count the Jam ABA title. I am even making a splash in some of the new statistics that have come along.

These days, coaches and basketball junkies are forever trying to come up with new statistics that will give them an edge or just settle a bar bet. Sometimes, they can get way out there.

Here's one that *The Sporting News* says basketball junkies have adapted from baseball statistician Bill James. It's called the "modified Pythagorean formula," and it is supposed to predict a team's winning percentage based on the number of points scored and the number of points allowed. Here's how a reporter explained it to me after reading about it in *TSN*. A team's winning percentage (WP) is equal to the number of points scored (PS) multiplied by itself 13.91 times divided by the same number added to the number of points allowed (PA) multiplied by itself 13.91 times. Or, in mathematical terms:

$$WP = PS^{13.91} /(PS^{13.91} + PA^{13.91})$$

Say what? I knew I should have shown up for that Algebra class. Here's another new stat basketball-reference.com calls the "Similarity Score." It compares how players performed when they were the same age. For example, when I was 35 and playing with the Bulls, the player I was most like, according to the "Similarity Score," was the 35-year-old Charles Oakley, the hard-nosed, power forward for the Knicks. How do they come up with this one? Basektball-reference.com explains using Carmelo Anthony of the Nuggets and Lebron James of the Cavaliers at 19.

First, here's a little background:

The P.E.R., "Player Efficiency Rating," which they talk about, is calculated by subtracting a player's "negative accomplishments" from a player's "positive accomplishments" to get a "per-minute rating of a player's performance." The "Usage Rate" is an estimate of "the number of possessions a players uses in 40 minutes played."

Got all that?

After comparing and ranking Carmelo and Lebron in 13 categories like rebounding, three-point shooting, this, that, the "differences" in the ranks were calculated. So here's how basketball-reference.com wraps up the Carmelo-Lebron comparison.

> The sum of the squared differences is 3037; adding in the penalties for P.E.R. and Usage Rate gives us 3047. The square root of this number is 55.2. The similarity between these two seasons is 1000*(1-(55.2 / 144060 = 855.) As it turns out, Anthony had the most similar season at age 19 to James, and vice versa.

I'm like, "Yeah, but can Lebron take Carmelo one-on-one?" I'm sure the "Similarity Score" is useful to somebody, somewhere, but it doesn't mean shit to me. But there is one new off-the-wall statistic out there that I've come to love. It's called the "Rebound Rate."

The Rebound Rate measures "the percentage of missed shots a player rebounded" when he was in the game. My percentage is 23.44. That means that when I was on the floor, I pulled down about one out of every four rebounds that came off the rim. That's fucking amazing. One out of four balls that pop off that rim, consistently, every night. That's unbelievable even to me. No wonder I rank number one, all time.

Who's second? This Dutch guy named Swen Nater who never started a college game, but still was drafted in the first round by Milwaukee in 1973. Seems Swen spent his four years at UCLA as Bill Walton's backup. Finally, coming in at number 12 all time for Rebound Rate, is Will Perdue, the seven-something center San Antonio got when they traded me to Chicago. When he was in the game, Will pulled down just short of one out of every five and a half balls coming off the rim. Maybe the Spurs were on to something after all.

Numbers don't lie. So let's get down to it with some tried and true, traditional stats that will tell you exactly where Dennis Rodman ranks. Bottom line? I am not the best rebounder of all time. That's pretty much a dead heat between Wilt Chamberlain, who reportedly averaged 22.9 rebounds per game for his career—unreal—and six times averaged 24 or more during the regular season; and Bill Russell, who averaged 22.5 for his career, including seven straight seasons of 23 or more. Again, that's unreal. These two giants got almost 10 rebounds a game more than I did. My career average of 13.1 puts me at number 12 all time, which brings me back to Rebound Rate, the percentage of available rebounds a player pulls down. How do Wilt and Bill Russell compare? Wilt places seventh, and—I find this hard to believe—Russell doesn't even make the top 50. Could be a mistake there. But if you're looking for somebody to crunch the numbers, this phys-ed major is not your boy. There's one number I do understand though: number one. And after 58 years of NBA play, that's where I rank for Rebound Rate.

Of course, new or old, there are many things that statistics just don't measure: heart, the energy level you bring to the floor, how well you can get into another guy's head, and the number of Redheaded Sluts you can drink and still get it up—all categories in which Dennis Rodman excelled.

✦ ✦ ✦ ✦

There's one last contribution I made to the game of basketball and sports in general. Now I don't claim to be a Joe Louis or Jackie Robinson. Those dudes didn't just revolutionize sports; they changed the world. I put them up there with Martin Luther King. But I did create another way to be a world-class athlete following in the footsteps of people like Muhammad "Float-like-a-butterfly, sting-like-a-bee" Ali and Joe Namath.

"Broadway Joe" started playing professional football back in the sixties when the great Johnny Unitas of the Baltimore Colts was the poster boy for professional football. Clean cut, poker-faced, forever polite and respectful, you could imagine Unitas teaching Sunday school when he was not mentoring Boy Scouts on the mysteries of the square knot and sheepshank. The closest thing to Unitas today is probably Tim Duncan. So Unitas was the role model, and then the brash, cocky, fur-coat wearing, hard-partying Joe Namath came on the scene. Booze and broads, baby! Namath was considered kind of out there until his way-underdog New York Jets beat the Colts in Super Bowl III in 1969—just as Joe had predicted. Suddenly this early bad boy was at the top of the heap, and there was a whole new way to be a football player. I did the same thing for basketball players, and I have photographic proof.

In the *NBA at 50*, there's this two-page color spread containing a dozen individual pictures of players from the Bulls and Sonics exiting buses in the bowels of some arena. I'm guessing this was before some game in the 1996 NBA finals, but I'm not sure. Anyway, on the left hand page, far left, top row, there's a shot of Michael Jordan looking very *Fortune 500* in his dark suit, white shirt, and gold tie. Bottom row, middle, on the same page, Scottie Pippen's looking a little more casual in his beige suit and matching brown print tie—not that he wouldn't look at home in the board room. In all, eight of the 12 guys pictured have on suits, and Chicago's Ron Harper has on a *GQ*-worthy tan blazer and brown slacks. Even Gary Payton, a guy who at times has made even me look tame, has on a spiffy suit. There are a couple of Sonics who don't toe the line: the fashion-challenged Detlef Schrempf and

Frank Brickowski—remember that name. Schrempf has on a white polo shirt and black slacks and Brickowski is wearing a denim jacket, black T-shirt, and jeans.

And Dennis Rodman? Let's start at the top.

I've got on this big, shapeless, turquoise and black hat—looks like a laundry bag sitting on top of my head—shades, earrings, nose studs, and a tattoo-revealing, white, Van Halen T-Shirt. The T-shirt features a black-and-white photo of a couple of weight-challenged female acrobats on front. They are head to head, one fat woman balancing the second, upside down, spread-eagled fat woman on the top of her noggin. I completed my ensemble with a pair of shapeless, gray-and-white-print pants—look like pajama bottoms—that match the gray tones in the black-and-white photograph. Oh, and I'd altered the T-shirt, cut out a V-neck, and in the "V," you can see four or five necklaces. Overall impression: this ain't a guy about to run through a Power Point presentation on quarterly earnings.

That photo spread pretty much says it all. At a time when Michael Jordan was everything the NBA wanted a player to be, the second most famous player in the game, one Dennis Rodman, was showing there was another way to be a world-class athlete—both on and off court. Like Wilt's old Philly teammate, Chet "The Jet" Walker said in the *NBA at Fifty*, "Dennis Rodman is bringing something different to the game, something the game has never seen before."

Oh yeah.

✦ ✦ ✦ ✦ ✦

So why'd I ask you to remember the name of my old pal, Frank Brickowski, from the Sonics? I wanted to share this slightly abridged blast from the past as reported in an Associated Press story dated June 10, 1996.

> Just like the rest of the NBA finals, the head games battle between Chicago's Dennis Rodman and Seattle's Frank Brickowski has been no contest. Brickowski was thrown out for the second time in three games Sunday after knocking Rodman down with a forearm to the Adam's apple.

"It breaks my heart that he has to leave the game," Rodman said.

Those were the days, baby. Those were the fucking days.

✦ ✦ ✦ ✦ ✦

Back at the Cedars-Sinai benefit, the waiters were hustling, kicking it into high gear. The salad plates disappeared and plates with a filet with all the trimmings—julienned vegetables and this potato casserole thing—were plopped down in front of the 11 people at my table. The reporter started digging in while the rest of our group nibbled around the edges—Symone eating a couple of bites of salad, Darren and Thaer eating a bite of this and a bite of that— holding out for the sushi we'd be having as soon as we bailed out of there.

On my right, four chairs over, Paul Westphal was chatting up Drew Gooden, inviting him to work out over at Pepperdine. "Make your friends before you need them," I was thinking. Westphal's name keeps coming up every time there's a NBA coaching vacancy, and the job in Cleveland, where Gooden plays, hasn't been the most secure position since the new owner took over.

On stage they were gearing up to present the "Lifetime Achievement Awards" to Pete Carroll, who had just led USC to two straight NCAA football championships, and Jerry Rice, who the program called the "greatest wide receiver ever to play in the NFL." Me, I like Jerry because he's been known to wear earrings, *and* he's appeared on a Wheaties box. That's a man who has it all. All this got me to thinking about the greatest this and the greatest that.

One time somebody at ESPN asked me, "If you had to pick the five greatest NBA players of all time, who would they be?"

I was like, "Dennis Rodman, Dennis Rodman, Dennis Rodman …" and so forth. But if I really had to pick a "Dennis Rodman Dream Team," I would put Michael Jordan number one. I'd put Scottie Pippen at the two guard, of course. As my center, I'd put myself, and as my small forward, I'd go with James Worthy from the Lakers. My power forward would be Kevin McHale from the

Celtics. As far as a shooting guard, coming off the bench, that would have to be Steve Kerr—that guy could shoot the fuck out of it.

Why James Worthy? I'm one of the best defensive players of all time, and I couldn't guard his ass.

"If you defended me three or four different ways," said Worthy in the *NBA at Fifty*, " … then I had three or four different moves."

No shit. He would be coming off a screen, and I'd be trying to figure out whether he was going over the top or underneath. Next thing I knew, he was at the rim. Now if we'd played those guys more, I might have figured out how to guard his ass. But there was nothing but frustration with James Worthy. Clever, quick, a great player—he's one of the few guys who flat pissed me off. I want him on my team just so I don't have to guard him.

Now if you ask me what real team I was on that was the best—a team I would like to be on today—that would be the team we had the first two years that I was in Chicago. Aside from all the talent, this was a team that was happy. Just happy. There was no bitching. I mean it was great. Of course, all that happiness might have had something to do with all the winning we were doing. In 1995-96 we won 72 regular-season games—best ever—and the NBA championship. Then we won another championship in 1996-97. You're winning baby, and the owner's happy, the GM is happy, the coach is happy, and the guys playing are happy. And the guys who aren't playing? They're not so happy, but they've got no grounds for complaining.

And me? I might have been the happiest motherfucker of all. Perfect coach, perfect team, perfect city. Today? I'm not so happy. Not after being kicked around by the NBA for four or five years. But as I looked around the Cedars-Sinai banquet table that night, I could see I wasn't the first guy to be abused by the NBA. Paul Westphal coached at the Phoenix Suns and Seattle Supersonics before ending up at Pepperdine, not exactly the college elite. Drew Gooden has been on three teams in four years. This league can chew your ass up and spit it out, and nobody exits unscathed. Even superstars get hurt, lose a step, get old, and then "there's no room in the inn," y'know? It's something you understand in your head. In your heart? That's another deal. I looked at the reporter. He played somewhere back in the sixties, and he was thinking he could still play—half-speed anyway—right up until about a year ago. That's when he blew out his ACL. Shit, anybody could have seen the son of a bitch shouldn't have been out there. What is he? 55? 60? I guess his body gave out before his heart. Maybe that's what they'll say about me one day.

But not yet, baby, not yet.

CHAPTER TWENTY-FIVE

THREE RUMORS, FIVE DENIALS

Some of the people around me think Michelle has been fooling around. A revenge kind of thing. They didn't tell me, of course. They told the reporter. So the guy came to me and Michelle with all this gossip, so off the wall it was almost funny.

Here's the big picture:

"Michelle has a boyfriend right now," a friend told the reporter. "She's had one for a while. But she has double standards. Dennis is not allowed to, but she is."

First, I was going to just ignore all this shit, but then I was afraid if I did, I would be accused of sweeping it all under the rug.

"The guy's supposed to be doing this tell-all book, and he leaves all the sleazy stuff out trying to protect Michelle. He's kissing Michelle's ass."

So instead of ignoring it, I've decided to put it all to rest. Let's take it one rumor at a time.

First up is the motocross "boy toy."

That was a fun night.

Me, Michelle, a couple of friends—the usual bunch—were hanging out at Josh Slocum's. Michelle got pissed at me for something—no news there—and she left with a couple of people to go to another bar. They came back. She didn't, so I was like, "Where the hell is she?"

I was the only one wondering; or so the story goes.

"We all had our suspicions it was that guy from motocross. Everybody knew something was going on with that guy," recalled a friend. "She actually had the balls to go to his [Dennis's] restaurant with this kid when he [Dennis] wasn't there to have a couple of drinks."

I ended up driving all over Newport Beach at like four o'clock in the morning trying to find her ass. Friends took this to be a sign that I was jealous. Meanwhile, a friend of a friend spotted her car parked at the motocross boy toy's house. Newport Beach is a very small town. So we drove over there. I let the air out of her tires, had a change of heart, pumped the tires back up. Then I went home and waited. Come daylight, she showed up. I called her on it, and she said she and the motocross boy toy were only friends. She was just trying to score some free riding lessons for our son D.J., who was maybe four at the time.

I bought it.

"I don't think he wanted to believe she was actually cheating on him," a friend told a reporter, "actually sleeping with somebody else."

So that's the rumor. Some of the basic facts are true. We *were* sitting around drinking at Josh Slocum's one night; and Michelle *did* disappear and end up with the motocross guy. I *did* go looking for her, but it didn't have anything to do with jealousy. The reason I was chasing around after Michelle is that I didn't want her to be driving drunk—didn't want her to get hurt. I was so pissed she had disappeared, that when I finally found her, I let the air out of her tires. The whole thing had to do with worry, not jealousy. I'm just not a jealous guy. There's not a man on the planet who can make me jealous. If somebody is trying to fool around with my woman, I just go up and shake the guy's hand, say, "How you doin'?" No big deal.

Here's what Michelle said when she heard the rumor.

"This motocross guy is 24 years old," she told the reporter as if the kid's age alone were enough to put it to rest.

"My [teenage] daughter's even friends with him," she continued. "I met him at a motocross event, and we all became friends. That was it. He was gonna teach our kids. Teach our little boy [how to ride]. That was it."

As for Michelle parading him around at Josh Slocum's: "This guy and his friends would come into the restaurant. Dennis had met them."

And what about the night in question?

"I was drunk. I walked down to Villanova, which is a restaurant down the street," said Michelle. "I called [motocross guy] to come get me because I was too drunk to drive. And I obviously didn't feel like dealing with Dennis—that's why I left the restaurant in the first place."

So the motocross guy and the man he worked for showed up.

"His boss and his wife drove my car. I rode with [motocross guy]," said Michelle, "We all went back to [his] house," where they all ended up sitting around in the living room.

"Where the cheating became a deal was [Dennis] slashed my tires. I wasn't able to leave blah-blah-blah-blah-blah."

So Michelle stayed for what was left of the night, and a rumor was born.

"They made a big deal out of that one night, me being drunk," continued Michelle. "But nothing happened. If I cheated on him, I'd tell you, 'I cheated on him.'"

And what did I say when the reporter asked me point-blank if I thought Michelle was cheating with the motocross guy?

"No. Not at all. Not at all. Not at all." So this was a really big deal with my friends, and I could have cared less—just another little ripple in the polluted pond of Dennis Rodman's love life.

Rumor two also involves motorcycles. Remember Michelle's overnight trip to Big Bear that ended badly and her week-long excursion to the Black Hills Motor Classic in Sturgis, South Dakota? Opportunities, so the story goes, for Michelle to fool around with "a lover," we'll call "motorcycle man."

"Bullshit," said Michelle.

"I know who you're talking about," she told the reporter. "You're talking about a friend of mine that I've been friends with for going on eight years. And he will be a friend of mine until the day I die."

The motorcycle guy sealed the deal with Michelle the night her husband allegedly beat her up.

"The actual night that happened, this guy put me and my daughter in a hotel—the very first night it happened. That's how long [we've] been friends," said Michelle. "I chose not to have him in my life for a while, because I was too busy chasing Dennis around and not being friends with my friends.

"And up in Big Bear, I was literally with him, another guy, and two of my girlfriends." Michelle continued. "So it was three girls and two guys. And all of us girls had a bedroom, and the boys had a bedroom in our friend's cabin. So there was nothing.

"In Sturgis, same deal," she said, speaking of the sleeping arrangements.

"He is a friend, and he will remain a friend for good," she continued. "There's just nothing to tell. And Dennis—it bothers the hell out of Dennis—he can't stand it."

"That you've got this old friend," said the reporter.

"He can't stand it. I turn to this friend because this friend is very intelligent. He's got his shit together. And I turn to him for advice. And it bothers Dennis."

She's right about that one.

"Anyway, no, I'm not cheating on him," continued Michelle. "And I would not see another man until we were completely separated or I was divorced. I won't go there. I just won't do it again [like she did with her first husband.] And the one time I did cheat on him, and Dennis knows about it … I was lonely. I wanted a man to treat me good, pay attention to me, and that was it."

Which brings us to the third rumor, somehow linked to the internal combustion engine. In this one, Michelle left me for some valet parker.

"Where do you get these stories?" Michelle asked the reporter.

So why'd she really leave me?

"He was screwing around with some chick," said Michelle. "That and because he wouldn't involve me in his life."

So after Michelle filed and we were "completely over," she started "seeing a guy that was a valet parker."

That one would have a happy ending, for me at least. After Michelle left the valet parker to come back to me, I went over to the restaurant where the guy worked. I figured Michelle had been talking his ear off for days, and I was like, "What do I need to do with Michelle that I'm not doing?"

He was like, "If you want to know what Michelle is about, just look at her back."

What he meant was, check out that big "Mrs. Rodman" tattoo.

"He was trying to tell Dennis that what I'm all about is my husband," said Michelle.

"And your husband is Dennis Rodman," said the reporter.

"Yep, damn it."

Going through all these rumors, I can see why some of my friends might have been suspicious. You stay overnight a couple of places with eligible guys, you go on vacation for a week with another man, it looks bad. But you can't build your life around what other people think. And sometimes when "it looks like a duck and it quacks like a duck," it's not a duck at all. It's just, say, an AFLAC commercial.

"I'd love to know who these people are who say that I'm the one that's cheating," said Michelle. "But I should expect it. Anybody's that's gonna talk, they're gonna say good things about Dennis, bad things about me. I've cheated on Dennis one time in six and a half years."

While she was in a denying mood, Michelle took exception to all of us calling her jealous, saying her blow-ups were more about disrespect.

"This guy is screwin' this other girl and then brings her in front of me," said Michelle. "I don't know if that's about disrespect or jealousy. I'm not quite sure. Or me being pregnant with his kid and he's got another chick over at his house he's messing around with, and I see it."

And as far as her knocking the shit out of me the day I came back from shooting the Super Bowl commercial in Houston?

"The guys is six-how tall, six-seven? Anybody with a brain would know that I couldn't knock the shit out of him. How am I gonna knock the shit out of Dennis Rodman?"

That's a question my jaw has been asking for about six years. To look at her, it doesn't seem possible. And I am happy to hear that Michelle has been holding back—that there are limits to her violence.

"I've pushed him. I've hit him in the chest. I've used like open palms, but I've never actually socked him. Even the time I caught him naked behind the door, and I broke down the door—I slapped him. I never hit him."

"So you've never hit him with your fist," said the reporter. "Is that what you're saying?"

"Exactly. Never with my fist. I don't know how I could ever knock the crap out of this guy."

"But you have slapped him."

"Oh, yeah. Oh, heck yeah."

"Upside the head?"

"No, on his face. And he deserved it, let me tell you."

"So if somebody said you slapped him in the face, then that probably happened. That could have happened?"

"Oh, for sure."

Reality Check: Sometimes, where there's smoke, there's smoke.

C H A P T E R   T W E N T Y - S I X

CITIZEN RODMAN

O n Tuesday, June 14, 2005, I drove down to my restaurant in Newport Beach to meet with the manager. There's no connection, but it just happened to be the same day the *Los Angeles Times* announced that Michael Jackson got off scot-free. "Jackson Acquitted on All Ten Counts" said the front-page headline. Inside there were *five more pages* of coverage. Un-fucking-real.

I pulled into the parking lot and parked across from the infamous black Ford 350 XLT pickup that had ferried my ass to Las Vegas just in time for the motorcycle pile-up at the Treasures Gentleman's Club. It was parked in the handicapped spot. Figures.

The restaurant hadn't been what you'd call a cash cow, and I had stepped in to get it back on track. Now that my drinking is no longer a problem, I can really help. Who better than a guy who, for years, spent most of his waking hours in one club or another? Out front, I talked with a couple of guys who were installing lights on the covered patio entryway, cardboard boxes and tools sitting around. I had been thinking about re-doing the entrance all together, make it like the ivy-covered trellis at Mimi's Café over in Costa

Mesa. I asked the guys to run by Mimi's later and check it out. Not that my place wasn't inviting to begin with.

The architecture is Victorian, and the building has a story-and-a-half cupola on the right with lots of bric-a-brac painted gold with red accents. The building itself is a soft green, the roof a darker green, done in hexagonal shingles with an occasional red shingle accent. Being California, there were a couple of palm trees out front and a dozen or so potted plants.

I walked inside, and the place was dark as a cave, smelled a little musty. But even in the dim light you could see the full bar on the left with stools and the tables in the main room, looking naked without their tablecloths. Several not-quite-to-scale statues of top-less women—not *Playboy* topless, Venus de Milo topless—were scattered around, two flanking the fireplace, one part of a room divider. There were Greek columns, gold woodwork, and heavy drapes. In back, down a couple of steps, several red couches backed up to large windows that looked out on the marina where white boats were bobbing up and down in their slips. The overall effect: comfortable, just short of elegant, like an upscale gentlemen's club.

I hooked up with the manager, and we settled in at a table. After I lit up a cigar and took off my sneakers, we got down to business. We talked about how much to pay a band; what the cover charge should be. We discussed whether we should spend $6,000 for an ad in a trade magazine for event planners, a target audience if there ever was one. We talked about hiring bartenders, and in the first and last "Dennis Rodman moment" of the meeting, I suggested we hire "three hot girls." As I said, a drinker knows drinkers. Does all this shit sound boring? Perfect. I have been trying to piece together a new boring Dennis Rodman for Newport Beach use. The kind of guy who is invisible to cops. The wild boy was ready to show a whole new side: respectability.

As a part of that, I had even changed the name of the restaurant six months before. Josh Slocum's was now "Rodman's." It was my way of announcing Dennis Rodman's "second coming" as a businessman, a citizen, and a human being. At the time of this meeting, it had been about a year and a half since, in the midst of the intervention in Vegas, Wendell had told me just how far I had fallen. He had called me a disgrace to my children, my family, my friends, and black people in general.

Other than that, things were good.

"What was the point in snatching all those rebounds and going down in history as one of the greatest rebounders if you're gonna go out like a fucking drunk?" Wendell said. "What's the point of being able to boast and brag about playing on one of the greatest championship teams with the greatest basketball player ever, Michael Jordan, if you're gonna go out like a drunk?"

At the time, I was getting similar "You're a loser—Fix it" messages from Michelle, Darren, and Thaer. So I made a decision to sober up. But that was just the first phase of my comeback. Now I had a reputation to live down. Needed to retool my image. Wendell had some ideas.

"You know what you need to do?" he told me. "You need to get you a tailor-made suit, something that Michael Jordan would wear. Dye your hair back to its natural color, take off the sunglasses and go on Oprah. You will blow people's minds. The same way you blew their minds when you put on a dress."

"Being wild and crazy has no shock value anymore," he continued. "When you're 44 years old and tell someone, 'Look at my new piercing,' they're like, 'What's wrong with you?'"

One final piece of advice: "Blame it all on alcohol," said Wendell. "People love comeback stories. Blame it all on alcohol because, guess what, Dennis? It's the truth."

Well, alcohol was the symptom and not the disease. The disease was basketball or maybe the lack of basketball. As Wendell told a reporter: "After he got cut from the Lakers, it all started crumbling down."

When L.A. dumped me in 1999, that led to a little mix-up with my sister Debra, who had been working for me, and I let her go. My agent, Dwight Manley, and I already had parted ways right around the time I signed with the Lakers. Now there was no basketball, no Debra, and no Dwight in my life, and Carmen was coming and going. So there were huge holes to fill, and I topped them off with alcohol, alcohol, and more alcohol. Wendell, who was my full-time bodyguard at the time, watched me go down the toilet.

"Once Debra was gone, his drinking went into overdrive, man," said Wendell. "It was like, 'My family's all gone, my old agent's gone, everybody's gone. I'm getting ready to party my ass off.' And that's when I quit."

When Wendell bailed out, that left another hole, and I filled it with still more booze. When I wasn't at the Club 4809 beach house, I was at Josh Slocum's. If it was after hours and I was still in the mood to party, I headed for Las Vegas.

"His life for a lot of years was a blur—just one long fucking blur," said Wendell.

At the time, I felt totally alone. No one was around to pat me on the back and say, Dennis, "I'll be there for you." No one. So I kept on keeping on. And, other than the blip that was Dallas, the non-stop partying went on for almost four years before I hit rock bottom in the Treasures parking lot. Then, after I quit drinking, I was looking to go to the next level. I was looking for respect. That meant I had to change my ways. And that's how I ended up ram-roding business meetings at Rodman's.

Thaer showed up late for the meeting with Bugsy, his way-ugly, tan bulldog, trailing along behind. While Bugsy wandered around in search of snacks and petting, Thaer fired up his water pipe—it's a Palestinian thing—and, between puffs, he brought up this idea we'd been kicking around for something called, "Arabian Nights" at the club. We'd feature Middle Eastern music to pull in the Arab crowd. Thaer even knew a D.J. who could do the spinning. So I was like, "Why not?", and we put it in on the calendar for the first two Tuesdays in July. Talk about your niche marketing.

Somebody went, "What's that smell?" and everybody was look-ing at Bugsy. It's not what you think.

"When's the last time this dog had a bath?" somebody asked, not really expecting a straight answer. Bugsy smelled so bad, nobody would be able to remember that far back.

Thaer shrugged, and Bugsy just kept waddling around, being a dog, totally oblivious.

"Insults don't bother his ass," said Thaer. "Fucker doesn't speak English."

◆ ◆ ◆ ◆

After I moved to Newport Beach to live full-time in 1999, people got to know me as this person who partied all the time—this drunk. Sure, they respected me as an athlete, as a famous person, and that was great, but as far as being a human being, that was a different story.

My thing had always been, "As long as I don't hurt anybody, it's all good." But after I sobered up, I saw I *was* hurting people: disgracing the community, doing all this crazy shit, disrespecting the cops. This is a town with a proud past, and I was kicking sand in their faces.

Humphrey Bogart and Lauren Bacall once lived here, as had James Cagney and that other "Michelle," Michelle Pfeiffer. And while the town had seen its share of wild boys—Errol Flynn used to raise a little hell—I hold the all-time record for dissing cops and pissing-off neighbors. So my new thing was to be less like Errol Flynn and more like Shirley Temple, also a one-time Newport Beach resident.

I figured since I had turned on the fucking craziness, I could turn it off. So that's what I did. In 2004, I shut down Club 4809—sold the beach house, moved to Huntington Beach, and got my life together. The bar was no longer open. And I was like, "You know what? Things are gonna be okay. Everything's cool. I'm back in control now."

It worked, and now people in Newport Beach look at me and go, "Wow! He actually did it. He's actually cleaned up his act." They saw me when I was down, and they were there to help me get up again. They were there when I needed them. Now when I walk the streets people say hello, they say, "Hey, Dennis, what's going on."

Today, I realize there were consequences to everything I did back in the day. Dominoes *do* fall. Scientists say the flap of a butterfly wing can eventually change the weather hundreds of miles away. I don't know about that, but I do know the closing of a door can shake things up much closer to home. Here's a retelling of the story of the "nice, clean girl," the "librarian," this time from the perspective of an eyewitness who saw things a little differently.

"This girl showed up and asked where he [Dennis] was. We're like, 'Oh he's upstairs sleeping.' And she freaked out," said the eyewitness. "Just hysterical. That's when she grabbed the knife from downstairs.

"It was a scary situation," the eyewitness continued. "A girl that's not right in the head at the time with a knife.

"Finally me and another person got her away from the door and got her down, and she ended up cutting her hand," he continued. "We had to wrap it up for her.

"Dennis eventually opened the door and tried to talk her down," said the eyewitness.

Here's the good part:

"He never has intentions to actually hurt anybody," the eyewitness said. "I guess some people don't realize what they do emotionally sometimes to other people."

I do now. Dominoes fall.

As for the other girl, the one on *my* side of the door? According to the eyewitness, she wasn't sympathetic.

"You haven't cut her off yet?" the eyewitness recalls Michelle saying to me. "I could've been stabbed."

✦ ✦ ✦ ✦

I have now made it through the worst time of my life, and I'm slowly working my way toward total respectability. I could've ended up in the gutter, but I caught myself just in time, made it back to my safe place, and things are good. I'm not bombed. I'm not broke. The kids are good. Michelle's good. My life's good. And I've learned a few life lessons along the way.

Reality Check: There's a price you pay if you go by the rules.

Reality Check: There's a price you pay if you don't go by the rules.

Going by the rules in Detroit led me to a rendezvous with a rifle in a parking lot at The Palace of Auburn Hills. Breaking the rules in Newport Beach led me to a rendezvous with a light pole in a parking lot at Treasures Gentleman's Club in Las Vegas.

The trick is to strike a balance somewhere in between.

Before Treasures, "just being Dennis" meant breaking all the rules: getting wrecked, bedding some slut, going hog wild. In the future, "just being Dennis" will allow room for being a good father and a good husband. So move over wild boy and make room for "Citizen Rodman." It's my new thing. Not that I'd take back my old thing.

No. No. No. No. No.

The wild boy had a hell of a ride—a *hell* of a fucking ride: a helicopter landing on the beach, rock bands blasting; a very large black man running naked in the street; lots of "surgically enhanced" women; gallons of booze; tons of barbeque; Madonna; Carmen; Michelle throwing bottles at me so hard they ended up as permanent fixtures in the beach house walls; women knocking down my bedroom door. (I don't know how many times I replaced that fucking thing. I do know I was keeping the local hardware store in business just buying hinges.)

But I understand now. I see. It was *not* all good. My eyes are open. I know that things went down in my beach house—the "librarian" with the knife, scumbags sneaking around doing drugs behind my back—that, with the flap of a butterfly wing, could've destroyed Dennis Rodman's life and "earned" me a Michael Jackson-like six pages of coverage in the fucking *Los Angeles Times*.

But my ass got lucky, and 20 years from now, all that negative shit will be forgotten. Instead, people will still be remembering that beautiful spring day back in May 2001 when Dennis Rodman turned 40.

"Remember the two rock bands?" they'll say. "The cops in riot gear? And, hey—how 'bout that fucking helicopter?"

Like I said, it was a hell of ride.

CHAPTER TWENTY-SEVEN

ROLL VIDEO

The video biography is not *like* having your life flash before your
eyes. It *is* having your life flash before your eyes.

Sometimes it's a highlight reel: "There it is! Rodman's first
career triple-double." Sometimes not: "Police say Rodman faces a
number of charges, including driving under the influence of alcohol."

There are fond memories—Carmen and me at Planet
Hollywood—and things I'd rather forget, like me exiting the paddy
wagon in Miami. These flashbacks are from FOX Sports Net's
Beyond the Glory: Dennis Rodman. They shot the video in 2004, close
on the heels of ESPN's *Rodman on the Rebound,* which had aired earlier that year. But unlike the two-part ESPN reality series, Fox had
no particular angle, producing a straight biography that ran 44 minutes and 32 seconds. (They filled out the hour with commercials.)
Here's a five-minute version, the highlights of the highlights, cob-
bled together by none other than Dennis Rodman himself.

Let's begin with the Dallas childhood:

"The girls kind of overshadowed him a little bit," my mother
says.

No shit.

Cut to stills of my two sisters, the basketball stars, wearing their orange and black high school uniforms: Kim holding a trophy, Debra a ball.

Cut to Dennis Rodman, the undersized loser with very large ears.

Roll video of the six-foot-eight, skinny as hell Dennis Rodman—lucky if I weighed two hundred pounds—playing ball at Southeastern Oklahoma State.

Dissolve to video of the 1986 news conference when Chuck Daly announced that the Pistons had drafted John Salley and me.

Cut to the "bad boys" and then video of me flying over the scorer's table, guarding Magic, dunking, blocking a shot, making a steal.

"The NBA's Defensive Player of the Year, Dennis Rodman!"

Cut to a close-up of me crying.

Cut to pictures of Alexis and Annie, and then video of me after the cops picked me up in the parking lot at The Palace of Auburn Hills.

Roll tape of the Pistons hoisting the trophy after winning a second title, a much younger David Stern running for his life.

Cut to a sign in the stands in San Antonio: "Dennis Rodman: To Dye For."

"I went and got my hair dyed, and that's when my life changed completely," I say.

"He went from a shy, unassuming kid to a megastar," my mother says.

Cut to a close-up of Madonna in the stands and then video of David Robinson and me.

"I was the devil. He was God. He was Jesus," I say.

Cut to a still photo of me, Michael, and Scottie.

"He plays. He does his job. He comes to practice. He keeps his mouth shut. He works hard every day. He's never delinquent. He's just a very easy person to have on a basketball team," says Phil Jackson.

Cut to me wearing a feather boa and silver make-up in Chicago, a wedding dress in New York—"Oh my goodness! Rodman just kicked a photographer!"—then to video of the Bulls celebrating a third straight championship.

"When you're flying that high, when you're [at] like the peak of all peaks, there's nowhere to go but down," says Wendell.

Cut to me announcing my signing with L.A.

Roll the TV news clip.

"In handcuffs, former Baywatch star Carmen Electra steps from a police transport van. Also inside, her on-again, off-again lover, Dennis Rodman."

Cut to Dallas. "A technical foul on Rodman. He's been thrown out."

Roll the voice over by FOX announcer, Chris Rydell. "His professional reputation was ruined, but the party was just getting started."

Cut to video of the Treasures Gentleman's Club in Vegas.

"We actually gave him an ultimatum, which was either you stop, or we're done," says Thaer.

"Everybody's worried about, 'Oh, is he gonna make the NBA.' I could care less. To walk away from that alcohol is *huge*," says Wendell.

"It's step by step—and we work on it every day," says Michelle.

Cut to me with a white, crinkle-permed, Don Quixote-looking hairdo playing for the Long Beach Jam.

Dissolve to the happy ending of me, Michele, and the kids in the park.

That's the abridged version of my life on video—an overview of the overview. So what did Fox leave out? They didn't even mention one low point: my arrest for stealing watches when I was a janitor at the Dallas airport. I was a nobody then, so there were no news cameras there, no video. If that happened today? I'd be all over *SportsCenter*. Leno and Letterman would be ragging my ass unmercifully. This brings us to the first really big-time thing FOX left out of the biography—Fame. They're all over what I'm famous for—but as for what that fame means—that's the 800-pound gorilla sitting in the living room.

Fame is what prompted FOX Sports to do my bio—what prompts them to do any bio—and it's with me 24 hours a day. And whether the complaint is the across-the-board trust issues I've already bitched about or personal privacy, fame is the water in which this fish swims.

Michelle is over it.

"I just don't want you to be 'Dennis Rodman' anymore," she told me one day out of the blue.

Sometimes I feel the same way.

"We can't go anywhere and do normal things," she said, "And it sucks."

Like last weekend.

"He [Dennis] took us shopping," Michelle told a reporter. "He's got his kids in his hands, people come up and say, 'Hey, can we get a picture with you and our kids?' They want him to let go of his kids so he can take a picture with them.

"And then the one time he said, 'No, I'm with my kids,'" Michelle continued. "They called him an 'asshole.' And he wasn't even rude."

This kind of shit happens all the time. Now there are ways around it: like when we took the kids to Disneyland. I paid an escort to walk around with us to keep the people away. The cost? Two thousand dollars.

Whatever the source of fame—sports, movies, television, politics—once a person becomes a national celebrity, that very fame is a huge part of what their life is all about, dictating where they live, where they eat, where they can go and not go. Then there's the ever-present bodyguard who, like it or not, is a part of the family. So it's not the big house, the fancy car, the starring roles, and the championship rings that make a celebrity's everyday life so very different from yours. It's the fame. And FOX is a part of that.

FOX—all the media—and celebrities are, like Fred and Ginger, forever in lockstep. It's hard to tell where one starts and the other begins. You can't become famous and stay famous without the cameras, the reporters, the media. So even if FOX wanted to do the Dennis Rodman fame angle, I'm not sure how they'd capture it on tape. Do they shoot video of themselves shooting video? No clue.

Anybody have a number for *60 Minutes*?

One last thing on fame and I will give it a rest. In the last few years, my celebrity status may have actually hurt my chances of getting back in the NBA. Whenever my name comes up, it's all over the newspapers, and the battle lines are drawn. This guy loves Dennis. That guy hates Dennis. If some GM is considering bringing me on, he knows at some point he's going to have to explain himself. I'm thinking a simple, "I want to win," would get it done, but what do I know?

There's a second way my fame has hurt my comeback. People accuse me of having my own agenda. They say I'm just trying to get back in the league to build my popularity, as some kind of publicity stunt. Well, I'm going to be famous with or without another NBA gig. Right now I can walk into any of these celebrity rat-fucks and—I don't give a shit who's hot—I'll walk into that son of a bitch, and they are all over me. Bro, I'm famous in—at random—Finland, Spain, Puerto Rico, Croatia, Mexico—even China. Trust me, Dennis Rodman doesn't need any more fame.

That's it. I'm finally done bitching about fame. As of now, I've been a nationally known celebrity for more than a decade, and I'm going to be a celebrity for the rest of my damn life. Sometimes I regret it, and sometimes I don't. Whatever. I have decided to just get over it and play the hand I was dealt.

✦ ✦ ✦ ✦ ✦

A second big thing given short shrift in *Beyond the Glory* is my failed relationships. (I guess I should be thankful for that.) From my mother and sisters, to my wives, children, and girlfriends, it's been one long fuck-up.

Not that it's all my fault.

Back in 1999, my mother and I weren't on the best of terms to begin with, and then, when I let my sister Debra go, the shit really hit the fan. Debra threatened to sue me, she wanted to take this, this,

this. Then my mother took Debra's side, and I'm like, "Oh wow, all I did was take care of you guys."

Back in the day, I spent close to a million bucks buying my mother and two sisters houses next door to each other down in Texas—they still live in those houses—and, as I said before, I send my mother $4,000 every month. But as the old saying goes, "No good deed goes unpunished." So Debra was demanding this, this, this; my mother jumped in on her side; and suddenly, I got my own family fucking me over. Welcome to my world. I resolved that one in my usual way. I cut a fucking check, just paid Debra the money, because I don't like confrontation with anybody, much less family. But even after all that, I can honestly say, I don't hate my sister; I don't hate my mother; we're just not close.

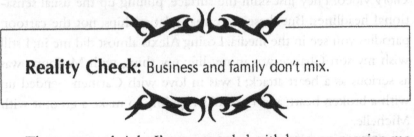

Reality Check: Business and family don't mix.

The amateur shrinks I'm surrounded with keep on nagging me about patching up the relationship with my family, especially my mother. Well, there's nothing to patch up. There never has been any relationship. One of my shrinks thinks that explains a lot.

"I personally think that it affects him more than anyone knows, including him," Michelle said in *Beyond the Glory*. "I think that has a lot of effect on how he treats people and how he is with people and why he's got such a wall up and not loving people. That's just my opinion."

Lately, Michelle and I have been talking about taking D.J. and Trinity down to Dallas so my mother can see them for the first time. This isn't an excuse for me to hook up with her. I'm still not ready for that. Someday, I hope my mother and I can have some kind of relationship, but as far as me finding a way to love her like a normal son loves his mother, I don't think that's going to ever happen. I'll keep on taking care of her every month, but that's about as far as it's going to go.

✦ ✦ ✦ ✦ ✦

If you think my relationship with my mother is fucked up, that's nothing compared with my relationships with women. It's one of my biggest failures in life. Sure, I've had sex with some of the most beautiful women on the planet—and like a comedian once said, "The worst I ever had was wonderful"—but as any guy will tell you, that don't mean shit at 2:00 a.m. on a Tuesday, when you just rolled over after having a go with some stranger in Bumfuck, Finland. At lunch the next day, a bar a year later, it may sound cool—"I banged Miss Fjord 2005." But the night of? Get my ass out of here!

My biggest flaw doesn't get much serious play in the *Beyond the Glory* video. They just skim the surface, pulling up the usual sensational headlines. But these were real relationships, not the cartoon parodies you see in the media. Losing Alexis almost did me in; I still wish my son Chance was in my life; my thing with Madonna was as serious as a heart attack; I was in love with Carmen—ended up with a broken heart; and I'm still struggling to make a go of it with Michelle.

"He gets caught up in a relationship. That's more important to him than any game or anything else," Thaer said in *Beyond the Glory.* "He's succeeded at basketball already, but he's never succeeded at a relationship."

Too true. So how does FOX handle this major sink hole in my life? They spend 58 seconds on Annie and Alexis, 18 seconds on Madonna, 52 seconds on Carmen, and don't even mention my son Chance and his mother. My relationship with Michelle gets 36 seconds, and she's the only woman who's taken seriously. They make no attempt to figure out what went wrong. Not that it's any big secret. It's like I said in that phone call to my mother after Michelle filed for divorce in 2004:

"I'm involved with a woman—a woman who wants a lot more than I can give her."

That's the story of my love life in a nutshell. What they want that I haven't been able to give is fidelity. That was the issue with

Carmen. And that is the issue with Michelle. Hell, that was the issue with the "librarian."

"He is who he is. And he always told her [Michelle] that 'I am who I am. I'm gonna be who I am, no matter what.' And that's how it went," a friend told a reporter. "And she accepted that until she didn't want to accept it. Then she caused problems."

After all these years, I'm guess I'm still looking for a woman who won't "cause problems."

"He's not gonna find her, either," a friend told a reporter. "He finds ones that say they will, but they always change their minds."

Then they leave, and I'm fucked.

"When he loves somebody and cares for people, and then they leave him, it hurts him, and he doesn't recover as fast as most people," my mother said in *Beyond the Glory*. "He doesn't move on. He can't move on."

Now I'm searching for a way to have a successful relationship with Michelle. Could happen.

While Michelle was at the Sturgis motorcycle rally, I took care of Trinity, and we ended up going to church together.

"And it just happened to be that service was about marriage and vows," Michelle told a reporter. "So it was really bizarre the one he picked—about being committed and being faithful."

I'll say.

Michelle took this to be a sign from God, and we are now scheduled to attend marriage counseling with the preacher. Hope springs eternal. Meanwhile it's been over a month since I told Michelle I wanted to renew our vows and buy a house together—still no answer.

So what's the big Dennis and Michelle wrap-up?

"That we'll eventually live happily ever after?" said Michelle. "Dennis and I are soul mates. We're never gonna be apart."

I hope so. But it's like I told the reporter: "Even though I'm with a woman who I think will give me that satisfaction, not just in bed, I still have my doubts. I'll still always have doubts. No matter what the situation is, I'm always gonna have doubts."

EPILOGUE

"**B**locking out," AKA "boxing out," is a technique defensive players use to keep the guy they are guarding from getting a rebound. It's taught by every basketball coach at every level of the game from coast to coast and continent to continent with drills, drills, and more drills that players have run "since they's babies."

Here's how one basketball writer explained the technique:

> When the ball is in the air, the defensive player gets between his man and the basket. Then all in one motion, the player pivots 180 degrees, crouches, makes contact, and backs his opponent away from the rim.

"You've got to sit on their legs and sit in their crotch," said the late Al Lo Balbo, a defensive guru, "and then use your elbows a little bit."

When should players use the technique?

"Block out on every shot," said Hall of Fame coach Bob Knight.

Blocking out is so important that some coaches have started keeping stats on it. Nothing is more fundamental to the game.

And Dennis Rodman? I rarely, rarely boxed out. First, I wasn't strong enough. Can you imagine me trying to back Shaq away from the rim? That was the "immovable object." I was like 220, and he was two pounds shy of a Hummer. He was a fucking load, man, a load. Crouch? I was a six-foot-eight guy surrounded by people six foot ten, seven feet. I didn't need to be giving away any height by crouching. They'd just reach over my ass and snag the ball. If I was body to body with anybody, it was back to back.

What I did instead of boxing out was get intertwined with the guy, got all wrapped up in his arms, legs. The ball came off the rim, and it was a question of who could get untangled and get to it first. That was usually me. It was like a judo move, y'know? I was using my leg strength for leverage, using his weight against him. It was wrestling without the take-downs. Some guys didn't know how to handle that, got frustrated, and if I was lucky, they would start playing me instead of the ball. Now the guy was more interested in whipping my ass than getting the rebound. But I was so quick, so fast, so elusive—it was like trying to box out a ghost—and the guy would end up putting a body on air. Next thing he knew, I'd be sweeping the boards and firing an outlet pass to Ron Harper. The guy was left running down court shaking his head.

"How did Rodman do that?"

And I was doing it every night, every fucking night, going against the great centers in the league—Patrick Ewing, Shaq, Hakeem Olajuwon—everybody. They are four, five inches taller, outweigh me by 40, 50, 60 pounds, and not one of them could stop me. And so Dennis Rodman, this small, skinny, wiry guy won seven consecutive rebounding titles playing against these guys with their own zip codes. That's unheard of—that's crazy.

So come the end of my Chicago run, Dennis Rodman, the greatest rebounder in the game, was sitting around waiting for the phone call offering me truck loads of NBA-elite-megastar cash. The kind of cash that makes strong men weak and weak women—let's say they're "sexually attracted." That call never came, and I was like, "What the fuck is going on?"

I guess once I left Chicago, I left my safe place, my home— where people really embraced me no matter what I did. And people in the league were like, "Fuck Dennis now. He's not with Chicago anymore. Michael, Scottie, and Phil Jackson are not there to protect him." When the dust settled, out of all the great players on that Chicago team, I was the only player who didn't get picked up—the only one who didn't get picked up. Everybody in the NBA turned their backs on me. Why is that? Here's one of the greatest rebounders of all time: why is he not playing? I still haven't figured it out.

So I ended up sitting on my ass.

If I'd played the full season in 1999, I would've won the rebounding title. If I'd played the next year, I would've won the rebounding title. But I didn't get that opportunity.

Even today, when coaches, owners, and GMs are sitting around talking about the kind of guy they'd like to play for them, my name always pops up.

"Dennis Rodman."

"Dennis Rodman."

"Dennis Rodman."

But it seems they don't want me to actually *play*; they just want to sit there and yap about my ass. Sometimes it can get downright weird. In the spring of 2005, after Cleveland owner Dan Gilbert chatted me up about a possible 10-day contract that never materialized, the Cavaliers denied ever talking to me. After I talked to Pat Riley about playing for the Heat, he called Darren, not me, with the bad news. He was like, "I have too much respect for Dennis to turn him down in person." What's that all about?

Everybody's always telling me, "You're a great player. You're this. You're that." But when it comes down to pulling the trigger—nothing. And I'm like, "Where are you?" I've got a suggestion: quit kissing David Stern's ass and give me a shot. I'll swallow my ego and try out. I'll come to rookie camp. I'll do anything except sweep up (can't handle the Dallas airport flashbacks)—or plug in your favorite disgusting sexual favor here—to get back on the court. What do you have to lose?

✦ ✦ ✦ ✦ ✦

Los Angeles, California, June 15, 2005. After weeks of speculation, it came to pass on the 55th day that the prophecy was fulfilled. "Lakers Turn to Hire Power," screamed the cutesy *Los Angeles Times* front-page headline. "Lakers Get a Re-Phil," read the even cutesier headline on the sports page. Yea, verily, visionary coach Phil Jackson was to return to the fold.

Hallelujah! Hallelujah!

The same man who had branded prodigal son Kobe "un-coach-able" only months before, was rehired to shepherd the 34-48, play-off-challenged Lakers back to respectability.

"There's some hope," Phil told the Associated Press.

I'll say—I'm thinking now I have an "in." Phil Jackson? One of my favorite people of all time. L.A. owner Jerry Buss? Same deal. Whether or not I end up playing for L.A., I know these two guys will be straight with me. And while we're talking comebacks, why not go for the whole enchilada? Get Michael and Scottie on board. I'm thinking a few people might turn out to see the three of us play in the L.A. home opener on November 3—best be booking the Rose Bowl for that one. Now all I've got to worry about is what to do with the hair.

✦ ✦ ✦ ✦ ✦

Sports reporters are forever asking me how I want to be remembered. Well, as a hell of a basketball player, certainly, but not just that. People come up to me all the time, and it's like, "Wow, you're not just an athlete. You're a pop icon." Yeah, I'm that and a role model and a piece of history, and most importantly, a symbol of hope for people everywhere who are afraid to open up and be themselves. That may be what I'm most proud of. People see the way I've lived my life so far, see how I took a lot of chances and not only survived, but thrived, and they're like, "Hey, I can do that, too." So I freed people up, showed people they could be themselves—say, feel, dress, and act the way they want to—and actually get away with it.

So I hope people will remember me for that.

I also hope my kids will remember me as a good father; my neighbors will remember me as a good citizen; and that some day, somehow, some woman will remember me as a good husband. But if I had to boil it all down and put how I want to be remembered on a tombstone, it might look something like this:

Here Lies
Dennis Rodman

A cool motherfucker
A down-to-earth, straight-up, in-your-face, son of a bitch with a big heart
A big, big, heart

And while I'm at it, if there's any room left, they can chisel this in stone:

Reality Check: Don't follow a path. Blaze a trail.

EPILOGUE FOR THE 2021 EDITION

It would be easy to look at Dennis Rodman's post-basketball life as a series of random occurrences. But they could also be recognized as an attempt by Rodman to discover something to occupy his post-basketball existence.

For the record, Rodman extended his basketball career as far as the game would let him. He played for the Brighton Bears of the British Basketball League in 2006, and also played with several former NBA stars in exhibitions in the Philippines. But he was truly scraping the bottom of the basketball barrel.

Rodman the personality was faring only slightly better. He allowed his name to be attached to unusual sporting enterprises like the Lingerie Football League. He appeared in a professional wrestling event. He worked as an actor, if you can call it that, playing the role of himself both in person and in voice (in an episode of *The Simpsons*). He participated in numerous reality TV shows and competitions, winning ABC's *Celebrity Mole* contest.

But nothing stuck.

In juxtaposition to his penchant for reality TV roles, real reality struck Rodman in odd ways once he survived into the second decade of the 21st century.

There were three main aspects that colored the life of Dennis Rodman once he completed his playing career:

His family relationships: Much of the last half of this book pertains in some way to Rodman's marriage to Michelle Moyer, whom he married in 2003. As noted earlier, she threatened him with divorce on innumerous occasions, and the divorce became reality in 2012, but not before they had two more children, Dennis Jr. and Trinity.

Trinity established herself as a soccer star, eventually playing with the U.S. Women's National U-20 team and the Washington Spirit of the NWSL.

In an interview with *The Guardian* in 2020, Trinity said being Dennis Rodman's daughter "has definitely been a thing my whole life. He is my dad, at the end of the day, and I don't think it's going to go away, so I just answer the questions and move on."

In the summer of 2021, D.J. Rodman was preparing for his junior year at Washington State University, where he plays small forward for the Cougars. In an April 29, 2020 interview with the *Seattle Times*, the younger Rodman said his father told him he would eventually receive Rodman's five NBA championship rings.

Rodman's relationship with his son (as well as with Trinity) was characterized as occasional and erratic. But D.J. Rodman did watch ESPN's 10-part documentary on the 1998 Chicago Bulls titled *The Last Dance*, and marveled at the story about Rodman flying off to Las Vegas midseason. "I did not know that could happen," D.J. said.

He was also pleased that the documentary pointed to his father's well-known shyness, which he overcame with his brash public persona.

"I think that's cool he was shy and still made an impact," D.J. said. "Because right now in my basketball career, I'm also not really an outspoken player. I think it's just cool I relate to him in that way."

The younger Rodman also said that he had researched his father's career and used his newfound knowledge to inspire his own basketball career.

For his role as a father, Rodman occasionally references his children's athletic successes on social media, including an occasional photo of them taken when he is with them.

His relationship with Kim Jong-un: That's North Korean leader Kim Jong-un, with whom Rodman created a friendship out of a love of basketball. The relationship could best be described as the capstone on Rodman's unusual personal history.

Rodman went to North Korea in early February 2013 along with a collection of American basketball players to take part in an exhibition for Kim, whose love of basketball was well known. During the exhibition game, which included numerous North Korean basketball players playing with and against the Americans, Rodman sat next to Kim and spoke with him in English without the use of a translator.

At one point, Rodman appeared at center court and made a speech to the crowd, then offered to Kim a promise: "You have a friend for life."

During that trip, Rodman was invited to Kim's home for a post-game dinner, during which Rodman again spoke to the group to relay his intention to maintain and extend his friendship with Kim.

Thereafter, Rodman made repeated trips to North Korea, representing corporate interests every time. But basketball was no longer the impetus for Rodman's appearance. His relationship with Kim grew to the point that Rodman requested the release of a Korean-American prisoner Kenneth Bae, and Kim quickly complied one week after receiving a 2014 letter from Rodman requesting the release. Afterward, Bae said Rodman was a "catalyst" for his release.

During a trip to North Korea while Barack Obama was president, Rodman made a public plea to the American leader to make contact with Kim to improve relations between the two countries. All the while, he denied that he was acting as a diplomat in any way, although his efforts were the most serious act that had ever been connected with Rodman.

When Donald Trump became president in January of 2017, Rodman's relationship with Kim grew. He met with Kim that month and gave the North Korean leader a copy of Trump's book *The Art of the Deal*, hoping that it would encourage further negotiations between the two countries. However, when President Trump began his own campaign to befriend Kim, he pushed Rodman aside as an unofficial diplomat. Rodman said he was discouraged from maintaining his relationship with Kim because it detracted from Trump's success at creating a dialogue with the controversial leader.

The Naismith Memorial Basketball Hall of Fame: At the end of a colorful basketball career, Rodman became one of the most unique members of the Naismith Memorial Basketball Hall of Fame.

Rodman, a player who often eschewed scoring, was named to the Hall of Fame on April 4, 2011, and the induction ceremony took place August 13, 2011.

Rodman earlier revealed that to be considered for the Naismith Memorial Basketball Hall of Fame, one must apply for consideration, and Rodman was putting that process off. Apparently, he got around to it.

Rodman was selected due to his five NBA championships, seven rebounding titles (in consecutive seasons), two NBA Defensive Player of the Year awards, seven first-team All-Defensive teams, and two All-Star appearances.

Considering his penchant for outrageous behavior and dress, Rodman was likely one of the most unusual members of the Naismith Memorial Basketball Hall of Fame. Considering also the manner in which Rodman played basketball, he is almost certainly one of the most unusual members in the Hall.

With a career scoring average of just 7.3 points per game, Rodman is one of the least offensive-minded players to receive Hall of Fame credentials. His play on the offensive end of the floor was concentrated around the rim, with an eye always at the basket, waiting for an offensive rebound to be made available by an errant shot from a teammate. Steve Kerr, the former Bulls player and current coach of the Golden State Warriors, opined that Rodman would eschew easy layups off of offensive rebounds, preferring to send the ball back out to a shooter, with the possibility that that shot would miss and another offensive rebound would be available.

Rodman averaged 13.1 rebounds per game. His average is a number that would have won four rebounding titles in the 21st century. During his reign as the rebounding leader in the NBA, he topped out at 18.7 rebounds per game, bested only by Wilt Chamberlain's 19.2 rebounds per game in 1971–72. And remember, Rodman played at a height of six-foot-seven, while Chamberlain was seven-foot-one. Rodman's lowest average for rebounds in a season during his seven-year span of rebounding titles was 14.9 per game.

On the defensive end of the floor, Rodman accepted every assignment given to him, from the strongest and tallest interior players (including Shaquille O'Neal), to the quickest and smallest point guards around. He took pride in defensive stops, and often celebrated them with a fist thrust into the air on the way to the offensive end of the floor.

Rodman's induction speech was expected to be unusual; what Rodman offered was heartfelt, touching, brash, and revealing.

He walked to the podium with a blue feathered boa draped around his neck, with his son and daughter walking in front of him. Before he took the stage, he removed the boa from his own neck and draped it over his son's neck.

Wearing a black jacket adorned with basketball team logos and the words *Pistons* and *Bulls* on the back in shiny letters, Rodman often stopped during his speech to deal with the tears he was shedding as he discussed his pre-basketball life and his basketball career.

In fact, it took him several minutes to get started on his speech. Three times, he turned to presenter Phil Jackson, his former coach with the Bulls, for emotional support before he began.

After a long list of thank-yous, including to the Rich family who raised him in Oklahoma, Rodman tried to talk about his playing career, but he stood at the podium and cried for half a minute before he could actually get any words out.

"I didn't play the game for the money. I didn't play the game to be famous," he said.

He made the large auditorium of Hall of Fame members and guests laugh when he thanked former NBA commissioner David Stern for "letting me in the building.

"I could have been anywhere in the world," he said. "I could have been dead. I could have been a drug dealer. I could have been homeless. I was homeless."

He spoke of his relationship, or non-relationship, with his natural father, and he spoke of his attempt to rebuild his relationship with his mother. But the most revealing statement he made during the 12-minute speech came when he said, "If anyone asks if I have any regrets in your career being a basketball player, I say I have one regret: I wish I was a better father."

The rest of the story: Without an apparent desire to forge a career of any sort, Rodman continues to live off of his fame, attaching his name to a variety of products that appeal to people that might be influenced by Dennis Rodman's endorsement.

In September of 2019, ESPN released the documentary *Rodman: For Better or Worse*, part of its *30 for 30* series. In it, Michael Jordan, Isiah Thomas, and John Salley notably offered their takes on the Dennis Rodman they knew or worked with. For his part, Rodman was mostly unapologetic and revealed little more about his life and its motivations.

Then, in May of 2020, ESPN's *The Last Dance*, during which an entire segment was dedicated to the addition of Rodman to that team, Rodman provided short bursts of insight in one interview for that documentary.

Rodman has already outlived everyone's expectations: Jordan said he would not live to 40, and Rodman turned 60 in May of 2021. Although Rodman retired from basketball years ago, he has not retired from the public eye. Whatever comes next in his life, it is likely to be unusual or unique, although it probably won't come as a complete surprise.

—Kent McDill